7 CORNERS

THE RECORDING HISTORY OF
DAVE GROHL & FOO FIGHTERS

SIMON KILMORE
FOOFIGHTERSLIVE.COM

Dedication

Dedicated to Dave Grohl, Foo Fighters and everyone else involved in recording the music that so many people enjoy. Without them this book would simply not exist.

Special Thanks

Hundreds of people have contributed to this book in some way, but I also want to give special thanks to the following people:

Hugo Berthier
Kirri Liepins
Gillian Gaar
Alex Roberts
Paul Brannigan
Barrett Jones / Laundry Room Studio
Paul / FooArchive.com
Rachael Gilliver

Preface

Make no mistake, '7 Corners' is not just another Dave Grohl and Foo Fighters biography. It's not a book exploring their personal stories, how many records they've sold or the general timeline of the band that you've heard many times before. This is a unique book focused solely on the music.

More specifically, the recording sessions which produced the songs now loved by millions of fans worldwide. Dave Grohl experienced his first real recording session in 1984, aged just 15 and in the 30+ years since, has recorded hundreds of songs, including nine studio albums with Foo Fighters.

That's not to say this book will just jump straight into what went on between the walls of any given recording studio without first setting the scene. Background into each session is provided, covering the reasons the session happened and the events immediately leading up to each session. Whilst the publication is logically formatted in a chronological manner each session is clearly presented as an individual entry, written in a manner that means they can be read independently, if you so choose.

The first edition of this book was published in August 2013 and as Foo Fighters are still an active band naturally a lot has happened in those five or so years. Two albums and a surprise EP were among the releases and all the recording sessions relating to those (and many more) are now detailed.

That surprise EP, 2015s 'Saint Cecilia' also brought with it a very special development. The release featured a selection of songs the band had crafted by delving into their extensive back catalogue of unfinished tracks and ideas.

One of those songs was none other than '7 Corners', the track which had given this publication its title. First recorded in 1997, the band attempted to record the song at least once around the recording of each album, without ever being happy enough with the results. In 2010, before yet another recording attempt, Grohl even suggested in an interview that if they didn't get it right on that occasion, it'd be thrown in the trash can forever. Despite it again being passed over on the next album, 'Wasting Light', they did give it one last shot in 2015. Grohl had renamed the song 'The Neverending Sigh', an obvious nod to the long history of the song, but nonetheless, the elusive track Grohl had titillated fans with for so long had finally been released.

Several years of research went into the first edition but there was still a lot of holes left to fill. In the years since yet more research has been carried out, including interviews with many figures involved in the recording sessions, from studio owners to engineers. This new edition corrects many inaccuracies of the first edition, adds brand new information to some past sessions and of course documents those more recent sessions.

All in all, some 77 recording sessions are now covered. Some in more detail than others, but with the same amount of effort put into each. I hasten to describe this book as "Exhaustive", as there is always more to add, more sessions we don't even know happened, but I believe it's certainly the most complete compendium you'll find on the subject to date. I hope you enjoy this dive into the recording world of Dave Grohl and Foo Fighters.

Simon Kilmore
Author

Contents

The Hardcore 80s

The Nirvana Era

Birth of Foo Fighters, early teething issues

The Troubled Early Noughties

Going Acoustic

November 11th, 1984
Laundry Room Studio, Arlington, VA, United States

Freak Baby

Grohl, Dave (Guitar)   Samuels, Brian (Bass)

Mason, Bryant (Guitar)   Smith, Dave (Drums)

Page, Chris (Vocals)

Recording Credits

Jones, Barrett (Engineer & Recording)

Tracks Recorded

1. No Words   5. Outta Town

2. Dead You Fool   6. Different

3. C.H.U.D   7. If You Think It's Right

4. Presidential Aids   8. 20/20 Hindsight

Recording Equipment

Tascam 34 ¼ Inch 4-Track Reel-to-reel tape machine

Peavey 12-channel Mixing Console

After a brief and unsuccessful dalliance with the trombone, Dave Grohl's musical career got a kick start in 1981. Aged twelve, he was given his first electric guitar – a 1963 Sears Silvertone – as a Christmas present from his parents. He had already been playing a borrowed acoustic guitar for a couple of years previous, and even took lessons, although he found the authoritarian method of learning boring. He instead preferred to learn by playing along to his favorite records by artists such as The Beatles and Rush.

By the age of 15, he had become proficient enough on the guitar to play publicly with friends, entering (and losing) several 'battle of the band' style contests in his home town of Arlington, Virginia. Unperturbed by the losses Grohl joined his first real band in the summer of 1984. At a local show he got talking to Brian Samuels, the bassist of a teenage punk rock four-piece by the name of Freak Baby which also featured guitarist Bryant Mason, drummer Dave Smith, and vocalist Chris Page.

Grohl and Samuels connected over their love of hardcore bands and the young guitarist soon convinced Samuels to let him join them on an upcoming band practice session. Rehearsals with the fifth member went well, the band enjoying the fuller sound that a second guitarist provided. Freak Baby was now a five-piece band although during the rehearsals they did quickly realize there was a small issue in that there were now two members of the band named Dave. To avoid any confusion Dave Grohl decided to go by the portmanteau 'Grave' in future, whilst Dave Smith similarly would be referred to as 'Smave'.

By late 1984 the band was as rehearsed as five teenagers could be and with a handful of songs in their repertoire they wanted to do what all aspiring bands do – record their first demo. The teenagers couldn't afford time in a large, professional studio but luckily for them, the brother of vocalist Chris Page was friends with a local musician who also recorded bands in his home-cum-recording space, Laundry Room Studio. Barrett Jones was himself only 18 but had just started experimenting with recording and had set up a studio of sorts in the basement of the Jones family home, the laundry room acting as a control room – hence the name. Freak Baby arrived at the studio on November 11th, 1984 and over the course of just one working day the band put eight of their best songs to tape, thus forming their first demo. The recording session was not without issue, Barrett Jones noting that the young band was still learning their craft - drummer Dave Smith, in particular, was struggling with the fast-pasted hardcore style drum work the songs called for. "They had the passion but needed some practice," said Jones. The young producer (a title he never attributed to himself until over a decade later) also noticed during recording that one member of the band was "way too hyper, bouncing off the walls, knocking stuff over" – that member was, unsurprisingly, Dave Grohl. Equipment was naturally lo-fi for the session, the band having to make do with just the four tracks on Jones Tascam 34 reel-to-reel tape machine, recorded onto ¼ inch magnetic tape. By this point, Grohl had upgraded from his Silvertone to a Memphis 'Les Paul style' guitar.

The group quickly dubbed cassette copies of the demo and created home-made J-card inserts in true punk rock DIY style, even convincing D.C. area music store 'Smash!' to sell the cassettes. Copies of this demo tape do not currently circulate widely in the present day.

Early 1985
Laundry Room Studio, Arlington, VA, United States

Mission Impossible

Grohl, Dave (Drums)   Page, Chris (Vocals)

Mason, Bryant (Guitar)   Smith, Dave (Bass)

Recording Credits

Jones, Barrett (Engineer & Recording)

Tracks Recorded

1. Mission Impossible Theme
2. Different
3. Love in The Back of My Mind
4. C.H.U.D
5. No Words
6. Butch Thrasher
7. Dead You Fool
8. Band Aid Theme
9. To Err is Human
10. 20/20 Hindsight
11. New Ideas
12. Life Already Drawn

Recording Equipment

Tascam 34 ¼ Inch 4-Track Reel-to-reel tape machine

Peavey 12-channel Mixing Console

With their first demo in the bank, Freak Baby continued as a band into the tail end of 1984, Dave Grohl still in his position as the second guitarist. It was a position he was enjoying, but in his heart, he knew there was somewhere else he'd rather be – with sticks in his hands, sitting behind the drumkit.

As had been the case with guitar, Grohl received little in the way of professional instruction to play the drums. At his first (and only) lesson, his tutor informed him he had gone wrong with the absolute basics – how to hold the sticks. His supposed incorrect technique was something he adopted whilst playing on the rather unconventional 'drum kit' he'd set up in his bedroom. "The house was pretty small, so we didn't have room to put a drum set anywhere, and I didn't have enough money to get a drum set for myself," Grohl recalled of the setup. "But I knew the configuration of a drum set, so I'd set up a pillow between my leg as a snare drum and I'd use my bed as a tom and a chair as a high hat, and I'd just play along with the records all day long, 'til there was sweat dripping from my windows." Unwilling to pay vast amounts of money to re-learn the 'correct' way to do everything, he instead carried on playing his own way.

Itching to make the instrument switch during one band rehearsal Grohl plucked up the courage to ask if he could try out on the drums. Ordinarily, this might have caused problems in a band but the then-current drummer, Dave Smith, only really got the position by virtue of the simple fact he owned a drum kit. His real talents, he believed, was with a bass guitar. Original bassist Brian Samuels had gone home during this particular rehearsal session and so Grohl jumped behind the drum kit, Smith grabbed the bass guitar and they started to jam.

The four were happy with how the re-jigged band was sounding which meant Brian Samuels had been effectively kicked out of the band. With a new lineup they decided they also needed a new name – Mission Impossible.

In early 1985 the band once again headed to Barrett Jones' Laundry Room Studio, happy with the unique lo-fi sound the studio produced on their earlier visit. Four of the songs recorded a few months earlier as Freak Baby were re-recorded with the new line-up - 'Different', 'C.H.U.D', 'Dead You Fool' and '20/20 Hindsight' as well as seven new original songs. Jones was impressed with the new look band, noticing a clear improvement from just a few months earlier. In particular, he was again drawn to the "still really hyper" Grohl. Now behind the drum kit, Jones noted that he had "never seen a drummer play so hard, fast and precise before. It was insane. He could focus that [hyper] energy on bashing the drums."

Also recorded during the session was a cover of their new namesake – the theme music to the TV show Mission Impossible. Equipment at the Laundry Room remained the same as the previous Freak Baby session, using a 4-track Reel-to-reel recorder onto ¼ Inch magnetic tape.

New song 'Life Already Drawn' was featured on a 77KK Records 12" album, a hardcore/punk rock compilation which featured one side of French artists, the other side American artists. Released in 1985, it is the first widely available commercial release to contain a recording featuring Dave Grohl.

April 1985
Laundry Room Studio, Arlington, VA, United States

Mission Impossible

Grohl, Dave (Drums)   Page, Chris (Vocals)

Mason, Bryant (Guitar)   Smith, Dave (Bass)

Recording Credits
Jones, Barrett (Engineer & Recording)

Tracks Recorded

1. Stand   6. Into Your Shell

2. Aware of It   7. I Can Only Try

3. Helpless   8. Paradoxic Sense

4. Immortality   9. Now I'm Alone

5. Wonderful World

Recording Equipment
Tascam 34 ¼ Inch 4-Track Reel-to-reel tape machine

Peavey 12-channel Mixing Console

Just a few months after their first visit to Laundry Room Studio in their new guise as Mission Impossible, the band were once again back there in April of 1985 to record further new material, working towards their ultimate goal of releasing a full-length LP. With eleven original songs recorded on their previous visit, on this occasion, another nine were put to tape, showcasing if nothing else their ability to write songs at a consistent rate as well as the ability to record them exceptionally quickly.

By the mid-eighties, the hardcore punk scene in and around Washington, D.C was thriving, with dozens of up and coming young punk bands appearing on the circuit alongside more established names such as Fugazi and Minor Threat. One such band was Lünch Meat, which like Mission Impossible was formed by high school friends and the two bands played a handful of shows together in the local area during the spring of 1985. Despite having well over a dozen songs now recorded in a studio the band elected against releasing a full-length LP at this stage and instead contributed just three songs to a split 7″ with their new friends in Lünch Meat. Released on the Sammich Records label, a subsidiary of the legendary Dischord Records, the 'Thanks' EP was pressed to vinyl with a run of 500, a relatively large number for such unknown bands. The three featured tracks from Mission Impossible were 'Helpless', 'Into Your Shell' and 'Now I'm Alone'.

The band also managed to get themselves featured on a compilation LP released jointly by WGNS Recordings and Metrozine, a local punk rock zine. Appearing alongside bands such as Gray Matter and United Mutation the band contributed one track from this recording session, 'I Can Only Try'. The record was mastered by Don Zientara, owner of the Inner Ear Studios in D.C., with 1,000 copies being pressed.

By 1986 copies of the 'Thanks' EP had all been distributed and so a second run was pressed with a new, somewhat less catchy title – 'Getting Shit for Growing Up Different'. 1,000 copies were pressed this time although again it was not long before all copies had been shifted.

The other five tracks from this recording session were never released although tapes of the entire session were widely circulated by the band in the local area. The session was recorded onto ¼ inch magnetic tape using Laundry Room's trusty Tascam 38 reel-to-reel tape machine.

* * *

January 1986
Laundry Room Studio, Arlington, VA, United States

Dain Bramage
Grohl, Dave (Drums)   Smith, Dave (Bass)

Radding, Reuben (Guitar, Vocals)

Recording Credits
Jones, Barrett (Engineer & Recording)

Tracks Recorded
1. In the Dark   4. Space Cat

2. Watching It Bake   5. Bend

3. Cheyenne

Recording Equipment
Tascam 34 ¼ Inch 4-Track Reel-to-reel tape machine

Peavey 12-channel Mixing Console

Mission Impossible continued playing together until the end of the High School year, summer 1985. Guitarist Bryant Mason and vocalist Chris Page both graduated but drummer Dave Grohl and bassist Dave Smith had already dropped out. With Mason and Page headed off to college Mission Impossible were effectively disbanded, leaving the two dropouts in musical limbo.

"Enter Rueben Radding" recalled Grohl. Radding was the bass player for another local punk band, Age of Consent, which had also recently disbanded. The trio headed to

Grohl's house one evening "smoked a whole bunch of pot, wrote four songs and Dain Bramage was born".

In this new band Grohl remained behind the drum kit, Dave Smith on bass and Reuben took on the traditional frontman role, guitar and vocals. Grohl was very impressed with the speed at which the trio was able to write new songs, and how he himself was growing as a songwriter - "We started writing song after song at an alarming pace. I really started to utilize my growing interest in songwriting: arrangement, dynamics, different tunings. We were experimenting with classic rock clichés in a noisy, punk rock kind of way," said Grohl of the bands early days.

With a small collection of songs under their belt, the band wasted no time in heading to a recording studio. For Grohl, the choice was obvious – "Like every other band I'd been in, we eventually recorded a few demos with Barrett."

By early 1986 Jones had moved out of his parents' house into a new place in Arlington, taking the recording equipment from the laundry room with him. Whilst the studio operation was no longer based in the laundry room at the new house (The bands would play in the living room and the control room was in a large closet) Jones had retained the Laundry Room name.

Five tracks were recorded in this first Dain Bramage recording session via Jones 4-Track Reel-to-reel recorder onto ¼-Inch tape. The master reels are currently in the possession of bassist Dave Smith whilst a recording from a dubbed cassette circulates among fans.

May 1986
Laundry Room Studio, Arlington, VA, United States

Dain Bramage

Grohl, Dave (Drums) Smith, Dave (Bass)

Radding, Reuben (Guitar, Vocals)

Recording Credits

Jones, Barrett (Engineer & Recording)

Tracks Recorded

1. Flannery
2. Give It Up
3. The Log
4. Eyes Open
5. Home Sweet Nowhere

6. We're An American Band
7. ...And There's A...
8. Success
9. Baltimore Sucks (But Booje Needs The Bucks)

Recording Equipment

Tascam 34 ¼ Inch 4-Track Reel-to-reel tape machine

Peavey 12-channel Mixing Console

Dain Bramage made another visit to Barrett Jones' Laundry Room Studio circa May 1986 to record a second set of demos. Nine tracks were recorded in total at this second session and whilst some tapes were spread and circulated at the time no complete copies are known to exist and circulate today. The ¼ Inch Master reels of the session are in the possession of Dave Smith.

July 20ᵗʰ to 24ᵗʰ, 1986
RK-1 Recording Studio, Crofton, MD, United States

Dain Bramage

Grohl, Dave (Drums)   Smith, Dave (Bass)

Radding, Reuben (Guitar, Vocals)

Recording Credits

Copeland, E.L. (Engineer)

Kozak, Dan (Producer)

Radding, Reuben (Producer)

Tracks Recorded

1. The Log   6. Flannery

2. I Scream Not Coming Down   7. Stubble

3. Eyes Open   8. Flicker

4. Swear   9. Give It Up

5. Drag Queen   10. Home Sweet Nowhere

By mid-1986 Dain Bramage were starting to make a name for themselves in the Washington D.C. hardcore punk scene. Their two demos recorded earlier in the year were widely shared among scenesters with the band also playing as many live shows as they could to further their reputation. One of those shows was at the 9:30 Club, a legendary venue in downtown D.C. After completing soundcheck for their performance Dain Bramage drummer Grohl was approached by Reed Mullin, a fellow drummer for heavy metal band Corrosion of Conformity. C.O.C. was already a well-established band in the North East of the United States with two full-length albums under their belt. The drummer was impressed by Dain Bramage and caught Grohl somewhat by surprise when he asked if they wanted to put out an album of their own.

Mullin was friends with the owner of a Maryland independent record label, Fartblossom Enterprizes, and assured Grohl and the rest of the band that he could hook them up so they could make their album. "Flattered beyond belief" Dain Bramage booked into RK-1 Recording Studios in Crofton, Maryland to complete recording. Frontman Reuben Radding had convinced the band to use what he believed was a real professional studio, instead of their usual jaunt to Barrett Jones more homely Laundry Room Studio but upon their arrival, Radding and the rest of the band soon realized they perhaps hadn't made the best decision. The 'professional' studio turned out to be nothing more than a soundproofed garage but nevertheless, they set up their gear and recording began. Just a few hours into recording on the first day the band ran into another issue - the local police turned up after noise complaints from a neighbor. That was soon followed by a power cut across the whole area, bringing the recording to a complete halt.

Power was restored by the next day, but the recording didn't get any easier - "The next day's dubbing/mixing session turned into an all-nighter. Little things seemed to take forever to accomplish," explained Radding.

Engineer for the session R.L. Copeland had similar recollections - "It was probably the worst first weekend of recording I've ever had in my life." He did, however, have a lot of praise for the band - "[They] were extremely organized and we quickly caught up. There wasn't a lot of fiddling around or double-takes, it was just boom! We blazed through the songs and it was over." He was also specifically impressed by the band's drummer, noting that he'd never seen someone "beat the living piss out of a drumkit" the way Dave Grohl did.

Over the course of five days (or rather four and a half after the interrupted first day), ten tracks were recorded with producer Dan Kozak. A number of these songs had been demoed by the band previously, whilst others were brand new, including 'I Scream Not Coming Down', which producer Kozak helped with on the writing process.

Engineer Copeland also mixed the ten songs and the album saw release by Fartblossom Enterprizes on February 28th, 1987. Pressed on 12" Vinyl, it was sold across the country for $6.

In 2010 Grohl attended a 30th Anniversary show at the 9:30 club and recalled the show which gave he and Dain Bramage the opportunity to record their first proper album. "He [Reed Mullin] hooked us up with a guy who had a record label called Fart Blossom and I made my first album. So, thank you very much 9:30 club!" said Grohl.

1987
Lion And Fox Studios, Washington D.C., United States

Scream

Grohl, Dave (Drums, Percussion, Backing Vocals)

Stahl, Pete (Vocals, Piano & Tambourine)

Lee Davidson, Robert (Guitar)

Thompson, Skeeter (Bass Guitar)

Stahl, Franz (Guitar)

Additional Musicians

Dr. Dread (Backing Vocals)

Pickering, Amy (Backing Vocals)

Lagdameo, Eric (Keyboards)

Zientara, Don (Backing Vocals)

Pea, Joey (Backing Vocals)

Recording Credits

Dr. Dread (Producer)

Joey Pea (Producer)

Fox, Jim (Engineer, Producer)

Scream (Producers)

Tracks Recorded

1. Hit Me

7. Something In My Head

2. No More Censorship

8. It's The Time

3. Fucked Without A Kiss

9. Binge

4. No Escape

10. Run to the Sun

5. Building Dreams

11. In The Beginning

6. Take It From The Top

Early 1987. Around a year after recording his first full-length album with Dain Bramage   a 17-year-old Dave Grohl is shopping for new drumsticks at a Virginia music store. As he was leaving the store, Grohl noticed an inconspicuous looking flyer by the door. It read simply "Scream looking for drummer, call Franz."

Scream was, as Grohl described, "Legendary in D.C." The band formed in 1981 during the explosion of the hardcore music scene in the area and had established themselves as one of the top acts. He'd seen the band live several times and considered their first two records as among his absolute favorites. It was safe to say Grohl was a fan of the band, and the teenager initially saw their vacant drummer position as an opportunity to simply play with his heroes. At just 17 years of age, he didn't initially consider he could actually fill the role full time, but he would be able to tell his friends "I got to play with Scream!" Grohl called the number on the flyer, explaining to Franz that he was a huge fan and that he wanted to "give it a shot". When asked his age Grohl decided to tell a white lie, adding three years to his true age in an attempt to improve his chances. The phone call ended, and Dave crossed his fingers.

Some months passed by with no further contact from Stahl, so Grohl took the initiative and called him again - "This time I convinced him to give me an hour or two of his time and scheduled an audition." At the audition, Grohl surprised the band by turning down the suggestion to play some classic rock covers and instead wanted to jump straight into the Scream back catalog. "Seeing as how Scream records were among those I used to play drums to on my bed when I was first learning, I knew all their songs by heart" he recalled. "I even had an advance copy of their latest demo."

The members of Scream were suitably impressed. More practice sessions soon followed, and it soon dawned on Grohl that things had gone way further than just something to brag about to his friends. "[It] was something that never entered my mind, the possibility of actually joining Scream." It left him with a choice to make - "Leave my two greatest friends in the dust and travel the world with one of my favorite bands ever. Or stick with Dain Bramage and hope it all works out."

Initially, Grohl decided to stay loyal to his friends, calling Franz and explaining his predicament. Then came a change of heart. "I think he understood and invited me to their next show a few weeks later," explained Grohl. "It was one of the greatest Scream shows I'd ever seen. I changed my mind."

Shortly after joining the band they left the well-known Dischord label and were signed up by Ras Records, a reggae label trying to break into the rock and hardcore market. In mid-1987 the band was thrown into a professional 24-track studio with a reggae producer to record what would become their fourth studio album.

The studio in question was Lion and Fox Recording Studios in Washington D.C., a completely different world in comparison to Barrett Jones' Laundry Room or the converted garage in Maryland. The studio had a generously large live tracking room, professionally installed sound dampening and everything else one would expect from a top-of-the-line studio.

The main creative force behind Scream were Franz and Pete Stahl, the brothers who founded the band, but during recording Grohl was also invited to give his input, far more involved than any of his previous bands. As well as playing drums on all songs, Grohl also helped on the arrangement of the song 'Fucked Without A Kiss' and was the sole writer on the track 'In The Beginning'. It may have only been 45 seconds of music, but it was a clear sign of Grohl's talents and a sign of what was to come. Another first during this recording session was his contribution of backing vocals to all tracks, marking the first time his vocals would be featured on a commercial release.

'No More Censorship' saw release in August 1988 on vinyl, cassette, and CD. In 2017 the album was reissued, having been remixed and remastered by the Stahl brothers.

* * *

October 1988
Laundry Room Studio, Arlington, VA, United States

Recording Artist
Grohl, Dave (Drums, Guitar, Bass, Vocals)

Recording Credits
Jones, Barrett (Engineer & Recording)

Tracks Recorded
1. Gods Look Down

Recording Equipment
Tascam 38 ½ Inch 8 Track Reel-to-reel tape recorder

Carvin MX2488 Mixing Desk

Throughout 1988 Dave Grohl was busy touring with Scream, including his first visit to Europe, but whenever the tour dates let up, he would return home to Virginia. Whilst his most recent musical adventures had taken him elsewhere Grohl had remained friends with local studio owner Barrett Jones and would find himself visiting more and more often in his downtime. Earlier in the year, Jones had relocated his Laundry Room Studio for the third time, now situated in the basement of a house on Upland Street in the city.

Dave would help Barrett with his solo project in the studio "sometimes [playing] bass or guitar on some songs" but with his creative input in Scream growing and being eager to write more of his own material he had a brainwave.

"That summer I realized that if I were to write a song,

record the drums first, then come back over it with a few guitars, bass, and vocals, I could make it sound like a band. So, I came up with a few riffs on the spot and recorded three songs in under 15 minutes." Excited by the possibilities Grohl started writing more material. Some of the ideas would be taken to his Scream bandmates, whilst others would be "hidden away for later use". During downtime in early October 1988, in the middle of a European tour, Grohl asked Barrett if he could record one of his newly written songs, which his friend duly obliged, finding space on one of his tape reels. 'Gods Look Down' is a song that would be later recorded with Scream, but this first version was all Grohl.

Grohl stuck to his initial idea of recording the drum track for the song first, his natural rhythm and timing impressing Jones. "[He] didn't use a click track at all. [He] was good at that." The guitar tracks were added next, with a clean, melodic track and a more dirty, rough track - both running through a Marshall amplifier. A simple bass track was added and then the final step – singing. Whilst he'd recorded backing vocals during recording for his first album with Scream and experimented privately, this would be the first time he'd properly record lead vocals on a song.

The vocals on the recording were double tracked with Grohl later remarking that he sounded "like a girl," joking that his "balls hadn't dropped yet." Barrett described this version of the song as "incredible" and "very raw", noting that whilst he was perhaps a little biased, he preferred this version to the later Scream recording. It wasn't perfect, but the pair knew they worked well together, with Grohl describing it as "the beginning of a beautiful friendship."

October 1989
Laundry Room Studio, Arlington, VA, United States

Dain Bramage
Grohl, Dave (Drums, Guitar, Bass)

Recording Credits
Jones, Barrett (Engineer & Recording)

Tracks Recorded
1. Linus And Lucy

Recording Equipment
Tascam 38 ½ Inch 8 Track Reel-to-reel tape recorder

Carvin MX2488 Mixing Desk

Dave Grohl would continue touring hard with Scream through 1989, returning home whenever possible to take a breather, often also dropping by Laundry Room Studio. As well as recording their own original material Grohl and Jones would occasionally come up with suggestions of songs to cover, just for fun. One such recording in October 1989 was what Jones describes as a "rock version" of the Vince Guaraldi track 'Linus And Lucy'. The original was first released by Guaraldi in 1965 with his band the Vince Guaraldi Trio but is perhaps better known after featuring in many Peanuts cartoons, such as a Charlie Brown Christmas. Grohl and Jones' version recorded at this time has never been released although Foo Fighters did cover the song many years later, during an appearance on the show Saturday Night Live in 2017.

December 17th to 19th, 1989
Inner Ear Studio, Washington D.C., United States

Scream

Grohl, Dave (Drums)   Stahl, Pete (Vocals)

Stahl, Franz (Guitar)   Thompson, Skeeter (Bass Guitar)

Recording Credits

Janney, Eli (Producer & Mixing)   Stahl, Pete (Producer & Mixing)

Stahl, Franz (Mixing)   Picuri, Joey (Producer)

Tracks Recorded

1. Caffeine Dream   6. Crackman

2. Sunmaker   7. Gas

3. Mardis Gras   8. Dying Days

4. Land Torn Down   9. Poppa Says

5. Gods Look Down   10. Rain

Recording Equipment

Fostex B-16 ½ inch 16-track tape recorders

Mixed down to Tascam 2 track

Before recording their fourth studio album 'No More Censorship' Scream had parted ways with local indie giants Dischord and signed with major label RAS Records. The move didn't go down well with many fans who felt the band were 'betraying' their punk roots. An album was produced, and the band toured in support of it, but as it turned out it wasn't just the fans not happy with the move.

"We'd always been really upset with the record itself, with the production and everything – we never really liked it," later admitted Franz Stahl. The band liked the songs, but not how they had turned out, partly as a result of working with an unfamiliar, reggae producer.

For their next album, the band ditched RAS and headed to more familiar territory. Scream booked into Inner Ear Studio in Arlington, the studio of choice for hundreds of Washington punk bands in the 1980s. Founded and operated by Don Zientara the studio was seen as one of the go-to places for recording in the D.C. area.

The band arrived in late December 1989 with a bevy of new songs to record, one of them being Dave Grohl's new track 'Gods Look Down'. Grohl had played the song for his band mates shortly after recording and to his surprise they were keen to use it on the new album.

Rather than passing vocal duties onto frontman Pete Stahl, the band encouraged Grohl to remain as the lead vocal on the song, marking the first time he'd ever done so in a band. The track remained largely the same as Grohl's demo version, the main difference being more guitar layers and his vocals were also slightly more refined with an extra layer of confidence, having received praise from the men he still considered his peers.

The band managed to record ten tracks over the space of three days, utilizing the studios Fostex-B16 ½ inch 16 track tape recorder, mixed down to a Tascam 2-track reel.

With recording complete, the band headed back out onto the road but a series of events in the first half of 1990 would lead to the demise of the band. Following a European leg in the Spring they returned home to find an eviction notice in

Pete and Skeeter Thompson's mailbox.

With the prospect of having nowhere to live they decided the best course of action was to get back on the road, living out of their trusty tour van. Another leg of the tour was booked across the summer but according to Grohl, more issues would ensue. "[We were] plagued with cancellations and low attendance. Something had to give". That something would be bassist Thompson, who went MIA halfway through the tour.

Scream looked for a new bassist but with nobody found, Dave Grohl would also soon make the tough decision to leave the band when offered the vacant drummer position with Nirvana. With half of their band gone and other issues surrounding them, the Stahl brothers were forced to officially disband Scream, leaving what had been recorded at Inner Ear in limbo. It would be almost three years until the Stahl's would be able to put the finishing touches on the record and get it released with 'Fumble' put out in 1993 via Dischord, featuring all the songs recorded during this session. The track 'Crackman' featured only on the 12" Vinyl release, however.

* * *

April 1990
Laundry Room Studio, Arlington, VA, United States

Harlingtox A.D.

Grohl, Dave (Bass Guitar, Guitar, Drums)

Nieuwenhuizen, Tos (Guitar, Bass)

Jones, Barrett (Drums)

Merkle, Bruce (Vocals)

Recording Credits

Harlingtox A.D. (Producers)

Jones, Barrett (Engineer & Recording)

Tracks Recorded

1. Treason Daddy Brother In Crime Real Patriotic Type Stuff

2. Orbiting Prisons In Space

3. Recycled Children Never To Be Grown

4. Obtaining A Bachelors Degree

5. Open Straightedge Arms

Recording Equipment

Tascam 38 ½ Inch 8-Track Reel-To-Reel Tape Machine

Carvin MX2488 24-Channel Mixer

Before heading out on what would be the final Scream tour in North America Dave Grohl would continue his regular visits to friend Barrett Jones at his Laundry Room Studio in Arlington. When he wasn't helping Jones with his band Churn or recording his own songs, the pair would experiment musically, merely for their own amusement. On this occasion, in April 1990, Grohl and Jones were joined in the studio by friend Tos Niewenhuizen, a Dutchman who had recorded backing vocals with Scream in 1986 and had also been touring alongside the band more recently, with his own band 'God'.

The trio recorded five instrumental songs which Jones would later describe as "intricate, risk-oriented and heavy." Owing to the experimental nature of the session (and the multi-instrument talents of the musicians), recording duties were split. Grohl recorded guitar, bass, and drums on one track, guitar on another and bass on the other three. Nieuwenhuizen tracked guitar on all five as well as bass on one. Finally, Barrett Jones drummed on four of the tracks.

A few years prior to recording Dave Grohl had met Bruce Merkle, singer of the band 9353. Despite forming in Washington D.C. during the hardcore heyday 9353 were somewhat different, with a sound that many at the time would describe as "love or hate". Grohl was seemingly in the former camp, and at some point, the pair had agreed to work together on a future project.

It was decided Bruce would be perfect to add his unique vocal style to these recordings and so he was tracked down and he agreed to give it a go. Merkle borrowed the master tapes of the instrumental recordings and went away to craft some lyrics, visiting Laundry Room Studio approximately a month later to track them. "[They] are what you latch on to," said Jones of the vocal additions to the tracks. "Lyrically it's really intense. It's been described as grindcore meets Zappa, but I see it more, musically at least, Melvins-y and heavy."

With Merkle's vocals added to the tracks, Barrett Jones began considering a public release of the experimental project. " I always wanted to, because I always liked it a lot." It would, however, be a further six years before he could make that happen, with the creation of his own independent record label, 'Laundry Room Records'.

The tracks were given a final mix by Dan Kozak at Squeaky Wheel Studio in College Park, Maryland and released on CD in 1996 as 'Harlingtox A.D.', a name conceived by Merkle.

* * *

October to December 1990
114 North Pear Street, Olympia, WA, United States

Recording Artist
Grohl, Dave (Acoustic Guitar, Vocals)

Tracks Recorded
1. Friend Of A Friend

2. Color Pictures of a Marigold

Recording Equipment
Tascam Portastudio One 4-Track tape recorder

The 1990s began for Dave Grohl with what would be a life-changing decision, choosing to leave behind the imploding Scream to join grunge rockers Nirvana. With just a few personal belongings and his drum kit in tow, he headed across the country and joined up with his new band-mates in Washington state. Dave was given little time to get settled, with the band soon heading across the Atlantic for a two-week tour of the United Kingdom.

After playing half a dozen shows the band returned home at the end of October. Without enough money to afford a place of his own, Grohl moved in with Kurt Cobain at his Olympia apartment. Just one further Nirvana show was booked for the rest of the year and with no friends in the area, life in the apartment in these months was tough.

"The apartment was a mess the majority of the time, and not knowing Kurt that well-made things uncomfortable, and also quite boring," Grohl would later recall. "There was a lot of time just spent sitting in the room totally silent reading or doing nothing, staring at the walls."

Following his trek across the country Barrett Jones' Laundry Room Studio was now almost 3,000 miles away, meaning regular visits to see his friend and record music were a thing of the past, for the time being at least. Thankfully for Grohl among the corn dog sticks and endless cigarette butts in the apartment was an acoustic guitar, as well as a 4-Track Tascam tape recorder that Kurt owned, giving him at least a limited option to record any new ideas. Two songs were written and recorded whilst he was at the apartment. The first of the two, 'Friend of A Friend', was penned as an observation about his two new band-mates. Apprehensive about what Kurt would think of the song, he recorded it late at night, whilst his roommate was sleeping.

"That was the first song I ever wrote on acoustic guitar," Grohl remembered. "There was just a TV and a few worn-out records, so I would sit up at night on this couch that I slept on and write music." The second track, 'Color Pictures of a Marigold', was recorded in similar secrecy, or so Grohl thought. "I just did a guitar track and some layered vocals, and Kurt was in his bedroom on the other side of the wall. I thought he was sleeping, and I was trying to be as quiet as possible," he recalled. "He came in while I was listening back really, really quietly and said, 'what is that?!' And I said, 'Oh, just something I just recorded.' He [was] like, 'Whoa, show me the guitar thing, show that to me.' We used to kind of jam on it in the living room. That was probably the first time I ever thought, 'Wow, maybe I can write songs.'"

Both songs would be re-recorded and released in several forms in later years, but neither of these original recordings has been heard by the general public.

December 19th, 1990
Laundry Room Studio, Arlington, VA, United States

Recording Artist

Grohl, Dave (Drums, Guitar, Bass Guitar, Vocals)

Jones, Barrett (Guitar, Backing Vocals)

Recording Credits

Jones, Barrett (Engineer & Recording)

Tracks Recorded

1. Throwing Needles

2. Friend Of A Friend

3. Pokey The Little Puppy

4. Just Another Story About Skeeter Thompson

5. Hooker

Recording Equipment

Tascam 38 ½ Inch 8-Track Reel-to-reel Tape Machine

Carvin MX2488 24-Channel Mixer

With no Nirvana shows booked across the festive period in 1990 Dave Grohl chose to fly home to Virginia, spending Christmas with his family. Whilst in the area he would take the opportunity to catch up with Barrett Jones at his Laundry Room Studio. Armed with new songs, including those recently penned and recorded in the Olympia apartment, Grohl arrived at the studio on December 19th, which was still set up in the basement of Jones' Arlington house.

Since first meeting approximately six years earlier Grohl and Jones had become good friends, working together on several projects and helping each other with their solo projects. During this time, the pair had developed a working process which meant they could record at an impressive speed. With amps and microphones quickly set up, Grohl would begin by laying down a drum track, then "listen to playback while humming [the] tune in [my] head to make sure [the] arrangement is correct." Next would come the guitar, with two or three unique tracks recorded dependent on the song. His weakest instrument, Bass Guitar, was left for last and only once instrumentals were recorded for all songs would he add vocals, if at all.

Following this method, nine songs were recorded by the duo over the course of just a single day – four of Grohl's, four of Jones' and the ninth a collaboration between the two. Tracked first were three Dave Grohl penned tracks - 'Throwing Needles', 'Friend of A Friend' and 'Pokey the Little Puppy'. 'Friend of A Friend' was written about Dave's first few months with new Nirvana bandmates Krist Novoselic and Kurt Cobain, the latter of whom he'd been living with the past two months.

"I probably have to talk about that song the most because everybody tries to make some sort of correlation to Nirvana out of almost every song I write," said Grohl in a 2008 interview. "I just tell them that there are lots of people in this world that I love and hate, not just two. But that song is about Kurt, Krist and me, and it was written that way. They were strangers. I had just joined that band and didn't know them at all."

Next onto the reel was one of Jones' tracks, 'Living on Command', for which Grohl recorded the drum track. Track five of the day was the final Dave effort. 'Just Another Story About Skeeter Thompson' featured a heavy metal style backing track over which he would recite a story about Skeeter Thompson, the bassist of Grohl's previous band Scream. The focus moved back to Jones music for the song 'For The Record' after which the pair decided to have some fun.

In the recording of 'Hooker' the pair first laid down a simple, funky instrumental and then when it came to the vocals Dave imitated the style of several high-profile singers - Perry Farrell of Janes Addiction, James Brown, Ian Astbury of the Cult and Neil Young. When airing the song on Seattle radio in 1994 Barrett Jones played along with the idea that all of the singers had been at the studio recording on the track, having been in town for a convention. The truth was of course that Dave just enjoyed mimicking the performers in a throwaway track neither really intended for anyone to hear. The lyrics, according to Jones, were all about "the evils of sex". The recording session was rounded out with two further Jones penned tracks, 'Be (Bad)' and 'Heal the Savior'.

At one point during the day Jenny Toomey (local musician and co-founder of the 'Simple Machines' record label) visited the studio and heard the music Grohl had recorded. "I thought it was great," said Toomey. As it happened Simple Machines were planning to release a cassette series focusing on music that was unfinished and rough around the edges, or by bands no longer performing. For Toomey, it made perfect sense to ask Dave to add his solo recordings to the series. Grohl was initially hesitant, apprehensive about people other than his close friends hearing his music, still shy about his voice.

"I hassled him for a tape. About six months later, he gave me one when I was visiting in Olympia," recalled Toomey. Having been worn down the tape he gave to Toomey featured his four original songs from this session, but not 'Hooker'. The songs (along with six others recorded at later sessions, detailed on the following pages) were released as 'Pocketwatch' under the pseudonym 'Late!. The 'Late!' name was something of a joke from Grohl, envisioning naming a band 'Late' so that when they played live shows he could walk on stage and say "Hi, we're late!"

The cassette was released in 1992 through the Simple Machines mail order service at a cost of $4 but very quickly demand was far outweighing the speed at which tapes could be produced, as word quickly spread about a solo release from "The drummer in Nirvana".

A few years after releasing the cassette it was still causing Simple Machines grief according to Toomey. "It's sort of been a thorn in our side. Each mention of the cassette in Rolling Stone or wherever translates to piles of mail, and for the most part, these kids have never bought anything through the mail from an independent record company," explained the label owner. "So when they haven't received their tape in two weeks they write us nasty notes about how we've stolen their $5 and their mothers are going to sue us," she recalled of the ongoing heavy demand for the tape.

Simple Machines did hope to get upgraded copies of the recordings from Grohl and release them on CD, along with bonus tracks, but it was not to be. "He went back and forth with the idea and then it fell off the face of the earth," Toomey said of the plans. "I think he's worried about the quality. Which I can understand and appreciate, but his modesty is killing us! I know he also thinks it's cooler to have it this way. Which it definitely is. But it's been a mixed bag as our cassette masters degenerate. It's really only a matter of time until the cassette gets removed from the catalog" said Toomey in 1997. An upgrade or re-release never materialized, and the cassette did indeed get removed from their catalog soon after.

The 'Pocketwatch' cassette is now long out of print and genuine copies are commonly sold on auction websites such as eBay for prices in excess of $200, making it one of the most expensive and sought after Grohl releases amongst fans.

* * *

February 16th, 1991
Laundry Room Studio, Arlington, VA, United States

Recording Artist
Grohl, Dave (Drums, Guitar, Bass Guitar, Vocals)

Jones, Barrett (Backing Vocals)

Recording Credits
Jones, Barrett (Engineer & Recording)

Tracks Recorded
1. Color Pictures Of a Marigold

2. Petrol CB

3. Kids In America

Recording Equipment
Tascam 38 ½ Inch 8-Track Reel-to-reel Tape Machine

Carvin MX2488 24-Channel Mixer

With another brief break in Nirvana tour dates, February 1991 saw Dave Grohl once again heading home to Virginia and Barrett Jones' Laundry Room Studio. With the help of Jones, three songs were recorded in a single day.

First to be recorded was 'Color Pictures of a Marigold', a song that Grohl had written and first demoed in Kurt Cobain's Olympia apartment a few months earlier. That initial recording featured only acoustic guitar and whilst now having the opportunity to further the song, he elected to keep it as a simple acoustic + vocals arrangement. Jones had, in fact, labeled it as 'Nice sweet acoustic song' on the tape reel box before Grohl had made him aware of the final title.

The second song to be tracked was another new song written by Grohl which would later be known as 'Petrol CB', but at the time of recording it was known rather vaguely as 'That Song'. As was now commonplace for Grohl all instruments for the track were recorded by himself, although Jones did add backing vocals.

Finally, the pair decided to let off some steam and recorded a cover of the Kim Wilde classic 'Kids In America'. The recording once again featured Grohl on all instruments with Jones on backing vocals. Towards the end of the song, a tambourine and bar chime feature, the pair having fun experimenting with different instruments.

The two original tracks were, along with eight others, given by Grohl to Jenny Toomey for her Simple Machines cassette series, although 'Petrol CB' would first see release on the labels 'Neapolitan Metropolitan'. The compilation released in early 1992 brought together songs from artists in Baltimore, Richmond and Washington D.C. with Grohl's contribution, now titled 'There's That Song', featured on the white Washington D.C. record.

Later that year saw the release of 'Late! - Pocketwatch', featuring both 'Color Pictures Of A Marigold' and now correctly titled 'Petrol CB'. The two tracks were however erroneously credited as being recorded at an earlier session in 1990, due to Grohl mixing the two sessions on one cassette given to Jenny Toomey.

Fans became aware of the Kim Wilde cover in the mid-2000s but it wasn't until 2015 that 'Kids In America' was released, featured on the special Record Store Day EP 'Songs From The Laundry Room'.

July 27th, 1991
WGNS Studios, Arlington, VA, United States

Recording Artist
Grohl, Dave (Drums, Guitar, Bass Guitar, Vocals)

Recording Credits
Turner, Geoff (Engineer & Recording)

Tracks Recorded
1. Hell's Garden

2. Winnebago

3. Bruce

4. Milk

Since the first incarnation located in his parent's basement, Barrett Jones' Laundry Room Studio had relocated three times, each being more accommodating for recording than the last. Moving from house to house, each had one thing in common – like the original, all were still located in Arlington, Virginia. In the summer of 1991 Jones decided to up sticks for the fourth time, but this time he was heading further afield, across the country to Seattle, Washington. With Dave Grohl now located on the West coast with Nirvana, and with the grunge movement starting to take off, Barrett decided it was also time to make the move. With no Laundry Room Studio for the time being, Grohl had to find somewhere else to record during his downtime from Nirvana.

Despite there being no shortage of recording locations on the west coast, and off the back of completing recording for the Nirvana album 'Nevermind' at the famous Sound City Studios, Grohl still chose to fly back home to Arlington and booked into another studio in the City.

That local studio was WGNS, although like Jones' Laundry Room it was far from being a bespoke recording studio. WGNS was initially created by owner Geoff Turner due to a lack of underground radio stations in the DC area, the acronym standing for 'We Gots No Station'. As time went on the operation evolved beyond broadcasting and allowed local musicians to record their music.

The studio was set up in a house rented by Turner with most of the equipment located in the basement. Recording took place using a Tascam 58 8-track reel-to-reel tape recorder which used ½ inch magnetic tape.

Dave Grohl arrived at the studio on July 27th, 1991 and with the help of Turner recorded four newly written songs - 'Hell's Garden', 'Winnebago', 'Bruce' and 'Milk'. Grohl once again recorded all the drums, guitar and bass tracks himself, also tracking vocals for all but 'Bruce'. The lyrics for all three songs were written swiftly by Grohl whilst he was at the studio, with Turner being credited for the words to 'Winnebago'. Grohl even saw fit to show his appreciation during the song itself, quickly singing 'Thanks for the lyrics, Geoff!' before the final lengthy instrumental section that closed the track out.

The four songs, along with six others earlier recorded at Laundry Room Studio, were given to Jenny Toomey of Simple Machines and released on the 'Pocketwatch' cassette, under the pseudonym 'Late!', in the summer of 1992.

January 3rd, 1992
Laundry Room Studio, Arlington, VA, United States

Recording Artist

Grohl, Dave (Drums, Guitar, Bass Guitar, Vocals)

Jones, Barrett (Backing Vocals)

Recording Credits

Jones, Barrett (Engineer & Recording)

Tracks Recorded

1. Rent (Jerky Boys)

2. Floaty

3. Alone + Easy Target

4. Empty Handed

Recording Equipment

Tascam 38 ½ Inch 8-Track Reel-to-reel Tape Machine

Carvin MX2488 24-Channel Mixer

Following the release of their album 'Nevermind' in September 1991 Nirvana had seen their popularity go through the roof in an extraordinary story that has since been retold many times. The tail end of 1991 saw the band embark on exhaustive tours in the US and Europe culminating in a New Year's Eve show with Pearl Jam and Red Hot Chili Peppers in California. The band were given New Year's Day off, but the following day saw them playing again in Salem, Oregon, after which they would finally have a week off before they were due to fly out to New York for several TV appearances.

The day after the Salem show Dave Grohl returned home to Seattle and wasted no time in heading to the studio basement in the house he now shared with Barrett Jones. "The explosion of my real band kept me pretty busy for a while, but I always managed to bring along a guitar so that I could write songs to record upon returning home," explained Grohl. "The 8-track studio was in the basement, at our disposal anytime we came up with an idea". Four songs were tracked on this cold January day, starting out with a very short effort given the title 'Rent (Jerky Boys)'. The track was a fast-paced punk song that as well as Grohl's vocals featured overdubbed audio from Jerky Boys, a comedy duo from New York City most well-known for prank phone calls. "We were on tour when that Jerky Boys thing came out. Someone gave us a cassette of it," Grohl said of the unusual addition.

Next came the very first recording of the song 'Floaty'. As with many of Grohl's other songs, this initial version was already fully structured and didn't change significantly in later re-recordings. Vocals were also largely unchanged, the main difference in this first version being rather feminine sounding "Ooh ooh" harmonies on the chorus, not replicated in the later recordings.

'Alone + Easy Target' was the next track put to tape for the first time. Once again, the structure of the song was already fully formed at this stage, and except for a few minor lyrical changes, the song was ultimately the finished article at this stage.

At some point during the day, Dave telephoned Kurt Cobain and mentioned that he was in the studio recording.

Cobain was staying in a nearby Seattle hotel and asked Grohl to bring over a cassette so he could hear the songs. "I went over to his hotel and I played him 'Alone + Easy Target'. He was sitting in the bathtub with a Walkman on, listening to the song, and when the tape ended, he took the headphones off and kissed me!" Grohl remembered of the experience.

Clearly impressed with what he heard Cobain would tell Grohl he was happy to have another songwriter in the band. However, due to modesty from Grohl and apparent nervousness from Cobain to ask about modifying the song, Nirvana would never record 'Alone + Easy Target'. They would, though, play parts of the song during soundchecks on several occasions according to Grohl.

The final song to be recorded on this day was titled 'Empty Handed', a short, frantic punk track that Grohl later described as "an experiment in singing, guitar playing, and recording." Speaking in 2015 Grohl said that many of the songs recorded during this era were "an experiment for fun" and a lot of these experiments, like 'Empty Handed', had been forgotten. When listening to them again for the first time in over twenty years Grohl noted that several songs he had "no recollection of, which is weird. It's almost like seeing a snapshot of yourself, passed-out drunk at a party. You're listening to a song like, 'Oh, my God, what was I thinking?'"

* * *

April 1992
Laundry Room Studio, Seattle, WA, United States

Allister Lob

Dees, Mike (Guitar)

Grohl, Dave (Drums)

Grohl, Lisa (Bass Guitar)

Recording Credits

Jones, Barrett (Engineer & Recording)

Tracks Recorded

1. Podunk

2. Make A Bet

3. I Don't Want Your

4. How I Miss You

5. Watered It Down

Recording Equipment

Tascam 38 ½ Inch 8-Track Reel-to-reel Tape Machine

Carvin MX2488 24-Channel Mixer

As 1992 went on the popularity of Nirvana was showing no signs of slowing off the back of their hit album 'Nevermind'. The band spent the early months of the year touring far and wide, with shows in Australia, New Zealand, Japan and culminated with two performances in Hawaii upon their return to the United States. With those duties fulfilled the band finally had a decent length of time to rest and reflect upon a crazy few months, with their next live shows not set to take place until June. In early April the band headed back into a recording studio, planning to record several songs for upcoming minor releases. Rather than head to another large facility like Sound City, the trio instead opted for something more down to earth.

By this time Barrett Jones had settled in after his move across the country to Seattle, with his Laundry Room now set up in a "little yellow house" in the city that he shared with Dave Grohl. It was upon his recommendation that Nirvana visited twice in April 1992, recording demos and cover tracks. The studio in this house was never really considered an official spot for Laundry Room by Jones, with only two other artists recording there. Buzz Osbourne of The Melvins visited to record tracks that would be released on his King Buzzo EP and the other, also in April of 1992, was a trio by the name of 'Allister Lobb'.

The makeshift band was, in fact, Dave Grohl on drums, his sister Lisa Grohl on Bass Guitar and Mike Dees, most well known as front-man of Washington punk band Fitz Of Depression, on guitar. Grohl and Dees had first met in Olympia, Washington with Nirvana playing on the same bill as Fitz at a handful of shows in early 1991. The pair also jammed together on a few occasions around this time according to Dees, usually at the Fitz Of Depression rehearsal space.

Dave invited the pair to join him at the house to help record yet more new songs he'd penned, with Barrett Jones on hand to record the session. Five songs were put to tape and according to Dees, they were so new that none had been given a title by Grohl. The songs were instead referenced as simply 'Song 1', 'Song 2', and so, on during recording.

Three of the tracks recorded were in actuality early versions of the songs which would later be known to Foo Fighters fans as 'Podunk', 'Make A Bet' and 'How I Miss You'. The songs were already well structured at this early stage with only minor changes made in later recordings. In the case of 'How I Miss You', this is the only occasion on which the song was recorded.

The remaining two songs recorded by the trio would also be unique to this session, although one would bear a passing similarity to the song 'Exhausted'. They were, again at a later date, given the titles 'I Don't Want Your' and 'Watered It Down'.

Mike Dees brought his own equipment to the studio and his 1961 Gibson SG Guitar left a signature mark on the recording of 'How I Miss You'. The guitar had a faulty jack connection and the noise heard at the very end of the song is Dees adjusting the jack to try and keep it connected. For amplification, he brought a 1980s Ampeg SS140C amp as well as a 1980s Mesa Boogie 2x10 Bass Cabinet which according to Dees "had some wicked low end". The Grohl siblings used equipment already present at the house since Dave lived at and stored most of his equipment there.

No vocals were recorded by Grohl during this April session although he would add them during another session at the studio later in the year (November 1992, detailed later in the book).

The vocals from that later session were added to these instrumentals and one track, 'How I Miss You', saw official release. The track was included as a B-Side on the 1995 Foo Fighters single 'I'll Stick Around', although neither Lisa nor Mike were given any credits on the release, something which Dees said did not bother him.

Whilst no other songs from this session have seen official release a tape containing all five instrumentals was shared online in 2004.

The moniker for this one one-off band, Allister Lob, was bestowed upon them by Barrett Jones, borrowing the name of a friend from his early childhood. The session was recorded on Barrett's Tascam 8 track tape recorder through a Carvin MX2488 mixing desk.

* * *

May 1992
Laundry Room Studio, Seattle, WA, United States

Recording Artist

Grohl, Dave (Drums, Guitar, Bass, Vocals)

Recording Credits

Jones, Barrett (Engineer & Recording)

Tracks Recorded

1. What I'm About

2. Butterflies

3. Back in Treatment

Recording Equipment

Tascam 38 ½ Inch 8-Track Reel-to-reel Tape Machine

Carvin MX2488 24-Channel Mixer

Following a raft of activity at the Laundry Room Studio in April 1992 Grohl again headed down to the basement in May to record yet more of his own songs, added onto the same reel that already contained four Nirvana tracks. Three more of Grohl's were put to tape on this occasion, starting with the first ever recording of the song which would later be known to Foo Fighters fans as 'Butterflies'. At this stage, however, it had the working title 'Red Pellet Guns', from a lyric in the song. Grohl would in later years describe the song as "kinda ridiculous".

The two other songs recorded on this occasion have something of a mystery surrounding them. Written on the box containing the reel, Grohl had titled them 'What I'm About' and 'Back in Treatment'. When asked about the titles in later years, Barrett Jones had no recollection of the songs, and in his digitized archive found no trace of songs with those titles. What these two songs sound like then, for now, remain a mystery.

* * *

November 8th, 1992
Laundry Room Studio, Seattle, WA, United States

Recording Artist

Grohl, Dave (Drums, Guitar, Bass, Vocals)

Recording Credits

Jones, Barrett (Engineer & Recording)

Tracks Recorded

1. Pretty Girl

2. Podunk

3. Make A Bet

4. I Don't Want Your

5. How I Miss You

6. Watered It Down

7. Slackers Password

Recording Equipment

Tascam 38 ½ Inch 8-Track Reel-to-reel Tape Machine

Carvin MX2488 24-Channel Mixer

The second half of 1992 saw Nirvana continue their meteoric rise to fame with tour dates across the world, including a now-iconic headline appearance at the Reading Festival in England. The final tour date of the year came on October 30th with another now well-known mischievous performance in Buenos Aires, Argentina. Exhausted, the band returned home for a much-needed break, but Dave Grohl wasted no time heading down to the basement with Barrett Jones to crack on with more of his songs.

On this occasion rather than starting entirely from scratch

with new songs he instead primarily spent his time going back over the instrumental tracks recorded earlier in the year as Allister Lobb. Vocals were recorded for all five songs recorded in April and with these, the tracks were given their final titles - 'Podunk', 'Let's Make A Bet', 'I Don't Want Your', 'How I Miss You' and 'Watered It Down'.

Whilst the lyrics recorded for the first five tracks were mostly a serious effort, towards the end of 'Watered It Down' Grohl switched delivery to imitate the style of B-52s singer Fred Schneider, something he would do on a few later occasions.

The five tracks from April 1992 were book-ended on the November reel by two new songs, entitled 'Pretty Girl' and 'Slacker's Password'. Whilst little is known about the former, the latter was featured in an outtake video initially recorded for the 2015 documentary series 'Sonic Highways'. In the clip, Grohl and Jones are seen listening to both 'Watered It Down' and 'Slackers Password', with Grohl showing embarrassment for the former and not even remembering the latter, initially.

The only song released in full of the combined results of these two sessions was 'How I Miss You', included on the Foo Fighters single 'I'll Stick Around' in 1995. Whilst the instrumental versions of the five songs recorded in April do circulate, only the aforementioned clips aired during the Sonic Highways documentary exist for the versions with added vocals.

January 19th to 21st, 1993
BMG Ariola Ltda, Rio de Janeiro, Brazil

Recording Artist
Grohl, Dave (Drums, Guitar, Bass, Vocals)

Additional Musicians
Cobain, Kurt (Backing vocals)

Recording Credits
Beloti, Dalmo (Assistant Engineer)

Beveridge, Ian (Engineer)

Montgomery, Craig (Producer, Engineer)

Tracks Recorded
1. Onward Into Countless Battles

Whilst Nirvana was in Brazil in 1993 for two large stadium shows they secretly booked time in a local studio to work on some new material, mostly songs that would end up on their third studio album 'In Utero'. Towards the end of the session, the band decided to have some fun, recording a cover of the Terry Jacks classic 'Seasons in The Sun', the trio also switching up their regular instruments which found Grohl playing bass. Before that, though Grohl recorded a track by himself.

He would record all instruments on a partial cover of the song 'Onward into Countless Battles', originally by the Swedish Death Metal band Unleashed. Vocals were also recorded but rather than attempt to match the deep, heavy vocals of the original, Grohl instead just grunted the word 'Meat' several times over, with Kurt Cobain also joining in the fun on backing vocals. This led to the song commonly being mislabeled as simply "Meat" or "Dave's Meat Song", with Universal even planning to release it as an original composition on the 2004 Nirvana box-set 'With the Lights Out'. Grohl caught wind of the plans and made it clear it was, in fact, a cover, and the song was therefore not released officially. It does, however, circulate among fans.

N.B. This book only covers Grohl's solo activities during Nirvana recording sessions. For more details on this and all further Nirvana recording sessions covered check out the following website, which documents all aspects of the Nirvana recordings in detail.

www.livenirvana.com/sessions

* * *

February 12th to 26th, 1993
Pachyderm Recording Studio, Cannon Falls, MN

Recording Artist

Grohl, Dave (Drums, Guitar, Bass, Vocals)

Additional Musicians

Cobain, Kurt (Drums)

Novoselic, Krist (Bass Guitar)

Recording Credits

Beloti, Dalmo (Assistant Engineer)

Beveridge, Ian (Engineer)

Montgomery, Craig (Producer, Engineer)

Tracks Recorded

1. untitled jam

2. Marigold (Take #1 – instrumental)

3. Marigold (Take #2 – instrumental)

4. Marigold (Take #3)

With touring for the mammoth hit Nevermind considered complete February 1993 saw Nirvana booking into the Pachyderm Recording Studio to begin recording the follow-up. Naturally, the two-week session focused on Kurt Cobain penned Nirvana material as well as some group efforts but owing to the speedy rate that he had recorded his drum tracks, Dave Grohl also found some time to record some of his own material. "We blazed through In Utero. I was done after three days. I had another ten fucking days to sit in the snow, on my ass with nothing to do," recalled Grohl.

Alleviating the boredom, Grohl took the opportunity to first record an untitled track described as "A quick minute and a half of heavy metal-style riffing," recording bass, guitar, and drums himself. Following this quick outburst, he then decided to re-visit one of the songs he'd first recorded with Barrett Jones back in 1990, 'Color Pictures of A Marigold'. This time, however, Krist Novoselic and Kurt Cobain got involved in the process.

Three takes were recorded of the song in all, with the first take featuring Cobain on drums, Novoselic on Bass and Grohl playing acoustic guitar. The recording was largely similar to Grohl's earlier solo effort but naturally, the professional recording studio and 24-track tape recorder meant production was far slicker this time around. The track had also slimmed down slightly, with one less verse meaning the running time was now some 30 seconds shorter.

For the second take, Cobain had vacated the drum stool with Grohl jumping back behind the kit. Both of these initial takes were instrumental but a third take then followed, with Grohl once again remaining behind the kit and then recording the guitar tracks.

Novoselic also remained on bass but for this final take, Grohl experimented with adding a fourth instrument to the mix. Kera Schaley had been hired by the band to perform cello on the Nirvana songs 'All Apologies' and 'Dumb' and taking advantage of her presence, Grohl invited her to perform on his track.

Grohl recorded vocals for this final take and in a surprise to many Nirvana fans at the time, the track was released as a

B-Side to the first single from the album, 'Heart-Shaped Box'. This would mark the first (and only) time a Nirvana release would feature a song neither penned by Kurt Cobain nor featuring the frontman on vocals.

The third take of the song was used for the release, although Schaley's cello was not included in the final mix. The track did however rather curiously feature the sound of a chair scraping on the floor at the start of the song, as well as some other quiet ambient noises. Novoselic's strong bass was also featured prominently in the mix.

The title of the song was shortened to simply 'Marigold' for the release and whilst he first instrumental piece of music was never officially released it was made available in an online 'leak' in 2017, as were the first two takes of 'Marigold'.

* * *

April 18th, 1993
Laundry Room Studio, Seattle, WA, United States

Recording Artist

Grohl, Dave (Drums, Guitar, Bass, Vocals)

Recording Credits

Jones, Barrett (Engineer & Recording)

Tracks Recorded

1. For All The Cows

2. Good Grief

3. Exhausted

4. Weenie Beenie

5. Ozone

Recording Equipment

Tascam 38 ½ Inch 8-Track Reel-to-reel Tape Machine

Carvin MX2488 24-Channel Mixer

There was seemingly no end to the supply of songs coming from Dave Grohl's mind and in April 1993, he was once again back at the Laundry Room Studio to put more of his ideas onto tape. The studio was however no longer in the basement of his own shared house. Grohl had moved out into his own bigger house and Barrett Jones had also moved, setting up the studio inside a house in the Lower Queen Anne neighborhood in Seattle. The new studio was still using Jones' trusty 8-track tape recorder but was fitted out with new outboard gear and DAT machines. Grohl dropped by the studio on April 18th, 1993 and put to tape four new original songs as well as one cover.

'For All the Cows', 'Good Grief', 'Exhausted' and 'Weenie Beenie' were all tracked here for the first time, songs which would all be later re-recorded for the first Foo Fighters album. When recording 'Exhausted' Jones suggested Grohl use what he described as a "weird no-name tube amp that was dying a slow death" to achieve the deep, dirty sound he was looking for on the track. "We were able to coax this wonderful sound out of it before it died," said Jones.

The final song to be tracked owing to Grohl's "growing love of recording covers songs" was his take on KISS guitarist Ace Frehley's song 'Ozone', from his eponymous 1978 solo record. Just six of the available eight tracks on the 8-track tape were utilized by Grohl – two each for drums and guitars, one for bass and one for lead vocals.

With a large collection of songs amassed up to this point, Dave did briefly have the idea of releasing some of his material independently, whilst still in Nirvana. "Around the summer of 1993, I had been talking to a fellow in Detroit about possibly releasing some of my stuff on his small label. I wanted to remain anonymous, but ultimately have something to send to friends and stuff," explained Grohl.

"Nirvana's upcoming tour put that stuff on the back burner, but I was genuinely looking forward to pursuing it once the band had some time off."

Whilst that plan did not come to fruition one song from this session, 'Exhausted', did get a public airing at a much later date. On January 8th, 1995 Eddie Vedder of Pearl Jam took to the airwaves with his nationally syndicated "Self-Pollution" Radio show, a four-hour broadcast in which Pearl Jam played live songs and Vedder played some music by other artists. One of those artists was Grohl, having given Vedder a tape with the song. Another Grohl track broadcast during the show was 'Gas Chamber', a further cover (The Angry Samoans) that he had recorded.

In 2004 a cassette was digitized and shared online by a Foo Fighters fan which contained generated recordings of 'Good Grief', 'Exhausted' and 'Weenie Beenie' from this session but none have to-date seen any official release.

The cover of 'Ozone' was released in August 1995, included as a B-Side to the Foo Fighters 'I'll Stick Around' single.

* * *

January 28ᵗʰ to 30ᵗʰ, 1994
Robert Lang Studios, Shoreline, WA, United States

Recording Artist
Grohl, Dave (Drums, Guitar, Bass, Vocals)

Additional Musicians
Novoselic, Krist (Bass Guitar, Harmonium)

Recording Credits
Bailey, Earnie (Guitar Technician)

Kasper, Adam (Producer)

Tracks Recorded
1. February Stars

2. Exhausted

3. Big Me

4. Butterflies (instrumental)

Shortly before embarking on what would be their final tour Nirvana booked into Robert Lang Studio in Shoreline, Washington. Three days were penciled in over the weekend of January 28th to 30th with the primary reason being that they just wanted to "do something" according to Krist Novoselic, having recognized that several of their past songs had come about by recording on a whim. Whilst they were far from the stage of getting ready to record a new album a few ideas were swirling around, written during touring of In Utero.

Kurt Cobain had initially suggested they booked into Studio X, location for the recording of a huge range of popular albums from Soundgarden's "Superunknown" to R.E.M's "Automatic for the People". Robert Lang Studio was instead chosen based on the recommendation of Dave Grohl. Just a stone's throw from his Seattle home, a member of the crew had informed him about the location – "You know, there's this guy, Bob Long, who's built a studio that's entirely underground, and it's the size of a gymnasium," Grohl was told. After scouting the studio and meeting owner Lang the band were impressed by what they saw and intended to visit over the course of a weekend.

Dave Grohl and Krist Novoselic promptly arrived on Friday afternoon and were expecting Kurt Cobain to arrive at some point during the weekend. The pair were not too concerned by his initial no-show, having become used to it over the past few years.

Whilst waiting Grohl and Novoselic took full advantage of the time and empty studio, recording some of their own songs or just jamming and experimenting. "It was just Krist and I screwing around with funny things, and I recorded a couple of my songs. We just tried to make do with the time we had," Grohl recalled.

Much of the material recorded over the first two days was instrumental and given basic descriptive titles. After several experimental jams (such as one experimenting with the sounds created by a Theremin plugged into an Echoplex tape machine) the pair recorded what was at the time simply titled as 'Dave/Acoustic + Voc'. The track was, in fact, a very early version of what would later be known to Foo Fighters fans as 'February Stars', released on the 1997 album 'The Colour And the Shape'. This embryonic version would include several alternative lyrics and featured Novoselic playing the Harmonium, which according to guitar technician Earnie Bailey "really made the song". Another guest on the song was a cat, a stray that had wandered into the studio adding some mewing noises at the start of the track. The morning of the final day arrived with Kurt Cobain still a no-show. Unsure when, or even if he would arrive, Grohl and Novoselic plowed on. Grohl elected to record a new version of 'Exhausted' and debuted another new song, 'Big Me'. These recordings were almost identical to later versions, although with Novoselic on the bass these initial versions were stronger in that regard.

Cobain finally arrived at the studio in the afternoon and Nirvana material could finally be recorded but with limited time only one proper song could be worked on extensively, 'You Know You're Right'. Following one further jam, given the rough title 'jam after dinner', Cobain left the studio. With the day almost at a close, there was just enough time for Novoselic to assist Grohl on one more of his songs, a rough instrumental version of the track 'Butterflies'.

Whilst 'You Know You're Right' would see release in 2002, with snippets of the jam following on 2004s 'With the Lights Out' box set, none of Dave and Krist's work at this session has ever been released.

* * *

March 9th, 1994
Laundry Room Studio, Seattle, WA, United States

Recording Artist
Grohl, Dave (Drums, Guitar, Bass, Vocals)

Recording Credits
Jones, Barrett (Engineer & Recording)

Tracks Recorded
1. Big Me

2. Mountain Of You

Recording Equipment
Tascam 38 ½ Inch 8-Track Reel-to-reel Tape Machine

Carvin MX2488 24-Channel Mixer

On March 1st, 1994 Nirvana was in Munich, Germany to play what would turn out to be their last ever show with Kurt Cobain. Whilst many more dates were scheduled across Europe morale in the band was low and "Kurt wanted to go home" according to Dave Grohl. "I think he intentionally blew his voice out so that any doctor in his right mind would look at his throat and go, 'It's kinda inflamed.' He intentionally blew his voice out so that we could all go home," Grohl believed. Whether intentional or not, Cobain was diagnosed with severe laryngitis and bronchitis after the show, with the last two dates of that leg of the tour canceled. At this stage, however, shows later in the month were still set to go ahead.

Grohl remained in Germany to film a promo video for the Backbeat Band whilst Krist Novoselic had already flown home to Seattle. Cobain, on the other hand, headed to Rome to try and recover but instead wound up in a coma following an overdose on Rohypnol and Champagne. The rest of the tour was immediately canceled and after waking from the coma on March 5th Cobain flew home, with Grohl also following suit.

With tensions between the band members already high before the overdose incident the future of Nirvana was uncertain. Grohl was relieved to hear that Kurt was OK but had no idea what would happen next. To take his mind off the situation, soon after arriving back in Seattle, he headed to a place of comfort – Barrett Jones' Laundry Room Studio.

Tape was running on March 9th with the first song to be tracked being 'Big Me', a song he'd first recorded with Novoselic just a couple of months earlier. This was instead another entirely solo effort with Grohl on all instruments, also recording vocals. Just one other song would be recorded on this day, entitled 'Mountain of You'. In 2004 a recording of the track, among others, was shared online by a Foo Fighters fan, albeit with the slightly erroneous title 'Mountain View'. Dave Grohl himself went online to correct the mistake, ending an unrelated message on the bands official message board with the postscript "it's 'Mountain of You', and it's old as fuck."

The recording of 'Big Me' from this session saw official release in 2015 on the special Record Store Day release 'Songs From The Laundry Room', whilst the generated cassette recording posted online remains the only release of 'Mountain Of You'.

Circa 1994
Inner Ear Studio, Arlington, VA, United States

Recording Artist
Grohl, Dave (Drums, Guitars, Vocals)

Grohl, Lisa (Bass Guitar)

Recording Credits
Zientara, Don (Engineer, Recording)

Tracks Recorded
1. Weenie Beenie

2. Alex's Pizza

3. We're At Home

4. Song #6

At some point during his post Nirvana career Dave Grohl headed to Inner Ear Studio in Arlington, Virginia, to work on some more of his own new songs. Rather than going alone he also invited his sister Lisa, just as he'd done in April 1992 when recording as part of the Allister Lob group. On this occasion there wasn't a third member to play guitar, just the two Grohl siblings, with Lisa playing bass and Dave recording everything else.

Four songs were worked on an Inner Ear by the duo in a session which owner Don Zientara described as a relaxed, fun time. It's unclear exactly when this session took place, Zientara unable to locate his notes for the session, but he did remember Dave talking to him about his future plans, including the Foo Fighters name, which almost certainly places the session in 1994.

Dave and his sister worked efficiently completing four songs over the course of a single day. The first of those was another version of 'Weenie Beenie', a track he'd first recorded alone in April 1993. The three other tracks were given the titles 'Alex's Pizza', 'We're At Home' and 'Song #6'. Whilst Weenie Beenie was the name of a fast food restaurant just a block away from the studio Zientara wasn't familiar with any Pizza establishments owned by Alex, unsure of where that title came from.

It's possible the other three songs were later recorded under a different, well-known title but as Dave Grohl left with the 2-inch master tapes, and with Zientara currently unable to listen to his copy, it's unknown as to what those three songs sound like.

June 19th, 1994
Laundry Room Studio, Seattle, WA, United States

Recording Artist
Grohl, Dave (Drums, Guitars, Bass, Vocals)

Recording Credits
Jones, Barrett (Engineer & Recording)

Tracks Recorded
1. I'll Stick Around

2. Watershed

3. Oh, George

4. X-Static

5. This Is A Call

Recording Equipment
Tascam 38 ½ Inch 8-Track Reel-to-reel Tape Machine

Carvin MX2488 24-Channel Mixer

Following the death of Kurt Cobain and resulting demise of Nirvana in April 1994, Dave Grohl felt lost. Grieving the loss of his friend, Grohl was unsure of where he wanted to go next in life, what his future held. "After Kurt's death, I was about as confused as I've ever been. To continue almost seemed in vain," Grohl believed. "I was always going to be 'that guy from Kurt Cobain's band' and I knew that. I wasn't even sure if I had the desire to make music anymore." In the immediate weeks following Cobain's passing the drummer couldn't even stomach listening to music, never mind make it, but his outlook was soon brightened by a simple yet powerful message of support among the many condolences he would receive.

One morning a letter dropped through Dave's post-box. The letter was from the members of fellow Seattle rockers 7 Year Bitch, an all-female band who had also suffered similar tragedies. "We know what you're going through," the letter began. "The desire to play music is gone for now, but it will return. Don't worry." On June 27th, 1992 guitarist and co-founder of the band Stefanie Sargent returned home from a party, having consumed alcohol and taken a small amount of heroin. Sargent passed out on her back and as a result of vomiting without waking, died of asphyxiation, aged just 24. 7 Year Bitch made the hard decision to carry on with a new guitarist but just over a year later suffered yet more heartache. Mia Zapata, frontwoman of The Gits and very close friend of the band, was brutally raped and murdered as she returned home from a bar in Seattle.

"That fucking letter saved my life," remarked Grohl. "As much as I missed Kurt, and as much as I felt so lost, I knew that there was only one thing that I was truly cut out to do and that was music. I know that sounds so incredibly corny, but I honestly felt that."

Buoyed on by the message of support Grohl made several public appearances in the summer of 1994, including a performance with The Backbeat Band at the annual MTV Movie Awards. More significantly, he would also start writing new songs again, the first time since Kurt's death. There was still no ultimate goal, but the first step was to do what he'd done for almost a decade previous – visit Laundry

Room Studio and record the new ideas with his friend Barrett Jones. Visiting the studio in mid-June 1994 five new songs were recorded for the first time - 'I'll Stick Around', 'Wattershed', 'Oh, George', 'X-Static' and 'This Is A Call'. With years of experience working together, the pair had "a good system down" by this point according to Jones, and recording was fast, an entire song laid down within an hour.

"I had these ideas in my head and just went into the studio and did it," said Grohl of the session. There was apprehension before the first playback of the song 'I'll Stick Around', Dave unsure of himself, if the music he'd written in an entirely new frame of mind was any good. After a few listens he was more positive, happy with what he'd produced. "I thought like wow, that's the kind of song that I'd always wanted to write but I was either too scared lyrically to express myself, or I was too afraid to have such a kind of bonehead, like a hard rocking riff or something. So after I finished it I thought 'wow, I'd actually accomplished what I was trying to do for a really long time." Barrett had also observed a difference in Grohl's writing with this song, noting that he "tried inventing a cool bass line, trying something different on the bass than guitar" as he'd always previously done.

For many years after its eventual release, Grohl would be asked about the subject matter of the song, with many journalists speculating that it was about Kurt Cobain's widow Courtney Love, linking the lyrics to Grohl's possible feeling towards her at the time - "I don't owe you anything". For over a decade Grohl would brush off the questions, giving vague answers and straight up denials, but in 2010 he finally confirmed what most suspected – "I've denied this for 15 years but yes, it's about her," he told journalist Paul Brannigan.

With five more songs committed to tape Grohl had now recorded over 30 different songs or ideas over the previous 6 years and had a decision to make on what he was to do with them. Less than a week later however Barrett Jones would inadvertently put the first piece of the 'Foo Fighters' puzzle in place. Jones visited the local Seattle radio station 99.9 FM KISW, as he would regularly, to give airtime and promotion to some of the artists he had recorded. One of those artists on this occasion was Dave Grohl.

Jones joined DJ Damon Stewart on his 'New Music' show and started out by playing a song by up and coming local band Monkey Finger before Stewart then prompted him on to talk about some of the higher profile acts he'd worked with. "My friend Dave, from back East, joined this band Nirvana and I had the pleasure of recording a couple of songs for them," Barrett joked, before playing one of the songs he'd recorded, 'Oh, The Guilt'.

More bands were aired before the conversation turned back to Grohl. Jones explained that he had recorded new material with him the previous week and gave a glowing review of his skills, noting that he recorded all the music by himself and that he "gets everything on the first take".

Jones cued up 'I'll Stick Around' although at this time he noted that the song didn't have a title; instead, Grohl had given it a symbol, one which resembled that of cymbal producer Zildjian.

Whether he realized it or not, this combination of a public airing and by specifically giving the song to Damon Stewart, Barrett Jones had set the wheels in motion. The reason Stewart was so key came with his other job – as well as being a DJ, he also worked in the A&R department for Sony Music and he naturally saw huge value in the new music from the former Nirvana drummer.

Stewart took the tape along to Sony and it also soon got around to other labels, with word of mouth about it soon spreading. Within days Grohl was bombarded with phone calls from various parties, all broadly asking the same thing – "What are you going to do?" Still unsure, Grohl consulted his manager John Silva and lawyer Jill Berliner for advice. "Do you have a band? Are you going to make a record?" they asked. Grohl didn't have a band, but he did make a decision on the other question and formed a plan, or at least the first part of one. "[I'm going to] book a week in a 24-track studio, choose the best stuff [I've] ever written out of the thirty or forty songs that [have] piled up, and really concentrate on them in a real studio."

It was time for Dave Grohl to record an album.

* * *

October 17th to 22nd, 1994
Robert Lang Studios, Shoreline, WA, United States

Recording Artist
Grohl, Dave (Drums, Guitars, Bass, Vocals)

Additional Musicians
Dulli, Greg (Guitar on 'X-Static')

Recording Credits
Culp, Steve (Engineer)   Jones, Barrett (Producer)

Tracks Recorded

1. This Is A Call
2. I'll Stick Around
3. Big Me
4. Alone + Easy Target
5. Good Grief
6. Floaty
7. Weenie Beenie
8. Oh, George
9. For All The Cows
10. X-Static
11. Wattershed
12. Exhausted
13. Winnebago
14. Podunk
15. Butterflies

With a large collection of songs in the bank and record labels biting at his heels, the tail end of summer 1994 saw Dave Grohl make the decision to record an album. Unlike past recordings this wouldn't just be a casual affair in friend Barrett Jones studio, he planned to book time in a professional studio and create a somewhat more polished record. The studio he settled on was Robert Lang Studios in Shoreline, Washington.

The studio was just a few blocks from his house and based on a recommendation he and the rest of Nirvana had visited the studio earlier in 1994 for what would ultimately be their last recording session. Happy with this past experience at Lang's studio it made perfect sense for Grohl to head there again to record his album.

A week was booked from October 17th to 23rd, 1994 and whilst they weren't using his studio this time, Dave still took along his friend Barrett Jones to produce the session. Around thirty or forty songs had been recorded by the pair over the previous six or so years and for this session, Dave had selected what be believed to be his best fifteen.

Day one naturally began with setting up and finding nice sounds, a simple process for the duo who'd been recording together for so long by this point. "[It] was a cinch for Barrett, whom I'd asked to produce since he was the one person in the world I felt comfortable singing in front of," recalled Grohl. After around four hours of setting up equipment and mics, the duo was happy and ready to record at around 5 pm. With a running order for an album already decided Dave planned to simply record each song in order, and so the first song to be tackled was what would be track one, 'This Is A Call'.

As with almost all his previous recordings with Barrett, Grohl recorded every instrument himself during the session, and the pair had perfected their own method to record quickly. Drums would be recorded first, Grohl's strongest instrument, giving each song a solid base for everything else to work around. "[I would then] listen to playback while humming the tune in my head to make sure the arrangement [was] correct", said Grohl. With the drum track locked in, next to be put to tape would be "two or three guitar tracks", before finally adding a bass track.

"Everything was pretty much first take, so he could do about a song an hour after setting up," recalled Jones of the process. Vocals would be saved for last, so once one instrumental was deemed fully complete, including overdubs, it was onto the next song.

Whilst Grohl did primarily record all the instrumental music himself, one other name did sneak onto the record. With Dave busy laying down tracks in the main live room Afghan Whigs lead singer and guitarist Greg Dulli visited the studio. The pair had previously worked together on the Backbeat Soundtrack in 1993 and initially, he just watched Grohl at work from the control room, in awe of his talents. "He'd do a whole song in about 40 minutes," recalled Dulli. "I was completely fascinated by it. He could do it because he has perfect time. He'd lay down a perfect drum beat and work off that. He'd play drums, run out and play bass, and then put two guitar layers over the top and sing it." Whilst watching Grohl surprised Dulli by asking him to contribute - "I was just watching him record, and he asked me if I wanted to play. I didn't even get out of my chair. He just handed me a guitar." Dulli's part was very minor according to Jones, a "sort of one note repeating thing."

One of the last songs to be tracked was 'Exhausted', a song Grohl had first demoed in April 1993. During that recording Barrett used an old, dying no-name amplifier to get a dirty, grungy tone to the guitar track but with that now completely dead Jones did his best to replicate the sound with other equipment. Using a Pro Co Turbo Rat and other distortion effects Jones said he "was almost able to recreate the sound on the album session, but not quite."

Equipment for the session was relatively limited by

choice. Dave used the same Tama drum kit he'd used during Nirvana and most of the guitar tracks were recorded with just two models. The first was a tobacco sunburst Gibson Les Paul which, with the help of his best friend Jimmy Swanson, had been stripped and sprayed silver by Grohl. The other main guitar of choice was Dave's treasured red Gibson Trini Lopez, with a Marshall JCM 900 used for amplification. For the 'grungier' guitar sounds, as well as the distorted vocal effects on songs like 'Weenie Beenie' and 'Podunk', a rather unique DIY solution nicknamed 'The Can' was concocted. A small battery powered Marshall amp was placed inside a gas can which would create a unique rough, distorted effect on both the guitar and the voice.

The instrumentals for all fifteen songs were completed by just the middle of the third day. "It became sort of a game," said Grohl. "I wanted to see how little time it could take me to track 15 songs, complete with overdubs and everything. I was literally running from instrument to instrument, using mostly first takes on everything."

The focus then turned to vocals and whilst most of the songs had written lyrics from previous demos, Grohl still found himself tweaking and re-working some of them in the studio. "By no means am I a lyricist," said Grohl. "But a lot of times, the things you write down spur of the moment are most revealing. Now I look at them and some of them seem to actually have meaning. I had seven days to record fifteen songs, I was just concentrating on everything being as together as possible, having everything be tight and in sync. There wasn't too much time spent sitting on a chair thinking." When recording with Barrett at his Laundry Room studio Grohl would usually double-track his vocals but during this session, with twenty-four recording tracks to play with rather than eight, he went one further and tripled his vocals on many songs, giving them an even fuller, more rounded sound.

Recording was complete by October 22nd with the final day at the studio dedicating to mixing. Barrett Jones lead the process which like recording, was lightning quick with no fancy gimmicks. By the end of the week, Dave Grohl had himself an album. Twelve songs were earmarked for the album itself, with the other three - 'Winnebago', 'Butterflies' and 'Podunk' – designated as 'bonus tracks'. Once the rough mix was completed Dave Grohl wasted no time in heading to a cassette duplication shop in Seattle and ran off 100 copies of the session, even including a J-Card with the name he'd chosen for his 'band' and album – 'Foo Fighters'.

The reason for the name was an attempt to try and hide his identity as the sole author of the music. At this stage, Grohl planned to create a low-key release and not put his name on it, so people listening would not know it was "that drummer from Nirvana" and be able to listen without bias or any preconceptions.

"I wanted to get an independent distributor to send it out into the world. Maybe 10,000, 20,000 copies, so that people would think, 'God, who is this band Foo Fighters? I've never heard of them before'. I just wanted it to be this real anonymous release."

His plans were unfortunately undone by his own generosity. Grohl handed out tapes of his album with the Foo Fighters name to friends, family and even fans in the street. It, therefore, didn't take very long until word got out that Foo Fighters was in fact just Dave Grohl. "That fucking tape spread like the Ebola virus, leaving me with an answering machine full of record company jive," recalled Grohl. "I'd give tapes to everybody. Kids would come up to me and say, 'Nirvana was my favorite band' and I'd say,

"Well here, have this!" By January 1995, with the cat out of the bag and songs being played on the radio from the tapes Dave himself created, a bidding war had ensued between rival record labels, all eager to sign Dave Grohl and be the one to release his debut album. David Geffen Company (the label Nirvana were signed to upon their demise) and Capitol Records were reported in the media as the two front-runners in acquiring his signature.

Whilst this was going on, Dave Grohl knew his plans for a small, anonymous release were out of the window. Talk soon moved to Dave forming an actual band of musicians to go out on the road and properly promote the record. Grohl was talented enough to record all the instruments himself in the studio, but even he wouldn't be able to manage the feat live.

Dave started jamming with a few people in casual auditions, including prolific session drummer Josh Freese and former Nirvana bandmate Krist Novoselic, but none were working out. In the case of Novoselic, the pair just felt it would be too weird being in a band together again without Kurt. Grohl, therefore, had to continue searching.

Sunny Day Real Estate was an alt-rock band from Washington, D.C. and in late 1994 rumors were rife that the band was set to split. These rumors were confirmed in early 1995 when the band announced they were disbanding. Dave Grohl's wife at the time, Jennifer Youngblood, was friends with the girlfriend of bassist in the band, Nate Mendel. Mendel and Grohl first met at a Thanksgiving party in November and once it was clear that SDRE was finished, Grohl invited Mendel to be the first recruit to Foo Fighters.

One of the people Dave Grohl gave his tape to was Pat Smear, who'd most recently played with Dave as the second live guitarist for Nirvana from mid-1993 through to the end.

"Not long after meeting Nate, I gave a tape to Pat. I knew that the band would need two guitars but didn't think that Pat would want to commit to anything (or that he would even like the music)." To Dave's surprise, Pat not only liked the tape, but he was also interested in joining up.

"After you've been in the coolest band ever, what do you do?" Smear asked himself at the time. "I sat on the couch with the remote control in my hand for a year. I didn't know if I ever wanted to be in a band again. I was just working on solo stuff. Dave and I had kept in touch and I had heard about his tape, but I didn't know what to expect. When I heard the tape, I flipped. Dave gave it to me at a club and I went home. After I listened to it, I went back to the club. But I didn't want to ask to join the band. I waited for him to ask me."

With guitar and bass roles seemingly filled and Dave planning to assume the frontman role, just one position was left vacant - drummer. "Enter William Goldsmith" proclaimed Grohl, referring to the drummer of Sunny Day Real Estate alongside Mendel. "Though I had never seen or heard them, I knew a little about them. I saw them play their last few shows in Seattle and was blown away by Nate and Will. So, you can imagine my first reaction when I heard the band was calling it quits. I gave the two of them tapes through my wife's friend and prayed they'd enjoy them," he said.

The four got together to jam and see if they would all gel together, but also just as important was for Grohl to lay out his vision for the band, and the role he saw his new colleagues in. "I didn't want this to be some ridiculous solo project. I sure as fuck didn't consider Pat, Nate and William my backing band. I realized this was a bizarre foundation for a band, but that's exactly what my goal was: to have another band. We got together and it was soon apparent that this was to be that next band. I wanted everyone to have the freedom to do whatever they wanted to do within the songs, each member as important as the next."

With plans far grander than ever initially planned, it was decided that the rough mix created during the final day at Robert Lang Studios needed a little more work. In February 1995 the band headed to Arcata, California and 'The Shop', a mixing studio in the town headed up by Rob Schnapf and Tom Rothrock of Bongload Records.

Mixing was completed on a 32 channel API DeMedio console, custom built by Frank DeMedio in 1972 for Wally Heider Recording's 'Studio 4', with a Stephen's 24 track 2" tape machine used for playback. Processors used in the mixes included an Eventide Omnipressor compressor for vocals and guitar solos, an Alan Smart stereo compressor for "squashing" the drums and mixing them back in as well as being used over the entire mix. Other processors included UREI 1176 and LA3A compressors as well as an Echoplex for delays and a "crappy digital reverb". Overall the final mixes were "nothing crazy" according to Schnapf, noting that he'd mixed the song 'Big Me' in just 20 minutes.

The eventual winners of the label bidding war were Capitol Records, however, with Grohl holding all the aces during negotiations, he was very shrewd in the deal he signed. Rather than simply handing over the rights to the songs to Capitol, Grohl formed his own record label, Roswell Records, who would retain 100% control over the music. Roswell would then merely allow Capitol to widely distribute the music, but never giving them full control.

The album saw official release on Independence Day 1995, available on CD, Vinyl and Cassette. As originally planned, the album featured twelve of the fifteen songs recorded, and whilst 'Winnebago' and 'Podunk' were used as B-Sides alongside the first single 'This Is A Call', the final song of the fifteen recorded, 'Butterflies', has never seen an official release. It does, however, circulate among fans thanks to being on the original cassettes Dave handed out.

Whilst William Goldsmith, Pat Smear and Nate Mendel played no part in the recording of the album they were featured on the artwork for the record and received a percentage of the royalties.

* * *

July 17th, 1995
Dave Grohl residence, Seattle, WA, United States

Recording Artist
Grohl, Dave (Drums, Guitars, Bass, Vocals)

Tracks Recorded
1. My Hero

Recording Equipment
8-Track Reel-to-reel tape recorder

After playing a handful of warm-up shows including a private keg party and benefit show for Mia Zapata April 1995 saw the newly formed Foo Fighters begin their first full tour to support Dave Grohl's recordings. Playing support to former Minutemen and Firehose frontman Mike Watt on his solo tour the band journeyed across the United States, undertaking a grueling schedule which saw them play twenty-seven shows in forty-two days. The band was a hit with crowds all wanting to get a glimpse of "The drummer from Nirvana" in his new position as leader of a band.

The band would only play for around forty-five minutes each night on this first tour but with only one album of music set-lists were still somewhat repetitive each night, something guitarist Pat Smear soon became frustrated with - "I'm playing the same songs two or three hundred nights a year!" the guitarist exclaimed.

Grohl was also very much aware of their limited repertoire, regularly telling crowds that "we don't have many songs." The band also avoided what many suspected (or perhaps hoped) they would play, Nirvana covers. They did, however, add a cover of the Gary Numan/Tubeway Army song 'Down In The Park'.

It wasn't just about having songs to play live, however. If Foo Fighters were going to continue forward, they were going to need to work as an actual band and be able to write new material together. When recruiting his future band members Grohl was very conscious that they were not going to be the Dave Grohl backing band, but a real band, working together. "I wasn't sure what was going to happen. Can Dave write more songs? How was this writing process going to work?" recalled bassist Nate Mendel. "I had no idea if this band had a future or not." With their busy touring schedule, the only real opportunity to work on new ideas in the initial months was during soundcheck for the shows, but respite and more time would arrive in the summer.

The band was booked on their first headline tour from July onward but with a six-week break beforehand Dave saw an opportunity to go home and work on some new songs. One of those songs was 'My Hero'. "When I wrote that, I had this house in Seattle and downstairs in the basement there was a laundry room and right next to the laundry room was this other, tiny concrete room." Grohl managed to squeeze his drum kit into the room, set up his 8-track cassette recorder and got to work.

With a simple drum track laid down, he headed upstairs to try work on the other parts of the song, coming up with the guitar riff whilst watching TV. A couple of guitar and bass tracks were added with vocals, as usual, left for last. He had nothing fully written but wanted his band mates to get an idea of what he had planned – "[I] just sang that over it, just as a temporary lyric and it stayed. I just wrote them super quick so you could hear what the vocal would sound like" recalled Grohl of the main "There goes my hero, watch him as he goes" line. The lyrics for the verses were mostly gibberish nonsense at this point, simple phonetics.

Dave took the rough demo to his bandmates who were instantly positive of the new track. "I knew that we were going to be ok after I heard the song 'My Hero' because it was great," said Mendel. Despite the lack of proper lyrics, the band wasted no time in testing out the song live, debuting it as the very first song of their first show on their summer tour, July 20th, 1995. Grohl told the crowd that the song had been written just three days earlier but despite its embryonic state, the song went down well.

* * *

January 24th to 26th, 1996
Robert Lang Studios, Shoreline, WA, United States

Foo Fighters

Goldsmith, William (Drums)

Grohl, Dave (Guitars, Vocals)

Mendel, Nate (Bass Guitar)

Smear, Pat (Guitar & Backing Vocals)

Recording Credits

Jones, Barrett (Engineer & Producer)

Tracks Recorded

1. Down In The Park

2. Enough Space

3. Butterflies

4. I'm Alone Again

5. My Hero

Recording Equipment - Guitars

Candy Apple Red Fender Precision Bass (Nate Mendel)

Ebony Gibson EDS-1275 Double Neck Guitar (Dave Grohl)

Ever since playing their very first shows in spring 1995 Foo Fighters had been on the road almost non-stop, with just a few breaks. The band covered most of North America, visited a large chunk of Europe and wound things up with a tour of the Australasia region towards the end of the year. The final stop of the schedule came with a performance at the Queen Elizabeth Stadium in Kowloon, Hong Kong, on January 22nd, 1996, supporting Beastie Boys alongside Sonic Youth.

The band returned home but there was no opportunity for immediate rest. Foo Fighters had been approached to record a song for the upcoming X-Files companion album 'Songs In The Key Of X'. Grohl, as a huge fan of the series and all things supernatural, jumped at the chance - "I was obsessed with The X-Files!" The band booked into Robert Lang Studios in Shoreline, Washington from January 24th to 26th 1996 in order to record a contribution. Grohl was by now very familiar with the studio, but this would be a first visit for the rest of the band. Barrett Jones was once again asked to produce the session.

This wouldn't strictly be the first time the four members of the band had recorded in a studio. They had convened at the famous Maida Vale Studios in London, England in November 1995 to record songs for the 'Evening Session' show on the BBC. However, on that occasion, the band only recorded new versions of songs Dave Grohl had previously recorded on his own. This session at Robert Lang Studios would be the very first time they would work together on brand new material.

The song chosen for the album was 'Down in The Park', a Gary Numan/Tubeway Army song the band had introduced into their live shows back in April 1995. "'Down In The Park' is a beautiful song. It's sort of eerie but at the same time it's really pretty," Grohl said when asked about his choice of song to cover. "What he's singing about is bizarre. It's a great song."As the band was already familiar with the song recording went smoothly, and quickly. "We were just trying to capture the essence of the song and make it a Foo Fighters song as well," said producer Jones. The original recording of the song heavily featured keyboards but in the change to making it a Foo Fighters song, these parts were all replicated on guitar. With the song for the X-Files album in the bag, focus then turned to work on some new original songs with the time they had left.

The first was 'Enough Space', a song written by Grohl specifically to open their live shows. "There were only a couple of songs that we had that were really good openers, I thought 'god I need to write an opening song for us'." Whilst performing in Europe over his career Grohl had noted that crowds behaved differently to those in America, electing to jump up and down rather than "beat the shit out of each other". He wanted to write a song that "everyone would start bouncing to" as an opening song - "So, I had a melody and a riff idea but I didn't know the tempo, so I jumped up and down and found a tempo by bouncing." The song was put together by Grohl in the Autumn of 1995 and learned by the whole band in soundcheck just a day before it was given a live debut in Stockholm, Sweden on October 16th, 1995.

The demo version recorded during this session was effectively the same as the live version, albeit with some parts tightened up and with more extensive, complete lyrics. The words of the song were in reference to the movie "Arizona Dream", a 1993 surrealistic comedy starring Johnny Depp, Faye Dunaway and Lili Taylor which Grohl enjoyed.

In the film, Dunaway's character Elaine dreams of

building a flying machine whilst Taylor's character Grace dreams of killing herself and being reincarnated as a Turtle.

In the song, Dave seemingly writes from the perspective of Elaine, with the lines "I was waiting for something, maybe flying machines", although he then references actor Lili Taylor, rather than her character name.

Next up the band decided to record 'Butterflies', an old song by Dave which dated back to May 1992 when it was known by the title 'Red Pellet Guns'. He'd recorded the song again during the session for the first album but whilst it was initially earmarked as a B-Side, never saw release. The band played the song semi-regularly during their live tour and saw value in attempting the song as a band in the studio. Structurally this new version was almost identical to the version recorded by Grohl in the same place just over a year earlier, the main difference being Pat Smear providing backing vocals during the choruses.

The penultimate song tracked was titled 'I'm Alone Again', a mid-tempo song of unknown origins. The song was structurally quite simple at this stage with repeated verse and choruses, as well as mostly repeated lyrics. This is the only known occasion of the song being recorded by the band, which has never seen an official release.

Finally, before their time at the studio was up, the band decided to put to tape a recording of 'My Hero', another song that had been given a live debut in the summer of 1995. Those initial performances highlighted the song still being in an early phase, with rough transitions and unfinished, placeholder lyrics. For this recording the song was much, much tighter with lyrics that were very close to that of the well-known version of the song released on their future 'The Colour And The Shape' album.

One rather interesting facet of this song is that it featured Dave using a unique Gibson EDS-1275 double neck guitar, which featured a 12-string guitar on the top neck and a regular 6-string guitar on the bottom. When the band was playing the song live in 1995 Pat Smear could be seen playing this model, using both necks at different points in the song. When it came to the studio recording, Dave played these parts with the guitar.

Whilst there have been rumors of the band working on a song titled 'Comfortable' during this session, producer Barrett Jones insists only the previously mentioned five songs were recorded at this time. On top of that Jones noted that only 'Down In The Park' was worked on extensively and given a final mix. The other four songs recorded were only ever meant as rough demos, the groundwork for a future second Foo Fighters album.

The X-Files album 'Songs In The Key Of X' was released just a couple of months after the session on March 19th, 1996. No other songs from this session have ever been officially released but a generated cassette containing all five songs does circulate among fans.

* * *

July 25th to August 8th, 1996
Robert Lang Studios, Shoreline, WA, United States

Recording Artist
Grohl, Dave (Drums, Guitar, Bass, Vocals)

Additional Musicians
Doe, John (Vocals)

Jones, Barrett (Keyboards)

Post, Louise (Vocals)

Richards, Eric (Slide guitar)

Recording Credits
Jones, Barrett (Engineer & Producer)

Warner, Aaron (Assistant Engineer)

Tracks Recorded
1. Bill Hill Theme
2. August Murray Theme
3. How Do You Do
4. Richie Baker's Miracle
5. Making Popcorn
6. Outrage
7. Saints in Love
8. Spinning Newspapers
9. Remission My Ass
10. Scene 6
11. This Loving Thing
12. Final Miracle
13. Touch

1996 saw Foo Fighters continuing a grueling schedule of tour dates supporting their debut album, culminating with an appearance at the Phoenix Festival in England, on July 19th. Upon arriving back in the United States, the band took a well-deserved break but less than a week later, Dave Grohl was back in a recording studio for a rather unique project. Earlier in the year Grohl had been approached by the producers of an upcoming feature-length film, offering him the opportunity to write and record the entire musical score, which would also serve as the companion soundtrack. "The movie people didn't want to have a soundtrack that was just 10 or 15 bands that all have records in the charts," explained Grohl. "They wanted to have someone actually score the movie and write incidental music for suspense and chase scenes."

The movie in question was 'Touch', a comedy-drama starring Bridget Fonda and Christopher Walken which was adapted from an Elmore Leonard novel of the same name. Having watched an early version of the movie and enjoyed it Grohl agreed to produce the score but did so with a jovial warning to the producers - "I haven't done this before – I could really fuck it up!" Grohl was provided with a copy of the film along with a list of scenes that required a musical accompaniment. "I sat down and tried to come up with some music that would go with the images, without being too in-your-face. The songs had to stay in the background," explained Grohl.

With no pressure or specific requirements from the movie producers, Grohl booked into his now favored Robert Lang Studio in Seattle and again took along friend Barrett Jones to produce.

Louise Post, vocalist, and guitarist for alt-rock band Veruca Salt was reportedly dating Grohl at the time and was an obvious choice after he'd decided he wanted to include a female vocal. Post sang vocals on the track 'Saints In Love' and was also credited as a writer on the title track. Also joining Dave at the studio was John Doe (real name John Duchac), bassist and singer of X, a band credited as being part of the first wave of punk in the late 1970s. Doe added his vocals to the track 'This Loving Thing (Lynn's Song)', also assisting with writing on the track.

Other than those, the only other track to feature vocals was 'How Do You Do', Grohl singing lead on a song he described as sounding "a bit like Foo Fighters". Producer Jones also got involved, playing keyboard on the track 'Final Miracle' and the final guest performer was Eric Richards, playing slide guitar on 'This Loving Thing (Lynn's Song). Grohl described much of the musical score as being weird, noting that he'd just use whatever he felt worked for the scene. "It doesn't sound like anything that I have ever done." Whilst, on one hand, writing a music score was less restrictive, he would have to write parts that matched the tone of the scene. "There's a scene with this redneck woman and her white trash trailer-park home, then you don't want a song that sounds like Gary Numan, you want a song that sounds like Hank Williams."

In comparison to writing songs with a classic poppy structure, he found writing what was effectively background music, less restrictive - "With a soundtrack, you can do anything, and the most important thing is, that parts don't have to be repeated continuously. You don't need a catchy chorus."

Dave got to see the finished film for the first time in early 1997 although admitted he mostly focused on his score, which he was very hard on himself about - "I just listen to the music and think that I fucked it up really bad!", echoing the warning he gave the producers. The recording session was completed in approximately two weeks and the film was premiered in the United States in February 1997, with the soundtrack following the next month.

* * *

October 1996
Robert Lang Studios, Shoreline, WA, United States

Foo Fighters
Goldsmith, William (Drums)

Grohl, Dave (Guitars, Vocals)

Mendel, Nate (Bass Guitar)

Smear, Pat (Guitar)

Recording Credits
Jones, Barrett (Engineer & Producer)

Tracks Recorded
1. Hey, Johnny Park!

2. Monkey Wrench

3. New Way Home (Take 1)

4. New Way Home (Take 2)

5. New Way Home (Take 3)

6. Wind Up

7. My Poor Brain

8. February Stars

9. unknown

10. Make A Bet

others

With the 18-month world tour for the first album complete and Dave Grohl's side project 'Touch' also finished focus turned back to Foo Fighters recording their first full album as a band. By late 1996 Grohl had many new ideas for songs, with several of them having already been demoed or played live. Before booking time in a costly professional studio to record the album for real Foo Fighters headed to Grohl's old haunt – Barrett Jones Laundry Room Studio in Seattle. Grohl had last visited his friend's studio in the summer of 1994, recording demo versions of then-new songs which he'd then re-record. Since then the preferred recording location had been Robert Lang Studios, although Dave did always take Jones along with him to engineer and produce. For pre-production work, this didn't make financial sense and so the band instead decided to spend around a week back in Jones studio, getting the music and themselves prepared for the real deal.

Demo versions of most, if not all songs later featured on 'The Colour And The Shape' were recorded. An early version of 'My Poor Brain', a song that was given a live debut in April 1996, featured a slightly longer intro and also ran at a slower tempo, but was otherwise a completed song at this stage, including almost final lyrics.

Three distinct takes of 'New Way Home' were recorded with one instrumental version featuring the louder, faster part as an intro rather than being towards the end. The basic melody was in place but the whole song structurally was very loose at this stage, at least in one of the three takes recorded.

'February Stars' is a song Grohl had first recorded way back in 1994 with Nirvana bassist Krist Novoselic and this demo version followed the same basic structure as the final recorded version, a soft intro gradually increasing in ferocity until the song fully came to life three-quarters of the way in. No vocals were recorded for the song during this session.

'Monkey Wrench' was another song already well advanced, with lyrics fully written. The song again simply lacked a final polish at this early stage. The joins in the screamed vocal section were far more obvious in this version of the song, Grohl not too concerned about it sounding like one complete take at this stage.

Recording took place in the last week of October 1996 with everything wrapped up by Halloween night. With a demo tape in hand, the next step for the band was to shop around for a producer to help them make their final album.

* * *

November 18th to mid-December 1996
Bear Creek Studios, Woodinville, WA, United States

Foo Fighters

Goldsmith, William (Drums)

Grohl, Dave (Guitars, Vocals)

Mendel, Nate (Bass Guitar)

Smear, Pat (Guitar)

Recording Credits

Farwell, Don (Assistant Engineer)

Hadlock, Ryan (Assistant Engineer)

Norton, Gil (Producer)

Tracks Recorded

1. Doll

2. Up In Arms

3. See You

4. The Colour And The Shape

5. Hey, Johnny Park!

6. My Poor Brain

7. Wind Up

8. My Hero

9. Monkey Wrench

10. Enough Space

11. February Stars

12. New Way Home

13. Dear Lover

14. Comfortable

Since the late 1980s Dave Grohl had recorded his own music almost exclusively in one manner – with friend Barrett Jones, and for the most part at his Laundry Room Studio in

Arlington and Seattle. However, for the second Foo Fighters album, and the first with an actual band of musicians, Grohl decided he wanted a change. "I've made punk records and they're fun and great, and it's quick and there's a passion. But I did that with the first record. I've never made a big, proper rock record before, so why not? People just don't seem to do it anymore, so we might as well take a shot."

The band approached Englishman Gil Norton to produce the record, best known for his work with The Pixies, producing the albums 'Doolittle', 'Bossanova' and 'Trompe le Monde'. "I admired Gil for a while," said Grohl. "I thought he'd be the right man for these songs because they've got the potential to be great pop songs, and a little polish can do no harm." He was specifically impressed with his work on 1991s Trompe le Monde - "I love it for the way you can hear the band falling apart, getting scattered, shooting off in a million different directions." He didn't realize it at the time, but 'band falling apart' would be a very apt description of future events, albeit in a more literal manner than he described.

Norton was sent demo recordings from their recent pre-production sessions as well as a copy of the first album and agreeing to work on their second record was an easy decision according to the producer - "When I first heard the first Foo Fighters album I got the sense of a really accomplished songwriter, and I really liked the raw power of it. I loved the demos that Dave had done for the new album, so I knew we had a great batch of songs."

One of the many reasons Grohl liked to record with Barrett Jones in his Laundry Room Studio was the privacy. The small home studio meant no prying eyes, and this was something he was keen to try and maintain as much as possible this time around. Potential recording locations were scouted and one that seemed to tick all the boxes was Bear Creek Studio. Located 30 minutes from downtime Seattle the studio was both close to home and secluded, situated within a 10-acre farm surrounded by woodlands. The studio itself is a century old barn converted into a recording studio with a large 60-foot by 40-foot live room, another 20×40 foot space with many isolation rooms and a large control room. Upstairs is an apartment to sleep six, fully kitted out with a kitchen and utilities, something the band would look to make use of during their stay.

Before entering Bear Creek Gil Norton and Dave Grohl spent several days together at a local hotel, Norton stripping the songs back to their basic components and challenging the songwriter to "pinpoint the essential truths and underpinning each one." This was a challenge for Grohl, a big departure from his "try and record songs as quickly as possible" approach of the first album. Wanting to make things with Norton work he took up the challenge over a few intense days in the hotel room. With that stage complete, the entire band then regrouped with Norton at a rehearsal space to further tweak the songs together. "[Gil] came in and we refined the arrangements with him. During this time many details changed, some guitar parts and bass lines got rewritten" Dave recalled. "It was like that the whole time, really, the tracks were never really complete," added bassist Nate Mendel.

Recording of Foo Fighters second album officially commenced at Bear Creek on November 18th, 1996. They had already suspected it was the case in the previous weeks but from day one proper the band realized that working with Norton was going to be vastly different to anything they had previously experienced. For Grohl, most of his recording had either been alone, with his friend Barrett Jones or with relatively laid-back producers like Steve Albini and Butch Vig. For Pat Smear, Nate Mendel and William Goldsmith they were also very much used to the loose, punk rock attitude to recording. Slightly out of tune? Not in perfect rhythm? No problem. For Gil Norton, the opposite was true. His ethos was that nothing less than perfection was required from everyone.

"Gil has a reputation as being a real taskmaster in the studio," as Dave Grohl put it. "He cracks the fucking whip and anyone who's ever worked with him will say the same thing. He accepts nothing but absolute perfection in what you do – whether that means dissonant, noisy chaos or a perfect pitch, perfect performance pop song, he needs it to be the best. So, working with him was really fucking hard."

Drummer Goldsmith and Bassist Mendel, in particular, were immediately feeling the pressure and questioning their own abilities. "I was fucking terrible and Will was having his own challenges," Nate recalled in the 2011 Foo Fighters documentary Back & Forth. "I could tell when I had to do something a million fucking times that it was taking longer than I wanted it to and it was sort of my first realization like 'oh, I'm not a fully formed musician', I've got to keep getting better," he added. The duo would be referred to in a now well-known put down as the "rhythm-less section" by Norton.

Mendel may have exaggerated when he stated the requirement to re-do something "a million times," but the real numbers were still extraordinary. Whilst tracking the drums Goldsmith would work for 13 hours a day and on one song was asked to re-do the take a staggering 96 times. "I gave everything I could. I couldn't believe at the end of it everything was done, and I had got through it" said the drummer. It wasn't just producer Norton that Goldsmith was feeling pressure from, however. Whilst they were now one cohesive unit it was still clearly established that Dave Grohl was the primary songwriter, in control of how the songs should sound. This would be the first time he'd be watching over someone recording the drums on his own songs, a fact William was very much aware of. The anxious drummer constantly felt that whichever song he was working on, Grohl "already had a drum part in his head" and that whatever he was doing would be "wrong". His feelings were very much correct. "When I've written a song, I have kind of a clear idea of where the basic root accents should lie. That's a fancy way of saying, I know what the drums should sound like in my head" Grohl later admitted.

Despite the problems progress was slowly being made, with basic tracks for previously demoed songs like 'Enough Space', 'Hey, Johnny Park!' and 'My Hero' being laid down, as well as new songs 'See You' and 'Wind Up'. Whilst progress was being made, tensions between band members and producer continued to increase as the days went on, morale inevitably heading in the opposite direction.

Musical ability and a perfectionist producer were not the only issues surrounding recording. Dave Grohl married Jennifer Youngblood in the summer of 1994 but by 1996 both had started to realize they may have rushed into things. "We were kids and honestly we just shouldn't have done it: even in the time we were engaged I think we both realized that we probably shouldn't get married". Rumors had circulated in the press that Grohl was seeing Veruca Salt frontwoman Louise Post and whilst he has never directly commented on it, Post claims that much of the album was written about her, and their relationship. 'Walking After You', 'Doll' and 'My Poor Brain' are all songs she is adamant are about her.

Whatever the truth, mid-December saw a visitor to the

studio – a legal representative of Jennifer Youngblood serving Grohl with divorce papers. It was yet another problem on top of everything else and producer Norton understood that it was naturally a distraction for Grohl. "Dave didn't get overly emotional about it with me, and I didn't see him crying or anything, but obviously it was a big part of his life and a concern at the time," said the Englishman.

Everyone agreed that a break was necessary and so just before Christmas 1996 recording was halted. The band members all went their separate ways for the holidays although with Grohl kicked out of his marital home, for him that meant returning to his mother in Virginia.

At the point of the time-out, the band had tracked fourteen songs, although none were considered finished, with many concerns from the musicians and producer alike. The band planned to re-convene in the new year to continue recording of the second Foo Fighters album.

* * *

December 1996
WGNS Studios, Washington D.C., United States

Recording Artist
Grohl, Dave (Drums, Guitar, Bass Guitar, Vocals)

Recording Credits
Turner, Geoff (Engineer)

Tracks Recorded
1. Everlong (instrumental)

2. Walking After You

Recording Equipment
Amek TAC Matchless 36 channel Recording Console

Tascam MS-16 1 inch 16-track tape recorder

With the recording of Foo Fighters second album halted for the holidays amid creative tension and personal issues the band members all headed home, which for the soon to be divorced Dave Grohl meant returning to Virginia. Temporarily homeless, Grohl found himself sleeping on the floor of a friend's house. Progress back in Seattle had been fraught with issues, the band struggling to adapt to producer Gil Norton's perfectionist approach. Nevertheless, Dave had a couple of new song ideas and decided to try and take his mind off his personal issues by increasing progress on the record.

In late December he headed across the Potomac River into Washington D.C. and rocked up at Geoff Turner's WGNS

Studios. The studio had relocated many times throughout its history, originally in Maryland, followed by several locations in Washington D.C. and then later Arlington, the incarnation Grohl had last visited in 1991 to record tracks with Turner. Through all these re-locations the studio retained the same WGNS name and by 1996 it was once again back in D.C.

He took the rough tracks from Bear Creek along with him and took stock of what the band had achieved in the three weeks they spent in Seattle. "It didn't seem right. The album had something missing," thought Grohl. To find that something Grohl recalled a riff that he'd so far not done anything with - "I had this one riff that I originally thought was a Sonic Youth rip off, but I decided it might be good to turn it into a song." That song was 'Everlong', and during this session, Grohl put together the basic tracks that would later help form arguably his biggest ever hit.

With his impending divorce and other problems temporarily put to the back of his mind Grohl got behind the studio drum kit and got to work. "I always enjoyed doing these one-on-one sessions with Dave," recalled studio owner and engineer Turner. "Just to get a chance to watch him play drums and to record him, which is so easy. You could record him with one mic or 10 mics. It wouldn't make any difference. It would just sound like Dave."

Grohl tracked the drums, guitar, and bass but recorded no vocals for the song at this stage, the focus being on just having a mostly complete arrangement of the song that the full band could work on once they re-convened in the new year. One new song in the bag, Grohl wanted to attempt another. 'Walking After You' was a song he described as an "emotional, sappy song about getting dumped," seemingly referring to his relationship with Jennifer Youngblood. As with almost any other song Grohl started by laying down a drum track, although owing to the soft, mellow nature of the song the regular drumsticks were replaced by "a mallet and drum brushes" according to Turner. Guitar and bass tracks were added and unlike 'Everlong', Grohl did record vocals.

Despite recording with him several times previously Turner was still impressed by Dave's natural ability to record an entire song alone. "It's the same as every other track I've made with [him]. From the vantage point of the engineer, it didn't come off as being this one-man band, one person's obsessive take on the song. It sort of came off as a live performance featuring one person in six positions."

Rather than capture the vocals in a traditional isolation booth Grohl sang everything from behind the drum kit, into an overhead mic. At the end of the take, he got up from the stool and headed to the control room to listen back to his work. The tape was still rolling and captured all the ambient sounds as he shuffled across the large live room and closed the door behind him. "I didn't know the tape was rolling and afterward I heard that at the end of the song and I thought it was corny, but it works!"

The version of 'Walking After You' recorded at WGNS would end up being included on the final album as-is, including the post-vocal ambient sounds. The rough instrumental version of 'Everlong' however remains unreleased in any form.

Happy with his work in the nation's capital Dave Grohl headed back to Arlington, with many decisions to be made in the coming weeks, both personally and with his band.

January to February 1997
Grandmaster Recorders, Hollywood, CA, United States

Foo Fighters
Grohl, Dave (Guitars, Vocals, Drums)

Mendel, Nate (Bass Guitar)

Smear, Pat (Guitar, Backing Vocals)

Additional Musicians
Post, Louise (Backing vocals)

Recording Credits
Boesch, Ryan (Assistant Engineer)

Burke, Todd (Assistant Engineer)

Cook, Bradley (Recording)

Norton, Gil (Producer)

Tracks Recorded

1. Up In Arms

2. See You

3. Hey, Johnny Park!

4. My Poor Brain

5. Wind Up

6. My Hero

7. Monkey Wrench

8. Enough Space

9. February Stars

10. New Way Home

11. Dear Lover

12. 7 Corners

13. Everlong

January 1997 saw Foo Fighters come back together to complete their troublesome recording for the second album. The band had spent approximately three weeks at Bear Creek Studios in Woodinville, but nobody was particularly happy with the results. Dave Grohl called the session "a bad experience", feeling that the band had perhaps jumped into recording too soon on the back of extensive touring for the first record.

The reclusive studio location was also expensive and so it was decided a change of scenery was in order, to a smaller and cheaper setting. Unlike Bear Creek, their newly chosen location was far from secluded – Grandmaster Recorders was in the heart of Hollywood, just off Sunset Boulevard. It was selected on the recommendation of engineer Bradley Cook, who was at the time working there as an in-house engineer. A former silent movie theater, the studio had been used by artists such as David Bowie and Red Hot Chili Peppers. According to Nate Mendel, the studio had also "occasionally moonlighted as a porn set" and "looked the part."

Initially, only Dave Grohl and producer Gil Norton were at the new location and Grohl wasted no time in playing the two new songs he'd written and recorded at WGNS Studios. "It wasn't a surprise to me when Dave came back from Virginia with two good new songs," recalled Norton. The producer was particularly impressed by the track 'Everlong', asserting that it "brought the whole album together."

With the two new songs given the thumbs up by Norton the pair then turned their attention to the recordings from the Bear Creek session - in particular, William Goldsmith's drumming. Norton made it clear to Grohl he was unhappy with Goldsmith's work and having heard Grohl playing drums on the two new songs, convinced him to carry out a 'test'. That test was to re-record the drum track for the song 'Monkey Wrench' so the pair could compare his and Goldsmiths takes. According to Norton, the result was "ten times better" with Grohl behind the kit and soon the rest of the tracks came under scrutiny.

More work was deemed to be required across the board and so Nate Mendel and Pat Smear were both invited to join Grohl and Norton at the studio. Crucially, William Goldsmith was not. He remained at home in Seattle over 1,000 miles away, oblivious as to what was happening in Los Angeles. The expectation from Smear and Mendel was that they would merely be adding some final polish and finishing touches to the work they had started in Woodinville but soon became suspicious of what was really going on.

"Dave comes in, he's like, 'Listen, we're gonna redo 'My Poor Brain' or whatever the song is. Drum track's not quite right. Actually, I'm doing the drums on this one. We're just gonna redo it," recalled Mendel. Smear had similar concerns, noticing that he kept getting asked to record guitar parts on songs he had already tracked and that more and more songs were being "done over". Eventually, it dawned on the pair that the whole album was essentially being re-recorded, without William Goldsmith.

One of the songs the trio worked on was the newly written 'Everlong'. Dave Grohl had tracked a rough demo version over the holiday break and with band members and producer alike enjoying the song, they got to work on recording a final version. The original demo was recorded only as an instrumental and in the meantime, Grohl had written some lyrics, although not alone; he had collaborated with Veruca Salt singer and guitarist Louise Post on the song she would later claim was about her. "Yes, Everlong was about me," she wrote on the Veruca Salt message board in later years. Whilst Grohl would not go so far as to state the song was about Post, he did reveal that the song was about "A girl that I'd fallen in love with. It was basically about being connected to someone so much, that not only do you love them physically and spiritually, but when you sing along with them you harmonize perfectly."

Post helped write the vocal harmonies during the chorus of the song, noting that the 'Doo-Doo Doos' were inspired by the Veruca Salt song 'Shimmer Like A Girl', from their 1996 EP 'Blow It Out Your Ass It's Veruca Salt'. Not only did Post help with the writing process, but she was also invited by Grohl to record the vocal harmonies on the song itself. There was something of a distance problem however, with Post in Chicago, some 2,000 miles away. Unable to fly out to Los Angeles, Grohl came up with the rather unique idea to record her vocals over the telephone. At Post's end she used her fax phone as a receiver to be able to hear the track and another phone as a microphone whilst at the studio engineer Cook simply pointed a microphone at the phone receiver.

The results were unsurprisingly lo-fi with Grohl using a vintage Astatic JT-40 microphone to give his harmonized vocal track some similar qualities. As well as recording the background harmonies the pair came up with the idea to record a conversation between themselves and include it in a quiet breakdown section of the song. Over the phone Post described to Dave a dream she had about the pair and whilst the recording method muffled much of what said, she could be heard mentioning 'and I saw you, and I didn't know how to get out'. She also recorded some additional very soft 'do do do' vocals which were overdubbed on top of it, further muffling the phone conversation. Despite Post's heavy involvement in the song, she has never been officially credited in any capacity.

With still no sign of Goldsmith and concern growing from Mendel he felt it was only right that he called to explain the situation. A shocked Goldsmith wanted answers - "I was like, what's going on? Should I book a flight? I should be down there?" With Grohl now aware Goldsmith knew they were at a studio recording without him, he too called to try and explain. According to Goldsmith, he was told that Grohl was re-doing just "a couple of drum tracks" and had told him not to come to the studio.

Suspicious, Goldsmith arranged to meet with Mendel in person who revealed the truth. "What's going on, Dave's redoing a couple of the tracks?" asked Goldsmith. "Is that what he told you? He re-did them all" was Mendel's response.

By January 20th rough tracks were once again complete for most songs, now with Grohl on the drums. Happy with the results, cassettes were made containing rough mixes of what they believed to be two of the strongest songs, 'Monkey Wrench' and 'Everlong'. The tapes were sent to management and their record label and everyone seemed happy with the songs - but there was one issue.

Several parties were not overly keen on the inclusion of Louise Post on 'Everlong', particularly the spoken word phone call section. Post herself noted that "[Grohl] was going through a divorce, and things were already difficult" and so it was decided the phone call would be replaced with Dave talking instead. Three tracks were recorded and blended together, the first of which was Dave retelling a story studio engineer Ryan Boesch had told everyone during recording. Boesch's father worked a night job when he and his brother were young children and if they were ever too noisy during the day, waking their father, he would force them into military style punishments – such as holding construction boots over their head. In Grohl's retelling of the story he can be heard mentioning how the children started crying because the boots were too heavy. The two other spoken word portions were of Dave reading a random textbook that was laying around in the studio, according to engineer Cook. Whilst the conversation with Grohl had been replaced Post's backing vocals were left in the song, albeit low in the mix and blended heavily with Grohl's own triple tracked voice.

With a few final tweaks and yet more re-recorded tracks recording at Grandmaster Recorders was completed by February 1997. The second Foo Fighters album was finally complete but as Grohl had unknowingly predicted before recording began at Bear Creek, the band were 'falling apart'. Drummer William Goldsmith never played any part in recording at Grandmaster and soon received confirmation that almost all his work in Seattle had been re-recorded.

Despite this Grohl did still want Goldsmith to remain in the band and tour the record, but this wasn't something the drummer could stomach. "As it is now, I have to rebuild my soul, or re-find it if you know what I mean. So, thanks, but no thanks" he told Grohl. Goldsmith officially quit the band in March 1997, announced to the press soon after.

Whilst Grohl had re-recorded much of Goldsmith's work, some of it did remain on the final master tapes which meant a great deal of stitching was required to put the album together. The first song on the album, 'Doll', was not re-worked at all during this second session, entirely using the original Bear Creek recording.

The first intricate stitching work came with the song 'My Poor Brain'. Rather than use either Goldsmith's or Grohl's drum track in their entirety, the decision was made to use the formers work on the verses of the song whilst the latter featured on the rest of the song. Next to be spliced was 'Up In Arms'. The opening slower paced 55 seconds of the song was taken from the first session whilst the second, fast tempo section was a Grandmaster re-record with Grohl behind the kit.

A different approach was taken for the song 'See You'. Rather than two different recordings of the song being book-ended together one part of the instrumentation (Bass and drums) came from the second session whilst an acoustic guitar track and Grohl's vocals were taken from the first session. The tracks were all joined together to form one coherent song on the album. A simple mix of the song featuring only the vocals and acoustic guitar were released on the 'Monkey Wrench' CD single.

Most of the finished songs were used on the album, but some out-takes were left on the cutting room floor such as the song 'Comfortable', a mid-tempo love song which picked up the pace in the final third.

Also discarded was the first attempt at a song titled '7 Corners'. This would be the first of many attempts at recording a complete song around a riff that Dave really enjoyed but it was at this stage not deemed a success. The titular track 'The Colour And The Shape' was only recorded during the first session and was released in complete form as a B-Side. 'Dear Lover' was also used as a B-Side as well as being contributed to the soundtrack CD to the movie 'Scream 2'.

Mixing was completed at Skip Saylor Recording, a studio situated less than two miles from Grandmaster Recorders. Owing to the tight deadline the band were operating under mixing actually took place concurrently with recording. As each song was completed at Grandmaster the master tape was driven the short distance to Skip Saylor for mixing to begin immediately. Chris Sheldon was the man in charge at Skip Saylor assisted by Jason Mauza and the duo would even return feedback to the band back at the studio if they felt something wasn't working. On one such occasion Sheldon thought the final mix of 'Monkey Wrench' would sound better with a third guitar track and so trusting his expertise, the master tape was returned, another guitar track was recorded, and then it was back to Chris and Jason for final mixing.

Sheldon mixed on an SSL 4000 G series recording desk which he said had "lots of outboard EQs". The drums and guitar were put through an old Neve sidecar desk with 16 channels and Teletronix LA-2As were used for the vocal compression, but Sheldon noted most of the big vocal sound on the record came from the fact Grohl triple-tracked his voice.

Recording of Foo Fighters second album had been extremely hard work, made several band members question their abilities and had ultimately cost them a drummer, but their hard work paid off and 'The Colour And The Shape' was released in May 1997 to strong critical reception.

* * *

Spring 1998
Sound City Studios, Van Nuys, CA, United States

Foo Fighters

Hawkins, Taylor (Drums)

Grohl, Dave (Guitar, Vocals)

Mendel, Nate (Bass Guitar)

Stahl, Franz (Guitar)

Additional Musicians

Haden, Petra (Violin)

Tench, Benmont (Hammond B3 Organ, Chamberlain)

Recording Credits

Foo Fighters (producers)

Kasper, Adam (Recording)

Raskulinecz, Nick (Assistant Engineer)

Tracks Recorded

1. A320

In 1997 Foo Fighters were approached by the production company behind a re-imagining of the 'Godzilla' franchise, interesting in having the band record music to accompany a new movie about the fictional monster. The band agreed and were, according to Grohl, paid "an astronomical amount of money" to write and record a song to feature in the movie, set to be released the following year.

Time was booked at Sound City Studios in Van Nuys, California to record the song, marking the first time Grohl had returned to the studio since recording 'Nevermind' with Nirvana in 1991. This recording session would also mark the first time that the new Foo Fighters line up had recorded together, including new drummer Taylor Hawkins and Franz Stahl, who'd replaced Pat Smear as guitarist in late 1997. Hawkins had previously recorded with Grohl and Mendel for a BBC Evening session in April 1997, but this would be the first time working in a studio with this incarnation of Foo Fighters.

The track they had chosen to record was titled 'A320'. The song had been written specifically with the movie in mind and the band was aware it was quite different from their usual sound. "It seems like it's almost for a movie score," said Grohl. Like many Foo Fighters songs, this one was written whilst the band were on tour and honed during sound checks. "We were writing the song at sound checks while we were on tour in Japan, ironically enough. And at every sound check, the song just got bigger and weirder. It's one of my favorite things we've ever recorded, just because it's so off-the-wall," Grohl enthused.

'A320' had an unusual structure, with three distinct sections rather than a usual verse-chorus-verse format. The first third was described by Grohl as "really beautiful and kind of mellow."

Three minutes in sees the song raise in tempo for the "big rock section" before exploding into the final section with a "crazy crescendo that you can almost see the credits rolling as you listen to," according to Grohl.

The first section of the song also featured all of the lyrics of the song, with the rest being entirely instrumental. "There's really not that many words," said Hawkins.

Owing to the unorthodox nature of the song and large departure from their regular sound Taylor Hawkins had reservations about how well the song would be received, surmising that people would either "love it or hate it", the drummer even going so far to say he believed the song was "pretty prog rock", a point Grohl agreed on.

As well as being the first studio recording for this incarnation of Foo Fighters it was also the first time the band had experimented with additional instrumentation by guest musicians. Benmont Tench, a founding member of Tom Petty and the Heartbreakers and prolific session musician was invited to the studio to record keys on the song. Specifically, he played a Hammond B3 Organ as well as the Chamberlain, an electric-mechanical keyboard capable of emulating various musical instruments and outputting special effects.

A second guest musician perhaps more familiar to Foo Fighters fans at the time was Petra Haden, violinist of the Los Angeles-based power pop band That Dog. Dave Grohl first met Haden whilst touring with Nirvana and asked That Dog to support Foo Fighters for a large portion of their 1995 and 1996 tour schedule. During those shows, Haden would occasionally join Foo Fighters during their set to sing lead vocals on the song 'Floaty', as well as playing violin occasionally. With 'A320' calling for strings, she was an obvious candidate for the job.

A third aspect of this recording session which makes it a key part of Foo Fighters history is that it was the first time the band worked with Nick Raskulinecz. A runner turned assistant engineer at Sound City, he helped during the recording of the song and hit it off with Grohl, bonding over their shared love of the band Rush among other things. Thanks to an opportune meeting in an LA car park three years later, he would go on to record and/or produce most Foo Fighters recording sessions between 2001 and 2005, including the albums 'One By One' and 'In Your Honor'.

Whilst Grohl has spoken positively of 'A320' as a song he was less enthusiastic about the movie for which it was recorded. "We were very proud of it, we submitted it and they gave us a cheque." The band was back on tour when the movie came out but found time to go and see the film, soon wishing they hadn't bothered - "we suffered the two and a half hours to sit in front of Godzilla," said Grohl.

Before a rare live performance of the song in November 1999, Grohl was even more scathing. "[A320] was on the soundtrack of the worst movie you've ever seen in your life," he told the crowd, before adding "but the song's good!". The song did not feature in the film itself but was included briefly in the closing credits, with the soundtrack CD releasing in May 1998.

Later in 1998 reports in the media claimed that the band had agreed to record a Depeche Mode cover song to feature on a tribute album to the band and that the song had been recorded at this session alongside 'A320'. The reports were however soon quashed by a statement from A&M Records, the label in charge of the release. The statement clarified the reports by revealing that whilst the band had indeed initially agreed to contribute to the album, they were not able to find time to record a track at short notice.

* * *

Spring 1998
Ocean Way Recording, Hollywood, CA, United States

Foo Fighters
Hawkins, Taylor (Drums)

Grohl, Dave (Guitar, Vocals)

Mendel, Nate (Bass Guitar)

Stahl, Franz (Guitar)

Additional Musicians
Harrison, Jerry (Piano)

Recording Credits
Derfler, Karl (Engineer)

Harrison, Jerry (Producer)

Tracks Recorded
1. Walking After You

Around the same time the band received the request to record a song for the Godzilla movie soundtrack another request came in. This time the interested party were Twentieth Century Fox who was at the time planning the production of a feature-length film of the TV series X-Files. Foo Fighters had in the past contributed a track for the sci-fi drama, recording a cover of the Tubeway Army/Gary Numan track for the 1996 soundtrack 'Songs In The Key Of X' and still being a big fan of the show, Dave Grohl couldn't refuse this second request. He would also joke that "They pay! And we just go for the cheques!"

At this point of the year Foo Fighters already had one eye on writing and recording their next studio album and so with one new song already given to a soundtrack release, for this contribution, it was decided they would re-record an old track rather than 'give away' another new one. 'Walking After You' featured on their 1997 album 'The Colour And The Shape' but was not recorded by the whole band, instead recorded alone by Grohl during a break in their troubling recording process. It was therefore decided that the new-look Foo Fighters would have another crack at the song.

Recording took place at Ocean Way Recording in Hollywood, California, a historic studio known for recording artists such as Frank Sinatra, Lionel Richie, and Radiohead. Producing the song was Jerry Harrison, keyboardist and guitarist for New Wave pioneers Talking Heads. The group disbanded in 1991 and from that point on Harrison decided to take on production work, operating as the in-house producer at Ocean Way at the time of Foo Fighters recording.

The band elected not to change too much about the track with the new recording, although they took the opportunity to tighten the song up, shortening the runtime by almost a minute in comparison to the original. More guitar tracks were also layered on the song, giving it a much fuller sound. Whilst working with Harrison the band couldn't resist asking him to contribute, the Talking Head adding piano to the already busy track.

In comparison to the Grohl solo recording which saw him record the vocal track in one take whilst still sat behind the drum kit, far more time and effort was put into the new recording, with Grohl noting that it had taken "seven or eight takes to get it right." The new recording of 'Walking

After You' was first included on the movie soundtrack released in June 1998 and was also released as a split 7" single alongside Ween's 'Beacon Light', also taken from the full soundtrack.

* * *

March 1998
Rancho De La Luna, Joshua Tree, CA, United States

Auto Environment

Catching, Dave

Drake, Fred

Grohl, Dave

Stahl, Pete

Tracks Recorded

1. 45-minute jam

During the recording of Foo Fighters second studio album Dave Grohl was feeling the pressure. By the time the band had moved proceedings from Washington to a studio in Hollywood he was homeless, facing divorce and drummer William Goldsmith had quit the band over the handling of the drum recording on the album. Working furiously at the studio to meet a deadline and under a lot of stress, Grohl decided he needed a day off and headed out of the city into the desert.

He and a friend drove out to Rancho De La Luna, the desert studio a couple of hours outside the city owned by Fred Drake and Dave Catching. Established in 1993 it had played host to many artists all looking to escape the usual LA madness. Grohl liked his first experience at Rancho, noting how different an environment it was from the almost authoritarian recording process he was in the middle of back in Hollywood.

"You pick up an instrument and just start talking and before you know it, Fred Drake just puts a microphone in front of you and someone's making dinner in the kitchen and you see that the tape machine's rolling," he said of the laid-back nature. "I was so used to sitting down and hearing, 'Are you ready? Okay, tune your instrument. Here we go: Take 1.' It was about capturing real moments. I was so blown away."

Having enjoyed his first visit out into the desert Grohl got invited back to the studio in March of 1998 to contribute to earthlings?, the band founded by Drake, Catching and Grohl's former Scream bandmate Pete Stahl. Whilst working on tracks for that album, as was so commonly the case at Rancho, the group would also just play experimentally, noodling on whatever came to mind as the beer flowed.

A 45-minute jam ended up being recorded utilizing synthesizers, drums, guitar and whatever else someone picked up in the studio. "It's funky, kind of," said Grohl of the jam. "It's good for driving." The four considered what to do with the experimental music piece before deciding on something a little left field.

'Auto Environment', as the jam had been titled, would be pressed to a limited-edition CD but it would not be sold via any regular channels. Instead, touring bands of musicians would apply for it. "In applying for 'Auto Environment', you will have to give your itinerary. We have to approve of your tour. And then you get 'Auto Environment' - the best driving music in the world," explained Grohl of the somewhat strange plan. "What we might do is, you send in the itinerary, and we'll record the song around the route of your tour," he continued. "So, say your tour starts in Scandinavia. Well! It's very cold and dark in Scandinavia. But by the end of the tour, you're down in Spain and Italy - some summer beach music", he added.

Whether or not he was completely serious about the release method, 'Auto Environment' never materialized and nobody has ever spoken about it again in the last twenty years. The only real clue to its existence is the master reel at Rancho De La Luna, seen in several 'studio tour' videos.

* * *

1998
WGNS Studios, Washington D.C.,United States

Recording Artist
Grohl, Dave (Acoustic guitar, vocals)

Recording Credits
Turner, Geoff (Engineer, Recording)

Tracks Recorded
1. Everlong

Recording Equipment
Amek TAC Matchless 36 channel Recording Console

Tascam MS-16 1 inch 16-track tape recorder

With their second album 'The Colour And The Shape' released to a positive reception in May 1997 the band hired a new drummer in Taylor Hawkins and headed out on the road once more. Much of their schedule would be filled with live performances around the world but another type of duty on their itinerary becoming more and more prevalent were radio and TV appearances. One such appearance came on March 18th, 1998 as Dave Grohl and Taylor Hawkins appeared on the Howard Stern show.

The duo took part in a lengthy interview with Stern but towards the end of the show, Grohl was due to perform a song with his acoustic guitar. When asked by Stern what he would choose to perform Grohl suggested 'For All The Cows', a song he'd performed acoustically on a few previous occasions. Stern, seemingly unimpressed with the choice asked what he was "really going to do", suggesting he perform a "hit". A member of Stern's production team suggested 'Everlong', with Stern agreeing.

Over the previous nine months of touring many of their new songs had already become fan favorites, including the singles 'Monkey Wrench', 'My Hero' and indeed, 'Everlong'. The song was a big hit at the live shows and the studio version of the song was also getting a lot of positive reception from radio airings.

Grohl explained that he'd never performed the song acoustically previously, this would be the very first time. The new rendition of the song became hugely popular with fans who began sharing recordings of the broadcast, and other radio stations were also soon aware of the new version.

With requests pouring in for Dave Grohl to release the acoustic version he decided that rather than the slightly sloppy Stern version be the one to put out, he'd quickly head to a recording studio to do a proper version. Not long after the Stern broadcast he headed to WGNS Studios in Washington D.C., the very same place he'd recorded the first demo of the song in December of 1996.

The recording was very fast, studio co-owner Geoff Turner describing the new version as "very quiet, almost withdrawn." Turner also noted that Dave was suffering from ill-health during recording, expressing surprise that it saw release - "I thought that version was kind of dead in the water because Dave had a cold and he was in a rush and it was very noisy." That noise he was referring to was the outside noise from the studio being picked up by the sensitive microphones, something he noticed the first time hearing it on the radio - "I was like, wow, I can still hear the

Metrobus rumble in the background."

The new recording was soon sent across the United States for radio airplay but curiously it was not featured on a Foo Fighters release at the time, despite further live performances in the same style and its strong popularity. A year after the initial performance, March 2000, Grohl was making another radio show appearance when a caller to the show asked about the 'Everlong' performance. 'Soon' was Grohl's response as to when it would be released. Despite that assurance, it would, in fact, be a further nine years until that happened, included as the final track on the Foo Fighters Greatest Hits compilation album in 2009.

* * *

March to June 1999
Studio 606, Alexandria, VA, United States

Foo Fighters

Hawkins, Taylor (Drums)

Grohl, Dave (Guitars, Vocals, Drums)

Mendel, Nate (Bass Guitar)

Recording Credits

Kasper, Adam (Recording, Producer)

Tracks Recorded

1. New Wave
2. Gimme Stitches
3. Breakout
4. Generator
5. Fuck Around
6. *They Never Threatened Us* *
7. *Human Fade* *
8. *Try Me On* *
9. Next Year
10. *Long E* *
11. 7 Corners
12. Learn To Fly
13. *Zombie Song* *
14. Ain't It The Life
15. Fraternity
16. *Call Me Up* *
17. Oh Yeah
18. *Echo In A* *
19. *Girl On The Moon* *
20. Have A Cigar
21. Stacked Actors
22. Headwires
23. Aurora
24. Iron And Stone
25. MIA
26. Virginia Moon

* *These are working titles applied to songs during recording. It is currently not known which final song title they apply to, if any. For this reason, the number of songs listed here is likely to be inflated*

Recording Equipment

Allen Sides' custom API Recording & Mixing Console

Neve Console Module

Studer A827 24-Track 2 Inch Tape Recorder

Foo Fighters spent the vast majority of 1998 on the road in support of their second album, 'The Colour And The Shape', culminating with a second appearance for the band at the Reading Festival in England. Since recording that album there had been significant changes - William Goldsmith and Pat Smear were out, Taylor Hawkins and Franz Stahl were in. Another change came in late 1998 when the band ended their distribution deal with Capitol Records. A clause in their contract allowed them to leave without penalty should the president of the company, Gary Gersh, ever leave Capitol. Gersh resigned from the company in June 1998, citing "philosophical differences", and the band duly took the opportunity to exercise the release clause.

Rather than immediately tie themselves down to a new deal with another label just before they planned to record a new album the band decided to instead focus on the said album. The lack of a record label gave the band almost complete freedom to do what they liked with no pressures or commitments. the only higher authority was their very understanding management team, a scenario Dave Grohl enjoyed greatly - "We were left completely to our own devices."

The band spent a large amount of their initial years on the road touring and as a result, many of the songs for 'The Colour And The Shape' were written whilst on tour, honed in soundchecks. This meant they went into the studio with many fully fleshed out songs but for their third record, that wasn't the case. "We hadn't played any of these songs live. We hadn't even done many of them at sound checks," Grohl said of the handful of songs he did have in place. "So, we went into a rehearsal space for about a month, coming up with ideas.

"That rehearsal location was Barco Rebar, a small independent space in Falls Church, Virginia. The band booked time at Barco in the fall of 1998 and began hashing out ideas but it didn't take long for Dave Grohl to realize there were problems with the relatively new look Foo Fighters - in particular, the latest recruit Franz Stahl. "When we started rehearsing, we were in a tiny practice space, and in those few weeks it just seemed like the three of us were moving in one direction and Franz wasn't," explained Grohl. "I think the problem with Franz is that he couldn't find his place within the three of us and... it just didn't work out. He was one of my oldest friends and we wanted it to work so badly, but it didn't."

Grohl was forced to make the hard decision to fire Stahl, leaving Foo Fighters without a second guitarist for the third time in three years. Knowing how much a problem hiring another musician right before recording an album might've been the band elected to continue onwards as a three-piece, at least for the duration of the recording process.

The band spent three months at Barco Rebar in total, usually spending between 40 and 60 hours there each week according to owner Richard Gibson. Foo Fighters choice of rehearsal space in Virginia rather than somewhere more glamorous on the West Coast had coincided with Grohl now once again living in his home state, buying a house there to get away from what he called "The Hollywood element."

In the spring of 1997 Dave Grohl was contacted by Verbena, an alt-rock band from Alabama who was at the time label mates at Capitol Record with Foo Fighters. The band wanted Grohl to produce their second record and despite admitting "I really don't know how to produce anything" he agreed, albeit with a stipulation – they also had to hire Adam Kasper to record it.

Grohl had first worked with Kasper during what turned out to be the final Nirvana recording session in January 1994. Three days were booked at the studio but for the first two days, Kurt Cobain failed to show up. "A lot of times we'd be waiting for Kurt [Cobain] to show up, so Dave would start doing these songs that ended up on his first album. We did about five or six of them," explained Kasper. "He'd run out, do the drums, run out, do the bass, and we'd be done in half an hour. I was joking with him, saying, 'Man, you should do a solo thing with this stuff someday."

In working with Verbena on the other side of the desk Dave Grohl was struck with an idea for his own future recording - "Verbena was given a budget to make their record that was just about enough to build their own studio, so I said to Adam, 'I'm going to build my own studio too!'" he exclaimed.

Fast forward approximately one year and with his new home in Virginia Grohl decided to turn that idea into reality, hiring Kasper to help. The pair worked together building and fitting out the studio in the basement of his house, a process Grohl found to be easier than people may envisage - "That was so easy. People imagine recording studios to be these, you know, gymnasium-sized technical nightmares. But building one is the easiest thing in the world. All I did was soundproof, put in hardwood floors, get a bit of equipment and that was it, job done. There was no acoustic engineering, no science to it at all. Why would you want to spend thousands on a studio in Los Angeles that'll suck all the life out of your record? Christ! If I can do it, anyone can." Grohl wasn't kidding. For soundproofing rather than use expensive material specifically made for the job, they used sleeping bags.

Costs couldn't quite be cut in quite the same way when it came to kitting out the studio with recording equipment, although most of what they bought was not brand new, state of the art equipment. "My tastes are usually along the vintage analog type of gear," said Kasper of his preferences. Not wanting to rush into any big decisions the pair spent several months touring different studios to find their perfect gear. Allen Sides' personal custom API recording console was acquired from his Ocean Way Nashville studio and a vintage Neve console was also bought but when it came to the tape recorder itself, an exception to the vintage devices was made - "We bought a Studer tape machine as well - Dave wanted to be able to do a lot of quick punch-ins, so he bought a fairly nice new Studer. That was the only thing that wasn't vintage, but it's a killer machine," Kasper explained.

In terms of outboard gear, UREI 1175LN Peak Limiter compressors were installed, along with a mixture of Manley and LA Audio tube amplifiers. A range of microphones were set up including Shure SM57s on the Amplifiers and Neumann u47 and u67 mics for vocals. Grohl was very complimentary of Kasper's efforts in helping him build and kit out his studio, albeit in a backhanded, jovial manner - "He's a really, really super nice guy. It doesn't seem like he's working. It seems like he's lazy, like he doesn't want to work, but there's something that he does, in just setting up microphones and letting you go, that brings out the most in your music, and the sound of your instrument. He's really great."

The trio of band members and Adam were all keen to record the album in an 'old school' manner, electing not to use any modern digital manipulation tools – they would instead record straight to old fashioned analog tape. "I didn't want to use any of the computer Pro-tooling or editing things that most people use because a lot of the time that will suck the life out of the song," believed Grohl. "The more you manipulate it, the farther away you get from the core of the music." This was in stark contrast to the perfectionist approach the band was asked to take for the previous album, where they would record take after take until it was just right. "This time we thought it would sound like a bigger record if we left the warts and all in it," said Grohl.

The DIY recording studio was christened with the name 'Studio 606', a favorite number of Grohl's that he would "see everywhere" and recording got underway in March of 1999.

As planned the band worked with no distractions or pressures of studio costs - "We told everybody to 'fuck off', built our own studio in my house in Virginia and took as much time as we wanted," Grohl bluntly described the scenario. Despite the months spent at a rehearsal space the band had only come away with a handful of songs, and so much of the work had to be done on the fly. "[Writing in the studio] is something we would never dare to do had we been somewhere we had to pay for. Having a studio in your house gives you the freedom of changing things at the last minute and re-recording and lets you spend time arranging. It gives you much more freedom."

Writing of the new songs began acoustically, just Grohl and his guitar. "I'd sit around with an acoustic guitar and come up with a melody, and then they'd wind up sounding like train wrecks," he joked. Grohl would then take these basic ideas to Mendel and Hawkins to work them into more fully formed songs. "Okay, which way are we going to fuck this song up?" he would jokingly ask the pair. "We wanted to see how far away from our original notion we could get. The most obvious and natural thing for us to do would be to put down a distortion pedal, have the pedal off during the verses, click it on during the choruses, play a little bit faster, and really bash it out," he recalled.

That approach had worked well on the previous record but this time the band wanted to experiment. Songs would be constructed that didn't follow the standard quiet/loud/quiet dynamic as well as songs that used the same riff throughout rather than a chorus 'hook'. "Tom Petty does it all the time, and it seems to work for him," Grohl joked. "So maybe we would try to create a contrast between a verse and a chorus by adding another guitar that complements the riff that runs through the whole song." Whilst their approach to instrumentation changed one thing remained the same – recording vocals was left until very last in the process. "I never sing the songs for the guys before we learn them, so they always begin as instrumentals. I can hear what I'm gonna sing in my head, but they have no idea – they're trusting me to be able to throw it together towards the end," Grohl explained, going on to describe the exact process for recording - "Once we get a song together, Taylor and I will come up with a good drum arrangement. After we put the drums down, I'll put down a couple of rhythm guitars. After that, Nate records his bass, and I start doing a couple of guitar overdubs here and there."

Thanks to the great chemistry between the trio this slightly unorthodox approach was not a problem. "Nate, Taylor and I have a wonderful relationship. I usually come up with a song and I don't have to tell Nate anything; Taylor and I have respect for one another because we're both drummers. I let him pull me in one direction because he's great at arranging music," Grohl recalled. "He always takes a song from A to B because I think he's spent so many years listening to Queen! I usually just give suggestions."

Grohl believed this to be one of the key reasons Franz Stahl had not worked out, unable to find his place with the other three members.

Nate was given almost complete freedom when it came time to record his parts to each song. The rest of the band would leave the room and without any direction, leave him to his own devices. Once finished, Mendel would casually head into the control room and simply declare "Okay, I'm done."

Unlike the last record, Mendel could work without any pressure, knowing that the results did not have to be perfect. Despite Dave and Taylor usually working on songs away from Nate they were always impressed with how quickly the bassist could add the finishing touches once he got to work. "He is a genius. He can sit upstairs all day long while Taylor and I are mapping out a song, and then he'll come in and tie it all together." Producer Adam Kasper was equally impressed with the work rate of Mendel – "The bass stuff is so non-standard, not root note kind of stuff; it's really cool parts, which you don't get with a lot of bass players."

A Vox AC30 was used for guitar amplification for most of the session as well as a Fender Twin Reverb, a Marshall JCM 900 and a Mesa Boogie Maverick. Shure SM57s were used to mic the amplifiers, a slightly unorthodox choice for work in the studio but with the band having used them extensively during live performances and enjoyed the results, it was decided they would also suffice in the studio.

In comparison to the almost military approach to recording guitar tracks for 'The Colour And The Shape', Grohl and producer Kasper stuck to the mantra of simple, and real. The human element. Spending just ten minutes getting a good tone, it was simply a case of throwing a mic up against the amplifier and playing. "Adam is so good and quick that he doesn't need to do any measuring, calculating, or science – he can just hear it" enthused Grohl about his producers' natural abilities. In the past, Kasper had worked with producers who'd spent three days getting a rhythm guitar sound, a scenario Grohl said would make him "Go postal."

"We'd do a take and walk away, bump into the mic, turn the amp off, bump into the knobs, come back to finish the guitar track, and not even really worry about it." Many of the songs they'd record would start with a guitar riff that had a rattling sound in the background, a noise they attributed to the Vox amplifier. "We kept promising we'd replace the tube, but we never did. And now I like that sound a lot," explained Grohl.

A variety of guitars were used by Grohl during the session including his treasured red Gibson Trini Lopez, a Gibson Explorer, and a Fender Telecaster. Rather than bundle on lots of effects and use several distortion pedals as he'd done for the last album Grohl elected to keep things simpler resulting in a "cleaner, fatter, more natural overdrive" tone.

"Sometimes we'd double a track using an old Pro Co Rat, and then hard-pan the parts so that a super-distorted guitar was in the left channel and a grindy guitar was in the right.

Then we'd sprinkle in lots of clean guitar overdubs. So rather than play through a distortion pedal and an amp with its volume at 5, we wouldn't use a pedal at all. We cranked up the amp to 10 so that it sounded like the speakers were screwed up. I enjoy the sound of a guitar breaking up because the speaker is getting its ass kicked" he explained.

Grohl recorded all his guitar tracks sat in the DIY control room of the studio, rather than in the 'live' room out by the amps. The reasoning being that he and Kasper could then work together to get the right sounds, able to hear what was really being committed to tape.

Most of the songs recorded used regular guitar tuning but for the song 'Stacked Actors' Dave experimented by tuning the low-E string down to A. Whilst 'Headwires' and 'MIA' were in a conventional drop D tuning for the latter the B-string was additionally tuned down to A. 'Stacked Actors' didn't actually began life as a Foo Fighters song, or rather was not written with the band in mind. Earlier in the year, Grohl had been approached to write a song for Ozzy Osbourne, potentially to be used by the Black Sabbath frontman on his next solo album. "I came up with the riff when I was asked to write some songs for Ozzy six or eight months ago" Grohl explained. "I was trying to come up with riffs that I thought would sound cool – Ozzy circa his 'Crazy Train' era – and I was just fooling around when I tuned the E down to A." The song was ultimately not used by Ozzy and enjoying the "sludge-heavy" guitar sound he elected to keep the riff for himself.

Like many songs the guitar tracks for 'Breakout' were recorded using his Trini Lopez, a guitar he described as "the world's most beautiful" which "sounds wonderful clean and wonderful dirty." The guitar ran through an Electro-Harmonix Memory Man Pedal and the AC30 amp. That combination was also implemented for the song 'Next Year', albeit with the treble on the amp boosted and volume kept low for a cleaner sound which Grohl described as the "Classic sound of the Trini Lopez – clean with just a slight touch of distortion." For 'Headwires' the main riff and harmonics were played with a Gibson Explorer through the same Memory Man/Vox AC30 setup. On the choruses, however, Grohl switched to a Gretsch Duo Jet and Pro-Co RAT effects pedal and for the "high, picking part in the middle eight" a Gibson SG was used, again with the Memory Man and AC30.

For the song 'Generator' Grohl used a Talk Box, a vocal effects unit that can shape the sound of the guitar, controlled by the mouth. It was made famous by Peter Frampton in the 1970s with the track 'Show Me The Way' and also used by artists such as Joe Walsh, Aerosmith and Bon Jovi. Owing to the origins of the device the song was given an early working title of 'Show You Better' before lyrics were written. Whilst the talkbox featured most prominently during that track it was also used during the bridge section of the song 'Breakout', in a much more subtle manner.

To achieve the correct tone for the laid back, mellow track 'Ain't It The Life' Grohl used a Gretsch Duo-Jet equipped with a whammy bar, something he'd never previously used. "That's the first time I've ever used one of those in my life" he recalled. "I never knew what to do with it, but that song just seemed like it had to have it." Whilst writing and constructing the song drummer Hawkins would tell Grohl it was going be great as he believed it sounded like a song by The Eagles, something he was not overly keen on - "Fuck it! I hate the Eagles!" Grohl exclaimed in response. To record the lead guitar part of the song two different guitars were utilized, the slide on a Fender Telecaster for the first section and then an acoustic guitar for the last section. By the time they'd finished recording Grohl likened it more to a Jimmy Buffet song rather than an Eagles one and whilst they thought the end result was a little cliché, they also believed "it worked".

Drumming duties during recording were split between Dave Grohl and Taylor Hawkins but only once Grohl had convinced Hawkins of his abilities and assured him he wanted him on the record. "I think it was important to him that I played some of the drums on that record because I was having a hard time in the studio" recalled Hawkins. "It was when I was still messing around with drugs and I remember just wanting Dave to play the drums on everything. And he wouldn't allow it. He really pushed me and pushed me to finish it and do the work. It's good that he did that because it really gave me confidence in the end. I was really lacking experience at that time, and I had no confidence being 'Dave's drummer'," he added.

With Hawkins clear on what Grohl expected of him, the pair agreed on who was doing what beforehand, wanting to avoid any repeat of the situation which led to original drummer William Goldsmith leaving the band. "We assigned songs to each other so that there wouldn't be any weirdness. Like, 'Hey, why don't you play on this,' 'Okay, well, why don't you play on this?'" Grohl played on "four or five" songs, leaving the rest to Hawkins. "There were just some things that Taylor does better than me and some things I do better than Taylor and we sort of met in the middle," said Grohl of the choices.

For the most part, Taylor and Dave played the drum tracks on an old Gretsch kit with a Drum Workshop kit also used for some songs. The snare drum on both kits was constantly being switched out depending on the song, including using some that were previously owned by Soundgarden drummer Matt Cameron.

"Dave had a few different ones too, and we would just change things up depending on the song. We'd mix it up as much as we could and recorded it with a lot of tube mics and compression here and there, to taste," explained producer Kasper. "Dave's room wasn't huge, but it was big enough to get a pretty roomy sound. I would place the room mics fairly close and low to the drums, and I used old tube mics and would compress those. If I wanted a roomier sound, I would use more compression" he added.

Despite many inquiring minds, the drumming duo has kept complete details of who did what a well-guarded secret, although some are known. 'Learn To Fly' is known to have been completed by Grohl, whilst Hawkins has mentioned he played on many of the softer songs - "Basically the more mellow or mid-tempo ones I played really well. I almost felt like handing Dave all the faster and crazier songs, and I wanted to do the jazzier, freakier ones," he explained. "I feel like I added some things, like on the song 'Aurora', which is totally me. It wouldn't have been like that if Dave played it. But I also listen to this record and hear things that I played that I feel were a little sloppy". 'MIA' was also confirmed to be the work of Hawkins and whilst fans with a good ear have long speculated on the other tracks, none have been officially attributed to either drummer.

Once a song was complete only then would attention turn to the vocals. Rather than construct a typical vocal isolation booth, all the vocals were recorded sitting on Grohl's couch. A few different microphones and effects were experimented with, but as with the instrumentation recording, everything was kept natural and simple. Grohl would double and even triple his vocals as he'd almost always done to date, but other than that no special effects were used.

The microphones used were Neumann's, u67 and u47 tube type mics, with Dave and Adam deciding which songs needed which treatment. "Usually I will get the track up in the headphones for myself and I'll sing something and make some noises to get the sound I think will work with the track, depending on if it's really bright or warm or compressed or not. Sometimes I'll put the effects right on it, which is what I did with some Soundgarden stuff," Kasper recalled. "We went right into an Echoplex and put it to the track that way, so when you're singing it, it is kind of close to what it will be. In this case, Dave would sing a take, listen to it and realize, 'oh, we need to make it thinner,' or 'We need more distortion,' and we'd tweak it like that. We'd go through and double things where they needed to be and stuff like that," he added.

With the vocals completed for a song a few overdubs sometimes followed and a full song would usually be completed within a day or two. With recording taking place over four months, songs would continually be re-explored days or weeks after the initial recording - "We would record a song and think, 'Wow! That's kind of cool!'. Then, a month later, we would think, 'Let's take another stab at it; I wanna change this one part,' and do it again. Or, we'd go in to mix it and think, 'You know what? Let's just record this one more time' and then spend another day and a half re-recording and mixing it," said Grohl of the iterative process.

Over approximately four months around twenty songs were recorded by the band. Ten of those would be included on their third album, 'There Is Nothing Left To Lose'.

Two cover songs recorded towards the end of the session, Pink Floyd's 'Have A Cigar' and 'Iron & Stone' by The

Obsessed were released as B-Sides to singles from the album. The original song 'Fraternity' was also relegated to B-Side status, although it was included with the album in some regions.

The remaining songs were in various stages of completion and not released in any manner. A track with the descriptive working title 'New Wave' had only drums and bass recorded before the band moved on whilst the song Grohl had raved about to the press before recording, 'Fuck Around', was fully recorded including vocals but was not deemed good enough to release. The same was true of '7 Corners' and both songs would be worked on at several further recording sessions in the future. A track with the title 'Oh Yeah' was abandoned even quicker than 'New Wave', with only a solitary guitar track being recorded.

One further song recorded during the session but ultimately abandoned was an early version of the song 'Virginia Moon', later released on the 2005 album 'In Your Honor'. It had a different working title at this stage but the song was still a soft, acoustic-styled song. Despite the overall feel of the record being more mellow than the previous one, Grohl still felt the song just wouldn't have worked on this album. "Something like that just didn't make any sense in the middle of a rock record," he believed. "We did one version where we tried to turn it into 'Everlong' but it didn't fucking work."

Recording wound up in Virginia in late June and whilst rough mixes were worked on at the house it was decided final mixing should be done in a professional studio. The band packed up their gear, grabbed the master tapes and headed back to Los Angeles.

July 1999
Conway Recording Studios, Hollywood, CA

Foo Fighters
Hawkins, Taylor (Drums)

Grohl, Dave (Guitar, Vocals, Drums)

Mendel, Nate (Bass Guitar)

Recording Credits
Kasper, Adam (Producer, Recording)

Tracks Recorded
1. Live-In Skin

2. Learn To Fly

With the recording of the music for their third album completed the band headed across to the West Coast and Conway Recording Studios in Hollywood, California. Bringing producer Adam Kasper along with them the plan at this studio was merely to complete mixing of what they had worked on in Virginia but as it turned out, more recording work was undertaken. Given a few days off before the mixing session was due to begin Dave Grohl found himself coming up with a brand-new riff and brought it to the studio for the rest of the band to hear. Despite having a solid number of songs ready for the album Grohl was eager to put to tape this new idea.

"Fuck it. Let's record this" he told his bandmates of the song which would be titled 'Live-In Skin'. In just a day and a half whilst also mixing the band recorded the new song with Grohl writing impromptu lyrics "about the place the band is in now". Explaining the lyrics further, he would note the song "has a lot to do with me going head-on with my hate and I'm amazed that I'm still standing, and I demand that we all blend in."

'Live-In Skin' was not the only song worked on during their time in Los Angeles. Seemingly unhappy with some aspects of the recording in Virginia, 'Learn To Fly' received further work with a new vocal track recorded as well as some guitar overdubs.

With the extra unplanned recording complete the focus of the session returned to mixing. Including the new song, a total of twelve were mixed by Adam Kasper - 'Stacked Actors', 'Breakout', 'Gimme Stitches', 'Generator', 'Next Year', 'Headwires', 'Ain't It The Life', 'MIA', 'Fraternity', 'Learn To Fly', 'Aurora' and the new 'Live-In Skin'. Assisted by John Nelson, Kasper worked with the Solid-State Logic SSL9000 console at the studio.

For reasons that have never been divulged three songs received a second mix by Andy Wallace at Larrabee Sound Studios in Los Angeles - 'Learn To Fly', 'Aurora' and 'Live-In Skin'. The final album featured Wallace's mix for those three songs and Kasper's original mixes for the other eight.

The original Kasper mixes of those three songs were never released and remained unheard until 2011 when 'There Is Nothing Left To Lose' was re-issued on 12" Vinyl. Rather than using the original masters used for the 1999 pressings, fresh lacquers were cut by Chris Bellman at Bernie Grundman Mastering and those new lacquers were cut from a master featuring Kasper's original mix of all songs.

December 1999
Studio 606, Alexandria, VA, United States

Foo Fighters

Hawkins, Taylor (Drums)   Mendel, Nate (Bass Guitar)

Grohl, Dave (Guitar, Vocals)   Shiflett, Chris (Guitar)

Recording Credits

Kasper, Adam (Producer)

Mathewson, Curtis (Engineer)

Tracks Recorded

1. Lonely Boy   5. Fraternity

2. Baby Hold On   6. MIA

3. Invisible Sun   7. Untitled #1 (instrumental)

4. Jet   8. Untitled #2 (instrumental)

In late December 1999 Foo Fighters had a few weeks off from touring and elected to head to Studio 606 to carry out some new recording. The primary reason for the session was to give an opportunity for new guitarist Chris Shiflett to work with them in the studio, having joined the band in September and played a handful of live shows.

Their intention was to record songs with Chris that could be used as B-Sides on future singles for their third album 'There Is Nothing Left To Lose'. Adam Kasper remained in the role of producer and engineer for the first week of recording and things got underway with some cover songs. Speaking after the session during a radio appearance Dave

Grohl revealed that they had recorded the Eddie Money track 'Baby Hold On', enthusing that "it turned out so great". Next up was a Foo Fighters version of the Andrew Gold song 'Lonely Boy', a song he described as "one of the greatest ever."

Two more cover songs were recorded in the first week, 'Invisible Sun', originally by The Police and 'Jet', the Paul McCartney and Wings song from their 1974 album 'Band On The Run'. Unlike the other covers which were seemingly set for release as B-Sides, there were different plans for the Wings cover. In early 2000 media outlets reported that several artists including Squeeze, Barenaked Ladies and Sloan had recorded tracks for a tribute album to McCartney. The report confirmed Foo Fighters had recorded 'Jet' and stated the album was set for release later that year but soon after the album was scrapped and never released. After a week Kasper left the studio and in his place as engineer stepped Curtis Mathewson. Mathewson was a friend of drummer Hawkins and had unsuccessfully tried out for the open Foo Fighters guitarist position earlier in 1999. He would occasionally help Hawkins with some of his demo recordings back in California and was invited across the country to assist with recording for the remainder of the session.

The first track the band worked on with Mathewson was a new version of 'Fraternity', a song they first recorded during the recording session for 'There Is Nothing Left To Lose' six months earlier but hadn't used on the record. It had however been included as a bonus track on Australian editions of the album. The band wanted another attempt at the song with Shiflett and had planned to include the new recording on a future single as a B-Side.

Another track first recorded during the spring session,

'MIA', was re-worked next. Rather than being a B-Side the band intended to release a new version of the song as a featured single, as they had done with 'Walking After You' in 1998. Sticking to their familiar recording format drums and rhythm guitar was recorded for the song before Nate added a bass track. One late night Grohl attempted to record a new vocal take for the song but after one or two beers during a dinner BBQ party earlier in the evening, nothing useful could be captured by Mathewson. New boy Shiflett recorded his guitar parts the next day but efforts on the song were soon abandoned, leaving the new version unfinished and subsequently, the release plans were scrapped.

During the same radio appearance that Grohl had discussed the cover songs he also revealed that the band had recorded two entirely new original songs, describing the experience recording with Shiflett for the first time - "He was reading my mind the whole time, he and I come up with very similar ideas for guitar parts" he said of the instant chemistry.

According to Mathewson both new "experimental" songs were recorded without vocals and described the first as "Slow, Led Zeppelin-esque open tuning ballad", sounding similar to songs from Zeppelin's Physical Graffiti. A CD of the album was sitting on the recording console in the studio throughout the recording. The second track he described as having a "mid-tempo droney Rolling Stones feel" with a repeating riff before "a Sonic Youth-like explosion" at the end of the track, running "seven minutes long or so".

Despite the various plans and ideas for releasing the songs recorded during this session none came to fruition, all recordings from this session remaining unreleased and unheard by fans.

March 5th, 2000
Allerton Hill Studio, Windlesham, United Kingdom

Foo Fighters

Hawkins, Taylor (Drums, Vocals)

Grohl, Dave (Guitar)

Mendel, Nate (Bass Guitar)

Shiflett, Chris (Guitar)

Additional Musicians

May, Brian (Guitar)

Recording Credits

Shirley-Smith, Justin (Recording, Production)

Foo Fighters & Brian May (Producers)

Tracks Recorded

1. Have A Cigar

March 2000 saw Foo Fighters once again in a recording studio, this time tasked with recording a song for the soundtrack of Mission: Impossible 2, the first sequel in the popular movie franchise. Despite having a half-dozen or more unreleased songs left over from the recent recording sessions for 'There Is Nothing Left To Lose', the band elected to instead do over a finished track from those sessions, their cover of the Pink Floyd track 'Have A Cigar'. That first version, recorded at Studio 606 in Virginia, was featured as a B-Side to the 'Learn To Fly' single, released in October 1999.

Rather than re-record the track as just a four-piece including newly installed Guitarist Chris Shiflett, the band also enlisted the services of Queen guitarist Brian May, or rather Taylor Hawkins did. "Taylor rings me up and leaves me a message on my answering machine every week," May explained. "We wanna do this thing, and you've heard the B-side. Let's do another version. We want you to be on it and its gonna be incredible," exclaimed an excitable Hawkins to May.

The recording session took place at Allerton Hill, the home recording studio located on the second floor of May's house in Surrey, United Kingdom. Foo Fighters were in Europe to play a handful of shows to promote their new album, including one at the Scala nightclub in London on March 4th. Recording in Surrey took place the next day – "They came down my house, which was great, I have my studio down there. Normally its fairly quiet down there but they came down and invaded" May explained. "We had a brilliant weekend just kicking stuff around and doing this track which was really no effort whatsoever, it just happened."

As with their original recording, Grohl and Hawkins switched roles for the Floyd cover, with Taylor on lead vocals and Dave behind the drum kit, a scenario which Brian greatly enjoyed - " I got to have Dave Grohl playing drums in my studio, which was a big thrill for me I have to tell you. I've recorded Cozy [Powell, drummer for various bands including the Brian May Band and Whitesnake] in there and I've recorded Roger [Taylor, Queen drummer] and a few damn good drummers, but God, the guy's unbelievable." May also had heaps of praise for Taylor's vocal performance - "He is a very good singer, isn't he? Yeah. Damned good as far as I'm concerned."

The track was produced collaboratively by the five performers as well as longtime Queen producer Justin Shirley-Smith, who also recorded the song. Despite being unsure about his own guitar part, seeking reassurance from Hawkins at one point, May was happy with the overall result of the session. "It didn't get the corners knocked off it, it didn't get over-produced, and actually what you hear is what we did."

New boy Chris Shiflett gave a brief comment on his first proper Foo Fighters recording session in an interview with Kerrang! Magazine, stating that it was like "living in a comic book, 'cos you always think of those people as superheroes when you're a little kid".

The movie soundtrack was first released in May 2000 as well as getting radio airtime. The track was also later re-released on the 2011 Foo Fighters compilation record 'Medium Rare', alongside a selection of other cover songs recorded by the band over the years.

* * *

March 2001
Studio 606, Alexandria, VA, United States

Foo Fighters
Hawkins, Taylor (Drums, Vocals)

Grohl, Dave (Guitar)

Tracks Recorded
1. All My Life

Recording Equipment
Allen Sides' custom API Recording & Mixing Console

Neve Console Module

Studer A827 24-Track 2 Inch Tape Recorder

On March 19th, 2001 Dave Grohl and Taylor Hawkins were in Cleveland, Ohio to induct the legendary Queen into the Rock and Roll Hall Of Fame. The pair joined remaining members Roger Taylor and Brian May on stage at the ceremony for a rendition of their classic track 'Tie Your Mother Down', as well as giving an official induction speech. Returning home on a high, Grohl and Hawkins headed to Studio 606 to record the very first version of what would go on to become a classic track of their own.

"Dave just had a riff. We jammed it out a couple of times, and then he said 'Well, let me change it here, here is the other part'," said Hawkins of the new track. The riff/song in question was 'All My Life' and the pair put the rest of the song together at a quick pace.

"We came up with that rhythm interplay thing in the middle and basically put that together in like an hour, and then recorded it really quickly," added the drummer. According to Hawkins, this initial version was "pretty close" to the final version of the song, released on their 2002 album 'One By One'.

When it came to vocals for the song Grohl would "always procrastinate with the lyrics", unsure of what he would sing. "I didn't know what the hell I was gonna sing over it, because it's not the most melodic riff. I thought 'How am I gonna turn that into a song? What's the chorus'?" Writing something the night before tracking, the two were unsure of the results - "Does that work'? We thought, Well let's keep it for now and if we need to change it, we can," thought Grohl. In the end, the original lyrics were indeed almost entirely the same as those of the final song.

Chris and Nate were not present during this demo recording session, hearing the song for the first time when this rough demo was presented to them a month later.

* * *

April 2001
Taylor Hawkin's Home Studio, Topanga Canyon, CA

Foo Fighters

Hawkins, Taylor (Drums, Vocals)

Grohl, Dave (Guitar)

Mendel, Nate (Bass)

Shiflett, Chris (Guitar)

Tracks Recorded

1. Halo	5. Lonely As You
2. Knucklehead	6. Tears For Beers
3. Spooky Tune	others
4. Full Mount	

With no live shows booked between April and August 2001 Foo Fighters went into productivity mode, working towards what would be their fourth studio album. Throughout their extremely busy touring schedule of 2000 the band had still managed to find time to work on new songs and ideas, even teasing some riffs during a show in Germany.

Dave Grohl preferred recording away from large, commercial recording studios and having converted the basement of his house in Virginia into a recording studio, he later convinced Taylor Hawkins to do the same thing.

"The whole idea of building a home studio is just to be in complete control of everything," explained Grohl. "I will never work another way again. There's just no way. There's no clock on the wall, it's your fucking house, which also means that you decide who's allowed to come by the studio and who's not."

The renovation work at Hawkins' house got underway in early 2001 and by April the basement studio was in a state suitable for the band to get to work. Fourteen tracks were recorded over a fortnight, most of which only had descriptive, working titles at this stage. Journalist Joshua Sindell of Kerrang! magazine was invited to the home studio during recording and he observed some of these titles scribbled on a piece of paper taped to the floor. The band have long had a habit of giving songs a working title that simply references the artist or musical style they believe the track most resembles - two such examples during this session being 'Tom Petty' and 'Tears For Beers', the latter being a play on the English pop-rock band 'Tears For Fears'. The track they believed resembled Tom Petty musically was, in fact, the song later released under the title 'Halo'.

Two further descriptive working titles listed on the paper were 'Spooky Tune' and 'Full Mount', the former being a clearer description than the latter. Two further titles listed were more familiar, 'Lonely As You' and 'Knucklehead', the latter title remaining attached to an unreleased song in later recording sessions.

The demos from this session were taken forward for further pre-production sessions later in the year.

July 15th, 2001
Conway Recording Studios, Hollywood, CA

Recording Artists

Grohl, Dave (Guitar)

Hawkins, Taylor (Drums)

Homme, Josh (Guitar)

Keltner, Jim (Drums)

Novoselic, Krist (Bass Guitar)

Sparks, Donita (Vocals)

Sweeney, Matt (Guitar)

Tracks Recorded

unknown

On July 15th, 2001 Dave Grohl and Krist Novoselic convened in Los Angeles at Conway Recording Studios to oversee mixing and mastering of the final song Nirvana recorded in 1994, 'You Know You're Right'. The song was initially due to be released as part of an anthology box set in September 2001, marking the 10th anniversary of their seminal album 'Nevermind', however, later disagreements and legal battles between the pair and Courtney Love would scupper these plans. The song would eventually see release on the 2002 compilation simply titled 'NIRVANA'.

Mixing of the Nirvana track didn't take too long and so with an entire room at their disposal, Grohl and Novoselic decided to take advantage of the situation. "We had a big room at Conway to ourselves for the day and we thought, let's run tape and invite a bunch of our friends over," Grohl recalled.

Those friends invited were an eclectic bunch – Foo Fighters bandmate Taylor Hawkins, Queens Of The Stone Age front man Josh Homme, session drummer Jim Keltner, L7 singer Donita Sparks, and Matt Sweeney, guitarist for several bands such as Chavez and Zwan.

The makeshift 'supergroup' spent the day working on various loose jams and ideas, with Grohl particularly impressed by Jim Keltner's work - "He's a legend you know, his meter, his vibe, he's a real vibe player you know. So, he comes out, sits down behind a drumset, and does everything sideways, and backward. And as we're jamming, I look over and he's got a stick and a shaker in one hand, and a brush and a frying pan in the other and he's playing the snare with his foot or whatever", he recalled enthusiastically. "It was fucking crazy what he was doing, but it had this sound. And I watched it and I thought, THAT is messed up! And then I listened to it, and I thought, 'THAT is genius!'"

Whilst tape was known to be running throughout the impromptu recording session, no music from this day-long jam session has been released to date.

* * *

September 2001
Taylor Hawkin's Home Studio, Topanga Canyon, CA

Recording Artist

Grohl, Dave (Drums, Guitar, Bass)

Recording Credits

Aloi, Michael (Recording)

Tracks Recorded

1. Halo

2. Come Back

3. Untitled #1

4. Lonely As You

5. Untitled #2

After a break of several months Foo Fighters returned to the live stage in August 2001 with a planned two-week tour across Europe but with just three of those shows completed drummer Taylor Hawkins was admitted to hospital following a suspected drug overdose. To the relief of his friends and family Hawkins quickly recovered from the incident but was in no state to play shows, the remaining dates all canceled. Along with the rest of the band, he flew back home to the United States, checking into a rehabilitation clinic on his arrival.

Whilst he was away receiving treatment Hawkins asked his friend Michael Aloi to keep an eye on his LA home and look after his dog. Dave Grohl would also drop in at the house from time to time and on one occasion in September, to take his mind off the situation, decided to set up some equipment in the recently constructed studio at the house to continue work on ideas for the next Foo Fighters album, despite not knowing when Hawkins would again be available to work on it.

With the help of Aloi six songs were recorded, Grohl returning to his one-man-band setup by recording all instruments himself, including the grand piano Hawkins had installed in his studio. No vocals were recorded for any of the tracks according to Aloi, all remaining instrumental.

Tracked first was a version of 'Halo', still known at this point by its working title of 'Tom Petty'. The overall structure of the song was largely the same as the version later released on the album 'One By One' but this early demo naturally lacked some of the final polish found on that finished version. The guitar tracks were simpler with fewer overdubs and a similarly simple bass line just mirrored the guitar parts. The drum track was mostly the same, with Taylor Hawkins just adding a few more fills in his later recording. The song was also slightly faster in tempo at this point in its life but otherwise, the song was largely finalized in this initial demo recording.

Next to be recorded was 'Come Back', a song that would go through a significant transformation before its eventual release in 2002. The final version would be a two-part song with complex dynamics and layering but this early version was in comparison a much simpler, straightforward rock song with heavy, sludgy guitars and uncomplicated drum beats.

The intro of the song featured a palm muted guitar over the drums, unlike the heavily distorted guitar intro on the final version.

Grohl didn't give a title to the third song he recorded but it was, in fact, a very early version of what would later become the song 'She's Giving In' by Jackson United, a side project of Foo Fighters guitarist Chris Shiflett. The Grohl composition recorded at this session was relatively bare bones in comparison to the Jackson version, with a much slower tempo and a more relaxed feeling in general. The guitar parts recorded by Dave were simple and clean with none of the frantic leads found on the later recording. Drums were similarly light and basic although this version did feature more pronounced hi-hat work during the intro. The bass guitar was again very simple, a straightforward walking bass line throughout most of the track.

The much-evolved version of the song recorded by Jackson United was featured on their debut album 'Western Ballads', released in October 2004.

The fourth song to be tracked by Grohl during this session was one more familiar to Foo Fighters fans, 'Lonely As You'. As with 'Come Back' recorded earlier, this version of the song was far rawer and embryonic in nature. The subdued introduction of the album version was not present, the recording instead jumping straight into the riff of the song with heavy drumming standing out, at least in the initial rough mixes. There was no guitar solo or any layered guitar tracks present at this stage, just the basic riffs, and repeated verses.

The fifth track was a second original Grohl composition that later became a Jackson United song, 'Sharp Edges'. This early version was again still very early in development, even more so than the first track. The drumming was much more subdued as was the guitar, featuring only a very simple rhythm track throughout with no heavy riffs as can be heard on the Jackson version. As with 'She's Giving In', the song was included on the 'Western Ballads' album.

Finally, Grohl recorded an early version of the track 'Burn Away', differing from the version on 'One By One' in several ways. The recording opened with a mixture of very light guitar and piano before exploding into life with Grohl's signature heavy drum beats. The tempo of the song was much faster and as was the case with other tracks recorded during this session, the overall structure was far simpler, Grohl just repeating the same simple chorus and verse. The palm muted guitar was not present during the verses however the main guitar melody was already in place, which would be matched with the vocal melody in the final recording. Despite the faster tempo, this version of the track ran for five and a half minutes, some thirty seconds longer than the album version, partly due to the bridge section being extended.

Rough mixes of the session were mixed down to DAT and CD so Dave could take the songs back to the rest of the band for further work, once Taylor had fully recovered. None of the recordings from this session have ever been publicly released.

* * *

October 2001
Studio 606, Alexandria, VA, United States

Foo Fighters

Hawkins, Taylor (Drums)

Grohl, Dave (Guitar, Vocals)

Mendel, Nate (Bass)

Shiflett, Chris (Guitar)

Recording Credits

Kasper, Adam (Producer)

Raskulinecz, Nick (Engineer)

Tracks Recorded

1. Win or Lose

Recording Equipment

Allen Sides' custom API Recording & Mixing Console

Neve Console Module

Studer A827 24-Track 2 Inch Tape Recorder

November 2001 saw the release of 'Out Cold', a snowboarding based comedy film starring Jason London and A. J. Cook. Along with bands such as Sum 41, Andrew WK and Jimmy Eat World Foo Fighters were requested to appear on the companion soundtrack.

As was the case with a handful of past contributions to movie soundtracks the band elected to re-record an older song rather than give away a brand new track. The song, in this case, was 'Make A Bet', a song first recorded by Dave Grohl in 1992 as part of the 'Allister Lob' project. The song was then later again recorded by Foo Fighters during pre-production recording sessions for their second album 'The Colour And The Shape'.

The band had re-convened at Studio 606 in early October following Taylor's overdose in August and quickly got to work re-imagining the song. The new recording was noticeably more produced than the earlier recordings with more layered guitar work and an overall slicker sound. The core structure of the song remained largely the same with a near identical runtime.

For reasons that have never been made clear, the track was submitted with the title 'Win Or Lose', rather than 'Make A Bet', both lines featuring as lyrics in the song. The track was first included on the movie soundtrack released in November 2001 and was then also included as a B-Side on two Foo Fighters releases in 2002 - on a CD single for 'The One' and then on the 'All My Life' single in various formats.

November to January 2001
Studio 606, Alexandria, VA, United States

Foo Fighters

Hawkins, Taylor (Drums)   Mendel, Nate (Bass)

Grohl, Dave (Guitar, Vocals)   Shiflett, Chris (Guitar)

Recording Credits

Kasper, Adam (Producer)

Raskulinecz, Nick (Engineer)

Tracks Recorded

1. All My Life   9. Tired Of You

2. Halo   10. Attica!

3. Gun Beside My Bed   11. Lonely As You

4. New Wave   12. Come Back

5. Bottomed Out   13. Burn Away

6. The One   14. Walking A Line

7. Asshole   15. Normal

8. Knucklehead   16. Have It All

Recording Equipment

Allen Sides' custom API Recording & Mixing Console

Neve Console Module

Studer A827 24-Track 2 Inch Tape Recorder

Towards the end of the 1990s and into the new millennium online communication was really starting to take off, with many bands operating a website. The official Foo Fighters website also had a message board feature, allowing fans around the world to chat with each other about the band. The board also had a special section where the band members themselves could post messages if they so desired.

On November 13th, 2001 Taylor Hawkins posted a message to the board to assure fans that he was back in good health following his overdose, contrary to many reports in the media at the time. He also revealed to fans that the band were back in Dave's basement studio in Alexandria, Virginia, and had begun recording material for their fourth studio album. Hawkins message mentioned that they had already started recording a new version of 'All My Life', a track he and Grohl had first demoed together earlier in the year.

Since recording 'There Is Nothing Left To Lose' in the basement studio some new recording equipment had been acquired, with new amplifiers including a vintage Marshall and a Hiwatt cabinet from the 1970s, formerly owned by Cheap Trick guitarist Rick Neilsen. The tape machine was however still the same Studer A827 24 track, recording onto 2-inch magnetic tape. Producing the session was once again Adam Kasper, who had worked in the same role on their previous record.

At the start of the recording session, the band had twenty-nine new songs that they were planning to work on, whittling them down to a suitable number for an album by the end. By mid-November songs already worked on extensively included 'Halo', 'Gun Beside My Bed', 'New Wave', 'Bottomed Out' and 'The One'.

The latter was almost finished by this point as it was

recorded for use on the soundtrack to the movie 'Orange County', starring Grohl's friend Jack Black. The track was also released to radio, albeit as an edited version. 'The One' became the first Foo Fighters song to be released with explicit lyrics - "You're not the one, but you're the only one to make me feel like shit," Grohl sang.

With the first song in the bag, work continued throughout November with Grohl sporadically updating online fans with their progress. At this stage, working titles were still commonplace, with one rather blunt label being 'Asshole'. "I think I might change [it] because I'm not so sure that Carson Daily will be able to introduce the video to all the little kiddies unless I do," joked Grohl. "Tentative titles are tricky because more often than not they stick. I guess we'll see what happens with this one....it kicks though." Another song completed in mid-November was 'Knucklehead', a track they had already worked on in the spring.

Whilst Adam Kasper had returned to produce, he was not the one pressing the record button this time. That (among other roles) was instead left for Nick Raskulinecz. Nick had previously worked as an engineer at the famous Sound City studios, first meeting the band in 1998 whilst they were at the studio recording the song 'A320' for the Godzilla soundtrack. He and Grohl hit it off on that occasion but it wasn't until a chance meeting in an LA parking lot some three years later that the two met up again. "He told me the Foo Fighters were getting ready to go back to Virginia to make a new record and asked me if I was interested in going back with him and engineering the record at his house," Raskulincez recalled.

Late November saw a short break in recording as the band headed to New York to film a music video for 'The One'. When recording resumed Grohl revealed in another online message that the band were "a third of the way done with the drum tracks" and revealed that the number of songs the band was working on had increased by three, to thirty-two. "The list of songs is getting longer. I keep remembering stuff that I wrote while we were out on tour for the last few years. Stuff that I never bothered to put on tape," explained Grohl. "Usually, if I think I'm onto something good, the least I'll do is call my voicemail and leave ideas there, but so many of them slip through the cracks. I really want to give every one of them a chance but I'm afraid if I do, we'll be stuck in the basement for the next year and a half."

As recording was taking place at Grohl's private house Foo Fighters were not restricted to a set time schedule, with recording going long into the night on some occasions. Drum tracks continued to be recorded and by the very last days of November work on the guitar tracks had begun, with scratch takes being put to tape.

The band was also still working through the list of songs, with another track started and given the tentative title of 'Get Up, I Want To Get Down'. The song according to Grohl was "a monster" with Hawkins adding that it was "The most kick-ass, motherfucking, ass licking, dick smoking song of all time." Whilst Foo Fighters did not ultimately release a song under the title, it was instead utilized by Hawkins on his 2006 side project 'Taylor Hawkins & The Coattail Riders', an entirely different song for which he 'borrowed' the title.

Recording continued into December and by the fifth, all drum tracks were finished. Grohl described one unspecified song as "the B-52's playing a Black Sabbath song.... or vice versa." By mid-December the recording of guitar tracks was in full flow, with Grohl extremely enthused by the work being completed - "We have entered uncharted territory here.... finding new ways to make a guitar sound like an angry old power tool, which is exactly how it should sound. Adam has cracked the code. Nick is mixing up some serious shit over on his side of the laboratory. It's getting weird. It's getting noisy," enthused Grohl.

The recording was progressing well according to Grohl, painting a picture of a well-oiled machine. "It's getting done a lot faster than we expected. That's a good thing. Last record we just set up a mike and hit record. This time we set up a mike, make the amp scream like a wild banshee, and run for cover." Work continued with the rhythm guitar tracks up to the third week of December before a break was called for the Christmas holidays.

When the band reconvened in the new year it was apparent to those at the studio that progress was not progressing as well as Grohl has publicly suggested. With the band spending day after day at the studio tensions were rising, disagreements were becoming more commonplace and progress was slowing. Only six songs were fully completed in two months and the decision was made that a change of scenery would be the best option. "[We] are going out to LA to do the rest. Need a change of scenery," Grohl calmly announced. "The basement was getting smaller and smaller. It's no fun feeling like a rat in the sewer, never seeing the light of day, only coming out at night to hit up the 7-11 for Slurpees and microwaveable pork cracklins."

Despite being previously adamant that recording at home, in your own time, was the only way to record an album the new location for recording was the exact opposite. Conway Recording Studio was a huge, state of the art professional studio in the heart of Los Angeles, with recording time coming at a premium cost. The band packed up their gear, grabbed their unfinished recordings and headed for Hollywood.

* * *

January to February 2002
Conway Recording Studios, Hollywood, CA

Foo Fighters
Hawkins, Taylor (Drums)

Grohl, Dave (Guitar, Vocals)

Mendel, Nate (Bass)

Shiflett, Chris (Guitar)

Additional Musicians
May, Brian (Guitar)

Novoselic, Krist (Backing Vocals)

Recording Credits
Kasper, Adam (Producer)

Raskulinecz, Nick (Engineer)

Tracks Recorded
1. All My Life

2. Halo

3. Come Back

4. Walking A Line

5. Have It All

6. Normal

7. Burn Away

8. Lonely As You

9. Overdrive

10. Tired Of You

11. Knucklehead

Foo Fighters arrived at Conway Recording Studios in mid-January 2002, hoping to be able to finish the work they had started in Virginia three months earlier. Despite Dave Grohl and Taylor Hawkins painting a picture of almost complete recording bliss via messages on the band's online message board, the truth was somewhat different. Tensions had been running high in the basement studio, with nobody entirely happy with how things were going. Grohl was critical of his bandmates, telling them he felt they were lacking enthusiasm. Hawkins later stated he believed nobody "had their studio chops on" and suggested that the band were too focused on perfect production, using the digital Pro Tools system for the first time. The mixes "sucked a lot of the life out [of the songs]" according to Grohl, suggesting that the results "sounded like another band playing our songs."

Hoping that the change of scenery really would help improve matters, the band got to work. On January 21st, a few days into recording, they were joined at the studio by Queen guitarist Brian May. Invited by Hawkins in an attempt to stifle some of the tension, May recorded guitar parts for two songs, 'Knucklehead' and 'Tired Of You', although the second was somewhat of an afterthought. "This is a really sparse one guitar and one vocal song – but then in the chorus, Brian May overdubbed these 4-part guitar harmony swells – it's fucking insane," Dave Grohl said describing his contribution to the second song. He's the only guest appearance on the record but you wouldn't even have to put his fucking name on the album because someone would hear that song and be like 'oh my god – that sounds like Queen.' It sounds like a string section, but he did it with a guitar and it's fucking amazing."

Whilst May was the only guest on the eventual album, he wasn't the only guest to arrive at the Los Angeles studio.

Grohl invited friend and former Nirvana bandmate Krist Novoselic to join them yet rather than recording bass, as would be expected, Novoselic instead recorded backing vocals for the track 'Walking A Line'. In the liner notes for a special edition of the album 'One By One', Nate Mendel described 'Walking A Line' as "a better-than-average punk rock sing-along" and noted that "depending on fader position" Krist Novoselic may or may not have participated, referring to the fact Novoselic's vocals were either very low in the mix or not included at all.

By the end of recording in Los Angeles ten songs were considered finished - 'All My Life', 'Lonely As You', 'Come Back', 'Overdrive', 'Halo', 'Have It All', 'Burn Away', 'Tired Of You', 'Normal' and 'Walking A line'.

Recording was completed at Conway on February 6th and the following day the band played a live show at Anaheim's House Of Blues, a benefit show for MAP (Musicians' Assistance Program, a program assisting musicians health needs including drug rehabilitation). During the show four of the new tracks were debuted live - 'All My Life', 'Come Back', 'Overdrive' and 'Tired Of You', with Grohl revealing to the crowd that the record was done. Despite the apparent enthusiasm from Dave and the rest of the band during the public appearance, the truth was far from different. Grohl considered the end product "far too clean, too tame and boring," and despite having thirty-two songs in the works at one point, just ten were extensively worked on at Conway.

Of those ten tracks, the band was happy with only half. "Five of 'em we liked. The other five we thought were okay, but we were basically just making songs that we thought people would want to hear on an album." Said Grohl.

Despite these reservations, a record was for all intents and purposes finished and ready to release, if they so wished.

"Our manager, John [Silva], actually made the call," recalled Grohl. "He said, 'you know what? I like half of it. The other half just sounds like singles to me. And I don't think that's what you guys are all about, and it's not what you guys should do'." With the band and their management in agreement, almost everything worked on during this session, including the earlier groundwork laid at Studio 606, was shelved. "At that point, that's when I sort of called it and said, 'okay, let's stop, let's back away from it, re-evaluate'," Grohl remembered. Taylor Hawkins would later refer to the failed recording as the 'Million Dollar Demos', hinting at the huge cost the band incurred during the process to that point.

Of the eleven tracks worked on during this session, ten were deemed finished, the exception being one of the two Brian May featured tracks, 'Knucklehead'. Whilst the band decided against forming an album from the complete recordings, three tracks were publicly released. 'Tired Of You', the second track to feature Brian May was included on all copies of the final album whilst 'Walking A Line' was included as a bonus track on special editions of the record. 'Normal' also saw release as a B-Side.

The remaining seven finished tracks have never been officially released however two separate 'leaks' have since given fans a chance to hear them. The first of those came before the final album was even released by way of a mix up at the record label. By 2002, internet file sharing peer to peer (P2P) programs like Napster and Kazaa were very popular, allowing users to illegally share the latest albums by top artists like Foo Fighters.

To hinder users of these programs, record companies would upload the albums themselves, except the songs would be incomplete and cut up, frustrating users who spent several hours downloading them.

As the decision to scrap the album came very late in the day a mix up occurred, with Sony BMG uploading the jumbled clips of what they believed to be the final album to these P2P programs. Despite attempts to remove the clips once their mistake was realized it was already too late, with thousands of fans downloading and further sharping the clips. Recordings of 'All My Life', 'Burn Away', 'Halo', 'Have It All', 'Lonely As You', 'Overdrive' and 'Come Back' were all made available, ranging in length from just twenty seconds of 'Have It All' up to almost a minute and a half of 'All My Life'.

A decade later saw a more extensive leak of the songs, with an anonymous source uploading full-length recordings of all seven songs not officially released. Fans were finally able to hear the 'Million Dollar Demos', with the unfinished 'Knucklehead' now the only track worked on during these sessions yet to be released in any form.

This scrapped version of 'All My Life' was structurally very similar to the re-recorded version although some differences were apparent. The soft, whisper-like vocals in the verses were quieter with fewer guitar dynamics in the breakdown section. The final 'done, done, onto the next one' vocals at the end of the song featured a moderate distortion effect on Grohl's voice, as if recorded through a megaphone.

'Burn Away', 'Come Back', 'Halo' and 'Lonely As You' were all mostly similar to the versions Grohl had recorded solo at Taylor Hawkins' home studio in September 2001.

Vocals had of course been recorded during these sessions, however, with 'Lonely As You' featuring some key differences over the final album version. After the brief, quiet intro the loud, crashing drums were accompanied by a shrieking "YEAH" from Grohl. At the start of each chorus,

Grohl would ask 'Is anyone out there?' and there was only one 'One more time for the last time' verse. That was followed by one further difference, a much more pronounced guitar solo from Chris.

'Have It All' was structured much closer to the way the band played the track live after the release of the album. For the most part, it was very similar to the album version but does have a heavier sound during the outro and fades out rather than coming to a natural end.

With their fourth studio album essentially scrapped Foo Fighters needed to regroup and decide what to do next.

* * *

April 2002
Taylor Hawkins' Home Studio, Topanga Canyon, CA

Foo Fighters

Hawkins, Taylor (Drums)

Grohl, Dave (Guitar, Bass)

Tracks Recorded

1. Low (instrumental)

2. Times Like These (instrumental)

3. Disenchanted Lullaby (instrumental)

Recording Equipment

Studer A827 24-Track 2 Inch Tape Recorder

Makie 32/8 Recording Console

With four months of work scrapped amid massive tensions within the band, the future of Foo Fighters was uncertain in the Spring of 2002. No clear plans were in place for what the band was going to do next, everyone "taking a break". The latest recruit to the band Chris Shiflett was in the dark, wondering if his tenure with the band would be short-lived. "Wait, are we breaking up? Is that what this means, like 'taking a break' is a nice way of saying breaking up?"

There was no clear roadmap for the future of Foo Fighters in place and Dave Grohl soon went off to join desert rockers Queens Of The Stone age. "I've known them for years and they invited me to play on this record. It's great music to play drums to. They're amazing live and they needed a drummer, so I thought I'd do it." Grohl saw himself back in the role of being 'just' the drummer in a band once again, out of the spotlight. "It's really about just playing the drums. I feel much more comfortable and confident doing this than trying to sing every night," revealed Grohl.

Despite Chris' concerns, Dave Grohl was in fact not ready to call it a day with Foo Fighters. When a short break appeared in the Queen's schedule, he reached out an olive branch to Taylor Hawkins. "I had this two-week period that was, like, downtime, so I called Taylor and said, 'hey, why don't you and I go to Virginia and record some shit? I have a couple of new ideas." Hawkins agreed but rather than going back to Virginia the pair convened at Hawkins' home studio in California, hoping to be able to move the band forward.

According to Hawkins, the pair demoed five or six new songs at his house, including 'Low', 'Times Like These' and 'Disenchanted Lullaby'. "They were just instrumentals," said Grohl of the recordings. "I wasn't really concerned with making the rest of the record. It was just, like, 'okay, let's get back into just fucking around, how about that? Let's just do it, because I live 25 minutes away from you, and I can come up to your house and we can put something to tape for fun.'"

Three of the six songs would go on to be recorded with the rest of the band and ultimately released on the album 'One By One', however, none of these instrumental demos have ever been released publicly.

* * *

May 6th to 18th, 2002
Studio 606, Alexandria, VA, United States

Foo Fighters
Hawkins, Taylor (Drums)

Grohl, Dave (Guitar, Vocals)

Recording Credits
Raskulinecz, Nick (Producer)

Tracks Recorded
1. All My Life	6. Have It All
2. Lonely As You	7. Burn Away
3. Come Back	8. Low
4. Overdrive	9. Times Like These
5. Halo	10. Disenchanted Lullaby

Recording Equipment
Allen Sides' custom API Recording & Mixing Console

Neve Console Module

Studer A827 24-Track 2 Inch Tape Recorder

Foo Fighters continued to try and move forward from the disastrous few months that had almost ended the band and with a handful of new songs demoed by Grohl and Hawkins, the pair were feeling a little more positive. On May 6th, 2002 the duo headed back to Studio 606 in Virginia and once again got to work. For this session Nick Raskulinecz had been promoted to the role of producer, following a call with Grohl a few weeks earlier. The pair had discussed the state of the recording up to that point and Nick was asked for his honest opinions on its quality. "Dave called me up point blank one day and asked if I thought the record was as good as it could be," Nick recalled. Deciding honesty was the best policy the engineer gave Grohl a clear answer - no. "I thought it could be better," he believed. Appreciating his honesty and knowing his abilities Grohl asked Raskulinecz if he felt he could produce a new version, a challenge he was up for.

Nate Mendel and Chris Shiflett were not present at the studio, nor were they even aware of what was taking place. Recording, therefore, got underway with just three men present – Grohl, Hawkins and the newly promoted Raskulinecz. "Taylor and I went back to Virginia, and we recorded the basic tracks for everything in like 12 days. All the vocals, all the guitars, and all the drums," Grohl explained.

Of the tracks previously recorded, 'All My Life', 'Lonely As You', 'Come Back', 'Overdrive', 'Halo', 'Have It All' and 'Burn Away' were all re-done by the pair. Tracks such as 'Knucklehead' were left on the cutting room floor whilst the original recording of 'Tired Of You' was deemed okay, Brian May's contribution on that first version helping towards that decision.

Proper versions of their newly demoed songs were also

put to tape, bringing the number of songs deemed finished to eleven.

The newly re-recorded tracks had a varying level of similarity to their initial versions in terms of structure, but the trio felt overall all of the new recordings were more akin to their previous record 'There Is Nothing Left To Lose', sounding more natural and organic. "'All My Life' we had for a long time, not necessarily with all the lyrics, but the basic structure. The same with 'Have It All'," drummer Hawkins explained. "We ended up making them better when we re-recorded them, because we did it without all the technology and ProTools, and went for more of a real human feel, as opposed to this quantized Limp Bizkit version."

The changes to two songs were very drastic. "Completely unrecognizable" is how Hawkins described the track 'Come Back'. The song had changed from a simple, 4-minute hard rock song into a 7-minute epic featuring an extended, instrumental breakdown section two-thirds in. The drummer described the changes to 'Lonely As You' in a similar manner, with more drastic changes undertaken. A quiet intro section had been added to the song with whisper-like vocals from Grohl and the lyrics later in the song had also seen big changes. The line 'Is anyone out there?' was gone and Grohl would sing 'One more time for the last time' several times more than the original. Overall the song length was cut down by approximately 40 seconds.

"Recognizable, but we put a big line of cocaine on top of it" was the somewhat odd way Hawkins described the changes to 'Overdrive'. "We did it in an early Police record fashion, as opposed to the sterile "Learn to Fly" fashion that it was originally."

A new version of their album was now recorded but there was, of course, a problem – half of the band knew nothing about it. With the problems causing by re-recording an album behind the back of one former drummer and the tension surrounding earlier recordings for this album, Grohl made the potentially difficult phone call midway through the session. "I called up Nate and Chris and said, 'hey, I think we just re-recorded the whole record here.' And they were, like, 'what?!' 'Yeah, we did three songs yesterday, we're doing two today, we're doing three songs tomorrow.'" Grohl explained to the pair how recording "just came together - there was no time to fuck around, there was no time to overanalyze, it was just all about making music because we were excited to do it and the energy was really there." Thankfully Mendel and Shiflett were understanding of the situation and Grohl told them he still needed them to record their parts for the songs, although there was another issue.

Dave Grohl was still drumming for Queens Of The Stone Age and after a short break was due back on the road with his side-band. This meant two things. Firstly, since Studio 606 was also Dave Grohl's personal home, they wouldn't be able to go there to record their parts without Dave present. Secondly, it meant they would have to record their parts without the band leader to oversee their work in any manner. "[They] were left to do all of their recording on their own. So, they were basically left to play the parts that they wanted to play," said Grohl of the situation.

The drummer for hire headed off, knowing that Foo Fighters fourth studio album was turning out to be extremely troubled, and now rather unconventional. "When you imagine a band making an album, you imagine four guys, in the studio, playing the song once, singing everything live and doing it. That seems like what you should do. But it doesn't necessarily work that way," he explained. Whilst the process for this album was strange, Grohl was very aware that previous Foo Fighters albums had not been created in a conventional manner either. "We've always had sort of a weird way of making records, whether it's someone else playing the drums, or recording it in three different places," Grohl said, describing the troubled recording of second album 'The Colour And The Shape'. "I think the way we made the album was a very healthy way, compared to the way a lot of other records are made these days. It almost seemed like an experiment that worked. But I listen to it, and I think it's a pretty good representation of the band. Warts and all, it's fuckin'--the band. And that's what it should be, I guess."

At the end of twelve days of recording Dave Grohl duly headed back out on the road with Queens Of The Stone Age, leaving Raskulincz to arrange the recording of Chris and Nate's parts of the album at a later date.

* * *

Late May 2002
The Hook Studios, Los Angeles, CA, United States

Foo Fighters
Mendel, Nate (Bass)

Shiflett, Chris (Guitar)

Recording Credits
Raskulinecz, Nick (Producer)

Tracks Recorded

1. All My Life	6. Have It All
2. Lonely As You	7. Burn Away
3. Come Back	8. Low
4. Overdrive	9. Times Like These
5. Halo	10. Disenchanted Lullaby

Having heard the surprise news that Dave Grohl and Taylor Hawkins had re-recorded much of the new album in Virginia, Nate Mendel and Chris Shiflett had the strange and unconventional task of heading into a studio alone to add their own parts. With Grohl heading away on tour with Queens Of The Stone Age his home studio was not a viable option for the duo and so they and producer Nick Raskulinecz instead headed to The Hook Studios, situated in the Woodlands Hill suburb of Los Angeles.

"It was a weird way to make a record" explained Shiflett. "We had made a version of it, but we shelved that and then came back and made another one pretty quickly. Dave was leaving the next day to go back on the road with the Queens so we sat down in the studio with Nick and listened to the demos."

Without Grohl to oversee proceedings it was up to producer Nick to take control and instruct Shiflett and Mendel. "He'd say things like 'I think you should play a little something in there. Play a little melody on that chorus'" recalled Shiflett. He and Raskulinecz went through each song, listening to the guitar tracks Grohl had already recorded and deciding which parts needed further work, either doubling Dave's parts for a bigger sound or adding some unique touches. "[Dave] just left me and Nick to record my guitars and that was that, and I didn't even know what was going to make it on to the disc or not. But a lot of it did, even though it was a weird, broken-up way of making a record. Everyone did their parts separately."

Recording at The Hook took place towards the end of May at which point the fourth Foo Fighters album was complete for a second time. This time the band were happy enough with the results and the album was mixed and mastered, combining the work from May with 'Tired Of You' from the earlier sessions. The Foo Fighters troubled fourth album, 'One By One', was released in October 2002.

* * *

Summer 2002
Taylor Hawkins' home studio, Topanga Canyon, CA

Foo Fighters

Hawkins, Taylor (Drums, Vocals)

Grohl, Dave (Guitar, Vocals)

Mendel, Nate (Bass Guitar)

Shiflett, Chris (Guitar, Vocals)

Additional Musicians

Bissonette, Greg (Drums)

Recording Credits

Raskulinecz, Nick (Producer)

Tracks Recorded

1. Darling Nikki

2. Danny Says

3. Life Of Illusion

4. Sister Europe

Recording Equipment

Studer A827 24-Track 2 Inch Tape Recorder

Makie 32/8 Recording Console

Recording for the fourth Foo Fighters album could best be described as troubling. Re-recordings and blazing rows had almost led to the end of the band but eventually they got themselves back on track, finishing up recording on the album in May 2002. Whilst the band had recorded enough material for a full-length album, they found themselves a little short on material to use as B-Sides on future singles, most of the outtakes from recording deemed not good enough. With that in mind, a few weeks after recording wrapped up they decided to get together once more to record a handful of cover songs, something Hawkins said the band usually enjoyed doing after recording an album anyway.

Rather than head to a professional studio or even Dave's own Studio 606 the band instead headed once more to Hawkins' house in Topanga Canyon, California. The home studio had seen a lot of recent use by Foo Fighters over the previous year whilst working towards the new record with early demos recorded there, Grohl using it as a place to work on recordings whilst Hawkins was in rehab following his overdose and then in April 2002 he and Taylor returned there to work on new songs after scrapping the first version of the record.

Working in the sweaty basement studio on a hot California summer day each member of the band chose a song they wanted the band to work on. Dave Grohl's choice was 'Darling Nikki', a track from Prince's critically acclaimed 1984 album 'Purple Rain'. According to Hawkins, his band leader found the song "really funky" but they had only really recorded it "as sort of a joke". The recording turned out well enough for the band to consider using it as a B-Side but Prince himself would, however, scupper that plan.

"We wanted to put it out here in the States, but Prince wouldn't let us," Hawkins said, adding "I heard that he didn't like our version. Or maybe he just didn't like us doing it." The drummer was seemingly unsure of the reason for the objection but the man himself cleared it up to some degree when asked if he liked the cover. "No!" was his blunt response, explaining that he didn't like anyone covering his songs at all - "Write your own tunes!"

Despite Hawkins insinuation that Prince blocked the release of the song, this was not entirely accurate. Under US Copyright law a songwriter is obliged to give a license to anyone wishing to cover their song although it naturally comes with the cost to the new performer of royalties. Under normal circumstances the writer/rights holder of a song - in this case Prince - would negotiate the royalty fee with the artist performing the cover, keeping them to a low and reasonable figure. With Prince refusing to enter any negotiations if Foo Fighters were to release their cover of 'Darling Nikki', they would have to pay the standard, extremely high royalty fee. As a result of this setback, the cover saw a limited release, featuring on only the Australian and European editions of the 'Have It All' single. Despite not seeing release in the United States not long after it became available elsewhere the song began to get serious airplay across the country. The cover became extremely popular, with many retailers in the US importing copies of the CD.

For Chris Shiflett, his cover of choice was 'Danny Says', a love song ballad by the usually raucous punk pioneers The Ramones. As well as recording guitar on the track Shiflett also sang lead vocals, the first time he'd ever done so in a studio and becoming the third Foo Fighter to sing lead vocals on a track, with Taylor Hawkins having previously taken the mantle on Pink Floyd cover 'Have A Cigar'.

Naturally apprehensive about his first vocal performance, Shiflett soon got into the swing of things - "Once I did it, it gave me a lot more confidence I was like, 'Wow, I can do this if I just double the fuckin' thing," referring to the technique of recording the vocal track twice and dubbing the second recording onto the first. As well as being the first Foo Fighters track to feature Shiflett on lead vocals another anomaly was with the man sitting on the drum stool. Instead of being recorded by Hawkins or even Grohl, prolific session & touring musician Greg Bissonette dropped by the studio to perform on the track, although he would not be credited when the song was released as a B-Side in 2003. It wouldn't be until the song was re-released on the 2011 compilation 'Medium Rare' the drummer would get his due credit.

Taylor's choice was the Joe Walsh track 'Life Of Illusion' with vocal duties once again switched up, Hawkins taking the role whilst this time Grohl would take the sticks. The Psychedelic Furs track 'Sister Europe' was last to be recorded, although whether the track was actually the choice of Nate Mendel is something of a mystery. Rumors among fans at the time suggested the bassist wanted to cover a Talking Heads song but had been shot down by the rest of the band. Whether true or not, it was the Furs track they would record, this time with every band member reprising their usual role.

All four songs were released in some form and with that Foo Fighters work in the studio was over, for the time being, focus switching to touring in support of their fourth album.

* * *

March 2003
Grandmaster Recorders, Hollywood, CA, United States

Recording Artist
Grohl, Dave (Guitar, Vocals, Piano)

Recording Credits
Raskulinecz, Nick (Producer)

Tracks Recorded
1. Times Like These

Recording Equipment
Studer A827 24-Track 2 Inch Tape Recorder

Neve 8028 Console

Towards the end of March 2003, Dave Grohl joined post-punk veterans Killing Joke at Grandmaster Records in Hollywood, invited along by the band's leader Jaz Coleman. The pair had met earlier in the year when both Killing Joke and Foo Fighters performed at the Big Day Out Festival in Auckland, New Zealand. Grohl spent around a week with the band at the studio recording drum tracks for their self-titled 11th studio album.

Whilst at the studio Dave undertook a completely different project, recording a new version of the 'One By One song 'Times Like These', produced once again by Nick Raskulinecz. Video director Bill Yukich also joined Grohl at the studio as it was planned to direct a music video around the recording session.

The new version of the song was acoustic, for the most part featuring only vocals and acoustic guitar. One further addition to the track came from the custom Yamaha grand piano at the studio, and whilst Grohl had never learned the instrument, was able to record some simple notes for the song. The recording was completed very quickly with the final mixed and mastered song being added to the footage of the recording shot by Yukich. The video, the third version for the song (Liam Lynch and Mark Klasfield each directed a video for the original recording of the song) was sent to broadcasters and was later released by the band on the 'DVD/EP' video release in September 2003.

After recording this new acoustic version of the song Grohl would begin performing the song in a similar manner in live performance, the first known occurrence being on the KROQ FM Kevin & Bean show on April 3rd, 2003.

* * *

* * *

November 2004 to February 2005
Studio 606 West, Northridge, CA, United States

Foo Fighters

Hawkins, Taylor (Drums, Vocals)

Grohl, Dave (Guitar, Vocals)

Mendel, Nate (Bass Guitar)

Shiflett, Chris (Guitar, Vocals)

Additional Musicians

Beebe, Joe (Guitar)

Clinch, Danny (Harmonica)

Haden, Petra (Violin)

Homme, Josh (Guitar)

Jaffee, Rami (Keyboards)

Jones, John Paul (Mandolin, Piano)

Jones, Norah (Vocals)

Raskulinecz, Nick (Double Bass, Bass)

Recording Credits

Raskulinecz, Nick (Producer)

Tracks Recorded

1. No Way Back
2. The Sign
3. Best Of You
4. White Limo
5. Resolve
6. 7 Corners
7. In Your Honor
8. World
9. DOA (Take #1)
10. DOA (Take #2)
11. DOA (Take #3)
12. The Last Song

13. Free Me

14. Resolve (Take #1)

15. Resolve (Take #2)

16. Resolve (Take #3)

17. Resolve (Take #4)

18. The Deepest Blues Are Black

19. End Over End

20. Spill

21. What If I Do

22. Miracle

23. Another Round

24. Friend Of A Friend

25. Over And Out

26. On The Mend

27. Virginia Moon

28. Cold Day In The Sun

29. Razor

30. The Sign

31. I'm In Love With a German Filmstar

32. FFL

33. Spill

34. Oh, Yeah

Recording Equipment

Neve 8058 recording console

Studer A827 24-Track 2 Inch Tape Recorder

Preparation for the fifth Foo Fighters studio album began in late 2003, immediately following the conclusion of touring for the previous album, 'One By One'. After almost 18 months on the road, Dave Grohl had several new songs written and headed home to Studio 606 to commit them to tape. Whilst their studio 'base' was still in Virginia most of the band members were now living on the West coast, thousands of miles away. This made arranging long-term recording projects an issue, with band members not wanting to be away from their family for extended periods of time. Another issue was with Studio 606 itself.

Whilst the band enjoyed the privacy and laid back nature of recording in Grohl's home basement the space was not particularly large, and had certain challenges and issues that came with having a recording studio in the basement of your house - "we'd have to stop doing vocals sometimes, because you could hear the crows outside through the microphones," said Grohl of one of those issues. "Or I'd have a couple of beers, go to bed, and then at two o'clock in the afternoon, I'd hear a kick drum coming through the heating vent. I mean - it's my fucking house". It was, therefore, decided the band needed a new private studio on the west coast with the greater Los Angeles area making the most sense.

So dawned a huge project for Dave and the entire Foo Fighters organization – relocate Studio 606 two and a half thousand miles across the country. Of course, it would not be literal, nor that simple. "My original intent was to create something really low-key like my basement studio in Virginia where we made the last two records," said Grohl. "It was homemade, low-budget and low-tech, but a lot of good shit came out of there. I thought that was our vibe."

His ambitions soon grew, and a much grander idea was soon devised with plans to buy a large, empty warehouse type building and within it create a huge space for the band. It would serve both a recording studio and a storage space for their ever-growing collection of guitars, drums, and other equipment. "We wanted a nice big control room where people could smoke if they wanted to and it wouldn't drive everybody else out," said Nick Raskulinecz of one aspect to the plans. "Then it just made sense, since Dave had tons of gear scattered around the country, to build a place big enough to store it all." As well as being physically large,

Grohl also had similarly ambitious plans for what they would eventually record there - "Let's buy an 8,000-square-foot warehouse, build the nicest studio in L.A. and make a double album in six months" said Grohl of the ambitious proposal.

Like the original low-key plans for the studio Grohl's vision for the first recording there wasn't initially quite so grand. His first consideration was a venture back into the world of movie scores, following his first attempt with the 'Touch' soundtrack in 1997. "After we finished touring for the last record I thought, Okay, I'm in my mid- to late-thirties now. Do I really want to run around festival stages screaming my head off every night?" he thought to himself. "So I thought that, rather than just jump back into the album cycle, I'd see if I could find a movie that needs a score." Grohl started writing some appropriate music but then had a light bulb moment. "After about a month of writing I thought, wait a second, this could be a killer Foo Fighters record. I'd hate to have pulled a solo album out of my ass in the middle of the best time of our lives as a band, so instead, it became a Foo Fighters project."

As well as the softer, score like music Grohl also re-considered that thought on dashing around on stages playing the big rock hits – It was a definite yes. "I wrote 14 or 15 [acoustic] songs, but then it occurred to me that there's something about drinking half a bottle of Crown Royal and jumping up on stage at Reading Festival. So I decided I should probably write some rock songs too."

Before the new studio could be built and with Studio 606 in Virginia being stripped out friend and producer of the previous album Nick Raskulinecz helped Dave to kit out his new Los Angeles home with a basic digital recording suite, so he could continue working on his demos. "I put a drum setup and a Pro Tools demo situation in Dave's garage," said Raskulinecz. "Then I gave him Pro Tools lessons. He ended up doing everything himself. He writes the songs on acoustic guitar, then plays all the instruments, working really fast. For demos, he'll lay down drum tracks and record a complete song - with vocals - in about an hour".

With a huge number of songs recorded, both acoustic and rock, Grohl then had to decide what he was going to do with all the material, striking a plan just as ambitious as the blueprints for the new studio. "At one point I was demo-ing this stuff at my house, writing riffs and little pieces of songs, and I downloaded it onto a hard drive and [realized] it was five hours of music. We've got to make a double album!" he declared. "We've been a band for 10 years now, this is our fifth record, and I thought it would be boring to just keep making album after album and making videos and playing festivals, so I wanted to do something special."

The master plan was now complete and step one was to find a suitable location for the new studio.

The band scouted the wider California area and in Spring 2004 happened upon a large building in Northridge, a small district in northwest Los Angeles most well-known for being the home to many of the major pornographic studios. The plot earmarked by Grohl was thankfully a good distance from those studios however, in a small residential area. The location, according to Grohl, was previously occupied by a large home owned by a woman whose stalker "turned up one night and burned the place to the ground". Since then, the basic shell of a building had been built on the land with structural walls and foundations in place but little else. Unperturbed by the checkered history of the location, Grohl decided it was the perfect blank canvas for his grand plans and made the purchase in April 2004.

Preparations for the album recording and construction of the studio started concurrently. As plans and blueprints were drawn up for the studio in July, the band booked into Mates Rehearsal Studio to start working on Dave's new songs as a band for the first time. The studio, located in North Hollywood, was a favorite of the band that they had used many times previously, including in 1999 when auditioning new guitarists. New songs were worked through including 'In Your Honor', 'No Way Back' and a song given the working title 'Flagger'. The latter was, in fact, the first time the band worked on the song which would later be known as 'White Limo'. The working title was a reference to their belief it resembled a song by Black Flag. Speaking of the material they worked on during these rehearsals Raskulinecz stated that they ended up with three or four versions of around 30 songs and that "In hindsight, we might have gone a little too far."

One reason for the lengthy time at Mates was due in part to waiting for the new studio. "Finally, it got to the point where I didn't want them to play the rock songs anymore. I was afraid they were going to get stale," said the producer.

As the band was rehearsing construction was underway across the city, working to turn the empty shell into a working studio and Foo Fighters base camp. In late July members of the crew traveled back to Virginia and began the process of loading all the equipment onto trucks, ready for a long drive across the country. Upon arrival, much of the gear was temporarily crammed into Dave Grohl's house, stored safely until it could be moved into its new permanent home. Rehearsals and pre-production work continued throughout August and September and the band was becoming increasingly restless, wanting to get into the new studio and begin recording properly. Unfortunately, despite all the best efforts of the contractors, work was still far from finished and in mid-September the band decided the best course of action was to head to the building site and start helping out themselves, taking members of the crew with them. "Hammering, stuffing insulation — [we were] doing whatever [we could] to speed the process," said Raskulinecz of their desperation.

Finally, by November, it was decided that the studio was in a suitable state for recording to commence, albeit still far from finished. The walls of the studio were still just insulation, very little acoustic soundproofing was in place and the control room was similarly unfinished. Despite this gear was moved in and recording began for the first time that month. With lots of construction work left to do a shift system was implemented, the band using the studio from 1 pm to 1 am each day and construction continued outside of those hours, mostly in the small hours of the night.

The band entered the studio with "five and a half hours of music" according to Grohl. "Writing ahead of time has an added benefit. We usually write during the recording sessions. Sometimes you walk into the studio and you throw down an idea that's spontaneous and new and fresh and exciting. But then you wind up a year later playing it live and you've elaborated on it, you've made it better," he said in explaining the different approach from the past. "So, we've done that already in the six months we've had to work on these songs before recording them."

It was decided that Foo Fighters would tackle the rock songs first, setting a rough goal of Christmas for completion before they would move onto the acoustic material. The process for recording was one the band were now most familiar with, beginning with drummer Taylor Hawkins laying down his tracks based off the pre-production demos.

Guitars would follow next saving bass guitar for last, a decision producer Raskulinecz would explain - "Bass is so important. By doing it last, you can really tailor it for tuning, parts, and sound. The traditional way is to do drums, then bass; you get this massive bass sound — the greatest thing you've ever heard. But then you put the guitars on, and they're small because the kick drum and bass guitar are taking up all the space. So, you pile on 25 guitar tracks. Whereas if you do the drums and then the guitars, you can fill the hole that's left with bass. And sometimes that hole wants a certain frequency that isn't traditional for bass, but you have to go with it, which is even more fun."

For Nate Mendel, this meant a long wait until he could get to work. Once the drums and guitar were complete, he would take home a digital ProTools file and work on his part. "I would run it by Dave and the producer, we'd talk about it, make changes, and then put it down" explained the bassist. "I would usually come in with this elaborate bass line—but over time, I've come to appreciate simplicity and what it can do for a song," he added.

When it came to recording drums for the rock material Taylor Hawkins was in charge, guided by Grohl. "Dave lets Taylor own the tunes," said Raskulinecz. "Sure, Dave could play all the drum parts if he wanted to, and he certainly has specific ideas about how they should sound and how parts should be played, but he trusts Taylor to do his thing. There was never one song where Dave said, 'Let me redo that, Taylor' or 'I don't think you got it, let me do it instead.' He really respects Taylor."

Although there was clear chemistry between the Hawkins and Grohl the process of recording the drums was "really labor intensive" according to Mendel, with both pushing for perfection which sometimes led to frustration for the bassist. "Sometimes they record a whole song and then decide that it's a beat-per-minute too fast or too slow, and we'll re-record the whole thing based on that. Or, they'll slightly change the kick drum pattern and that may or may not dictate having to redo all the music." This kept Mendel on his toes, sometimes only needing to alter his bass lines in a small way but for some songs, starting from scratch was the only option.

For Hawkins recording of this album marked the first time he had a drum tech working with him in the studio. Gary Gershunoff (Known as Gersh within the band), a veteran session drummer based in LA had previously worked with Dave Grohl during the recording of Queens Of The Stone Age album 'Songs For The Deaf' and was brought in to help out Hawkins. "He understands how to tune drums and make them sound good. It's a real art and meant that all I had to worry about was playing," said Hawkins of the assistance he offered. "I'm the first to admit that I am more comfortable on stage than I am in the studio, but I felt like I had a great support system around me this time. I'm sure I will become more comfortable with each record that we do, but when I'm in the tracking room and all eyes are on me, I'm just desperate to get it right! Drums are tough because they are the first thing to be recorded and they are the foundation of the song. We used a click on most of the tracks on the new record," he added.

A wide range of drum kits and accessories were used during recording and the kits were also moved around the work-in-progress studio, experimenting to find different sounds. "Gear-wise, we have used a real mixture of stuff," explained Hawkins. "Gersh got a conglomeration of mine and Dave's Zildjian and Tama stuff; and some vintage drums, and we would mix and match for different songs.

Sound-wise, we have experimented more on this record than ever before, and we have tried to make every song different." One constant was a 22-inch black Slingerland kick drum, the same one used during the recording of previous album 'One By One'. A Sennheiser 602 microphone was placed inside with a Soundelux 251 outside.

Breaking down the different songs recorded for the rock album, Hawkins described the drum rolls on the track 'In Your Honor' as "Very Who-esque", referring to English mod rockers The Who. 'No Way Back', the first song the band tracked featured a "big, wide open sound" with "bouncy, upbeat tempo". The song 'DOA' had two very different takes according to the drummer, with the first version having a "lo-fi, indie rock sound." A little unhappy with the results and with a desire to make the song a little bigger another version was recorded which had a "much harder, rock feel" according to Hawkins.

Not every drum take was recorded to a click track. For the song 'Hell' it was preferred for the tempo to fluctuate throughout the short song - "It starts off in one tempo and moves up – perfect for someone like me who tends to speed up!" joked Hawkins. 'Free Me' and 'The Deepest Blues Are Black' were two songs Hawkins was very proud of, describing the former as "the proggiest [Progressive Rock] out of all the songs" and explained there was a "nice grace note on the snare" in the latter - a term describing an extra note specifically added outside of the melody of the song. Both tracks were recorded in the slightly unusual 6/8 timing with 'Free Me' transitioning to 3/4 time towards the end of the song. A lot of time was spent on the track 'Resolve' with three or four distinctly different versions recorded. "we wanted to get the best out of it, but we maybe started over thinking it a little bit," explained Hawkins, noting that they ended up reverting back to the second version recorded as the following takes had started to sound like "A fucking Bon Jovi song!"

Hawkins described 'The Last Song' as being "what Breakout should have sounded like," adding that "A lot of things on this record to me are what a lot of old past songs should have sounded like. With this record we worked on everything without beating the hell out of it; just getting the best, most intense, energetic performances."

Another song attempted for the rock side of the record was an early version of the track 'You Can't Fix This', although at this stage the song had entirely different lyrics and working title. Grohl had written the song for Foo Fighters and a fully fleshed out recording of the song was finished during this session but the band elected against using it because they believed the music "sounded too much like Fleetwood Mac". The song would re-surface eight years later in 2013 when Grohl recorded a new version with Fleetwood Mac's Stevie Nicks for the Sound City soundtrack, deciding it would be perfect for the Mac band member.

By early December the studio had reached almost full functionality although "by no means [were] we done" according to guitar tech Joe Beebe. "The big room sounds great, but the small room has some standing waves in it that are making it sound funny. Our control room is so fucking awesome it's unbelievable." he continued. The control room had been modeled on Polar Studios, a studio in Sweden made famous by ABBA as well and Led Zeppelin, the latter recording their album 'In Through The Out Door' there.

At this stage much of the structural work was complete with painting well underway, carpets being laid in the office, tiling being laid in the upstairs lounge and kitchen cabinets due to arrive for fitting in the new year. The band soon started covering the freshly painted walls with various items of memorabilia including gold and platinum records awarded to both Nirvana and Foo Fighters as well as Zeppelin Gold records and various other items from the band's personal collections. As the year ended recording for the rock record was close to completion, just a few guitar overdubs and vocal tracks were left to record before they would move onto the acoustic material.

The equipment installed in the studio was a mixture of analog and digital, the centerpiece being a classic Neve 8058 recording console hooked up to a Neve BCM10, a 10-channel analog mixing console. Also installed was the 32-input mixing desk shipped from the old studio in Virginia. The band operated in a somewhat unorthodox manner, recording the basic tracks on analog 2-inch tape which were then bounced over to a digital Pro Tools setup for overdubs and editing. One reason for this half and half approach was a shortage of analog tape at the time, not having enough to record and store everything recorded. Sixteen reels of 24-track Quantegy GP9 tape were ordered which they intended to continually re-use during recording but they hit a rather large snag mid-way through recording. Quantegy went out of business leaving them short of tape in a world which was by now digital dominated. "When we got the e-mail about them shutting their doors, we started frantically calling around all the guitar centers in the area, but they were all out because Rick Rubin bought it all. It's like insider trading or something," Grohl said jokingly of the situation. Thankfully a new supplier was eventually located and recording to analog could go ahead as planned.

Recording of the acoustic material began at the end of January 2005 although there were some reservations as things got underway. "We were in a panic when we recorded the acoustic record. We'd spent about two months on the rock disc, and then one day I thought, Okay, I know when our deadline is, and if we don't start on the acoustic album we might be fucked," explained Grohl. "Having never done anything like that before, I didn't know how long it was going to take. So, we had a little meeting where I sat everyone down and said, 'Here's what we have to do: Everyone has to be here all day, we need to do one song a day and no one's leaving until that song is done."

The band worked to a simple schedule which involved Grohl starting most songs off on his own with an acoustic guitar. Working from a simple click track in his headphones, the bandleader would quickly find a tempo and "just roll an arrangement" in an off the cuff manner. The rest of the band would then add their parts whilst Grohl went off to write the lyrics. The regime was tough, but the band "pulled it off" according to Grohl.

Owing to the different requirements for recording the acoustic material several changes were made with regards to the equipment. To capture the acoustic guitars on most songs a Soundelux 251 microphone was positioned near the sound hole of the guitar with an RCA 77 on the neck itself, near to the 12th fret. A couple of songs required a different approach however, with the RCA microphone moved over Grohl's shoulder and a Coles mic placed high in the room. For the track 'Friend Of A Friend' even more microphones were utilized with a pair of Royers on each side of the guitar and a further pair of Earthworks mics farther out, but all pointing towards the same sound hole.

The Soundelux 251 was also used to capture the Mellotron, Piano and all of Grohl's vocals. "We used it into a Martek preamp and a DBX 160XT compressor," said producer Raskulinecz, noting that the combination was "kind of funny" – the microphone and pre-amp cost in the region of seven thousand dollars whilst the compressor could be acquired for just two hundred.

When it came to guitars for the acoustic tracks a wide variety was utilized including an old Silvertone that had been laying around in Raskulinecz's van for several years, Grohl describing it as looking like "A fucking Cello!" A rather more expensive range of Gibson guitars was also used for various songs such as the Country Western and Dove models. Another guitar of note was a Martin acoustic from the seventies which Grohl had bought in London.

Owing to a large number of microphones pointing at his guitar every little sound would be captured, including potentially unwanted noises. On the track 'Over And Out' the sound of Grohl's fingers scraping against the strings could be heard, an early worry in the recording. Different ideas were concocted to stifle the noise, including rubbing a stick of butter along the neck, but the rest of the band convinced him that it sounded natural, as a recording of someone sitting in front of a microphone playing the guitar should sound.

For drummer Hawkins, his contributions to the acoustic tracks were done very quickly, most completed within 20 minutes. On the track 'Miracle' he and technician Gersh utilized a technique formerly used by The Beatles drummer Ringo Starr, putting T-shirts on the drum skins to get a sound they described as "dead, dry and dirty". The song also featured only a floor tom and snare drum.

The first acoustic track recorded was 'Still', a song with a very dark meaning but one that Dave liked. "When we listened back to it, I remember saying, 'That's my favorite thing we've ever recorded'. It's beautiful, and it was so new to me." The lyrics of the song describe a child who sat on train tracks in Grohl's hometown of Virginia when he was a youngster, committing suicide. Grohl and his friends rode their bikes to the scene and "saw pieces of his bones", among other gruesome sights. "It's heavy man, but you know, I was listening to the music, and that's what it was," he explained in the choice of lyrics.

Whilst the rock disc had been 100% Foo Fighters the band decided that the acoustic disc would be an opportunity to invite some guest musicians to contribute. "Ah, my famous friends!" quipped Grohl in an interview. "Yeah, we had a long list of people that we wanted to ask. I thought it'd be fun to have guests because we'd never done it before." Names that Grohl had shortlisted included Jim James of My Morning Jacket, multi-instrumentalist Ry Cooder, Greg Norton of Hüsker Dü, John Paul Jones of Led Zeppelin and Norah Jones.

One other important name on the list was Rami Jaffee of The Wallflowers who became a large contributor to proceedings, recording keyboards for five different songs. "It was almost a learning experience for him, seeing what in the keyboard world will work for him," Jaffee said of the experience being teacher to Grohl. "He's pretty focused on what he wants in his songs, and this was a weird area for him. When I first got to the studio, he wasn't sure how it was going to sound with his songs." Instructed to just experiment with ideas, Jaffee soon learned of what was going to work and what wouldn't.

"He doesn't like pretentious ideas and sounds. I had a few wacky keyboards, some pump organs, and accordion organs and when I got to the more eclectic stuff, he was kind of weary, he didn't want too much of that," explained Jaffee.

John Paul Jones of Led Zeppelin fame agreed to

participate and was the first big name to arrive at the studio on February 11th. "That guy is like royalty, but he was so down to earth and cool it was incredible" guitarist Chris Shiflett enthused in a post to the band's official message board the following day. "Of course, we managed to sneak in a few Zeppelin trivia questions and he even riffed Kashmir [Led Zeppelin track] on the mellotron for a minute. we are pretty fucking blessed," he added. Grohl, a huge Led Zeppelin fan was also very excited for his arrival. "He walked in with his mandolin like a minstrel, [and] immediately went into 'The Rain Song.' I was worried, [because] I have all these pictures on the wall down there of Jimmy Page and John Bonham".

Foo Fighters Bassist Nate Mendel initially had reservations upon hearing about the guest slot, wondering if he would be surplus to requirements on the record. "Okay, how many songs are not going to have my bass on them?" he nervously asked Grohl. As it turned out Jones only featured on three tracks and none of them involved a bass guitar. He first recorded piano on the track 'Miracle' and then used a Mellotron on two songs, 'Another Round' and 'Oh Yeah'. "He's an arranger, a composer. He came in, listened to the song, put it on piano, played it a few times and it was done" said Grohl of his work on 'Miracle'. Whilst two of the tracks made it to the final album the other, 'Oh Yeah', did not.

The song had first been worked on back in 1999 for the band's third studio album 'There Is Nothing Left To Lose' but never finished. This new version featured Jones on the mellotron and Grohl on drums but it was decided the song just "didn't fit" the album but Grohl was still happy, seeing the song as "the closest I will ever get to playing in Led Zeppelin," a fact which was true at the time but would not be the case a few years later.

On Valentine's day 2005, February 14th, the second-high profile guest arrived at the studio, Norah Jones. When Jones got the call from Grohl requesting her to feature on the next Foo Fighters record she was hoping it would be a chance for her to stray from her usual genre and style. "I was like, 'Cool, I get to rock'". Unfortunately for Norah, that dream was soon shattered when Dave told her the band was recording a rock disc and an acoustic disc. "Let me guess which one you want me on," Jones joked.

The song Grohl had earmarked for her vocals was 'Virginia Moon', another old composition the band had also first worked on during recording for their third album. "It never made sense on any of the records we'd made previously because it's hard to put an acoustic song in the middle of a rock record," Grohl said of the track's history. "So, I thought, 'Now that we're doing this acoustic record, maybe it can see the light of day'".

Whilst the song itself was old the lyrics were very new, something Jones was surprised by - "When I got to the studio, Dave was like, 'I just wrote the lyrics this morning,' and it was good. [I said] 'Wow. I can't really work like that myself, but I'm surprised you did this so quickly!" Grohl had selected Jones specifically to feature on this song after listening to one of her records before recording, thinking to himself "This is her vibe, she does jazz."

Believing her smooth, warm voice would harmonize well with his own the pair spent just three hours recording the vocal takes, Grohl impressed by her natural abilities - "She was playing dog-ear stuff, where you cock your head in disbelief," he said. "It was perfect on the first take."

Norah Jones was not the only guest musician to feature on 'Virginia Moon'. Grohl envisioned the song having a jazzy,

Bossa nova guitar lead to match the vocals but nobody in the band knew how to play jazz leads. In stepped guitar tech Joe Beebe who did have the necessary skills, a talented guitar player himself. 'This thing needs a lead and nobody in our band knows how to play jazz leads. Will you please do it?" Dave had asked him. A slightly nervous Beebe asked for a copy of the track and said he would take it home and "write the baddest lead you've ever heard!" but Grohl had other plans. "No. You know what, dude? We're gonna go upstairs and have some dinner, and we'll cut it when we come back down."

Beebe sat down at the Pro Tools rig, ran the track in a loop and wrote the guitar lead in less than an hour. Writing on his website he believed the track had turned out well but that it had "definitely put [him] on the spot". The band continued to work on the song but were forced to backtrack at one point as it headed in an unintended direction – "We put an organ on the song, and it turned into something that you'd hear in an elevator. We had to tread lightly around some of these songs. That one, in particular, could have gone south real quick," Grohl said of the misdirection. Even with the organ removed he still had reservations about including the song on the album, believing it may have been just "too fucking weird" for a Foo Fighters record.

In the end, Nate Mendel was the man to convince him – "That's exactly why we should put it on the record" he quipped. Drummer Hawkins was also happy with the song's inclusion, arguing that it wasn't just included because it featured Norah Jones but that simply "It works".

Another old composition revisited for the acoustic disc was 'Friend Of A Friend', a song Dave had written back in 1990 shortly after joining Nirvana and moving into an apartment with Kurt Cobain. The track was first released on the 'Late! - Pocketwatch' album in 1992 and Grohl had performed the song a handful of times live since, most notably for a BBC Evening Session in 1997. Despite that, it had never been released under the Foo Fighters name and so it was decided this double album was the perfect opportunity to do so. This new recording again featured only Grohl on acoustic guitar and vocals, just as the original, but with much higher production quality. As had been the case with 'Virginia Moon' Grohl had concerns about including the song given its history and subject matter but decided to go for it. "I thought 'Goddamnit, I don't know if I want to field a load of crap about that song for a year and a half', but it's a great song'."

Another song recorded during the acoustic sessions to partially come from Grohl's "work-in-progress" bin was 'Over And Out'. He'd first written and demoed the song around five years earlier in his Virginia basement but hadn't done anything with it since, describing it as "an experiment in doing something more mellow." Like 'Virginia Moon' and 'Friend Of A Friend', Grohl now saw this as the perfect opportunity to finally release the song with the full band this time featuring on the song.

January 17th, 2005 saw Dave Grohl joining other musicians including Eddie Vedder, Josh Homme and Tenacious D at the Wiltern Theatre in LA for a benefit concert, supporting victims of the Earthquake and resulting Tsunami that occurred in the Indian Ocean on December 26th, 2004. During Grohl's set, he gave a debut to a brand-new song entitled 'Razor', telling the crowd he'd written the track that same day. "I sat up all night trying to write this song, and it didn't work. I woke up early and started writing lyrics and got it right as the car was coming to pick me up. I was up in the dressing room practicing it and Josh and I were sharing a room. I said, 'There's a second guitar harmony in this song, try it out.' The pair played the song during the show and after getting a positive reception from the crowd Grohl also invited Homme to visit the studio to perform on the album version of the song.

Homme's sense of timing threw Grohl off somewhat when he decided to take him up on the offer. "Josh called me at like, one in the morning, going, 'Hey – I wanna come down and play that song'. So, I was like, 'Uh, okay'. And then, of course, we're here until six before finally, I was like, 'Okay, you're a genius – let's go home'. I mean, I have so much respect for that guy – he's a dear friend and an inspiration, really. He fucking rules", said Grohl of the inconvenient but fun guest recording.

In what was turning out to be a record of many firsts another would come with the track 'Cold Day In The Sun'. Whilst both Taylor Hawkins and Chris Shiflett had in the past sang lead vocals for the band, they were neither tracks on an album nor Foo Fighters originals.

The drummer had written the song a few years previous in a "rough sketch form" and showed it to Dave, something he'd always been apprehensive about doing - "It's hard playing a demo for Dave because he's like my older brother – I know when he thinks something sucks." Fortunately for Hawkins, the man he looked up to did enjoy the song and was keen to work on it with Foo Fighters.

The band initially attempted to record it as a heavier track for the rock side of the album but ultimately decided it made more sense for the acoustic disc, one of the very few songs that would be attempted in both styles. As Hawkins was set to perform lead vocals on the track it was decided that Grohl would then get behind the drum kit, the pair exchanging playful banter during recording. As Dave was recording a drum take Taylor would be listening from the control room and head out into the live room when he wanted to suggest a change. "No, I like what I'm doing" Grohl playfully quipped. A tambourine featured through many of the songs on the acoustic disc which was played by Grohl, not Hawkins, as he hated playing it. He did, however, make an exception for 'Cold Day In The Sun'.

Due to the speed at which the band was required to record all the acoustic tracks bassist Mendel also had to work faster in constructing his parts of the song. "We were running low on time and I didn't have a chance to go and write bass lines, so they ended up being much simpler," he explained. For some of the tracks, Mendel would not even have an opportunity to hear the song before going to record his bass. "Dave and Chris would put down their guitar lines and I'd be in a room with the bass, and Nick Raskulinecz would go, 'Okay, let's run it a couple of times and see what happens'."

In total fifteen acoustic songs were recorded, ten making it to the final album and five not, including the third song featuring John Paul Jones as well as 'Fuck Around', another older idea which was again not finished during this session.

As recording for the acoustic disc was nearing completion Grohl began having reservations about the rock songs recorded months earlier and decided they needed to go back and work on them further. "We listened to the rock stuff and realized the acoustic stuff was kicking its ass. We knew we needed to stay loose instead of always trying to perfect everything," Taylor Hawkins recalled of the situation.

Almost all of the tracks first recorded in late 2004 were re-worked in some way, including some that the band had put on the shelf - one of those being the song 'Best Of You'. "I'd kind of forgotten about it," said Grohl. "[It] was one of the first songs we wrote for the album. It was inspired by seeing people stand up in the face of struggle. It's meant to make you feel empowered. It's about the refusal to be taken advantage of by something that's bigger than you, or someone you're in love with. It's the fight in the face of adversity," he said of the song's meaning. "I didn't really think of an interesting melody; I just wanted to scream the whole way through. And the first few times we rehearsed it, I thought, 'There's no way I'll be able to play this live. There's blood in my throat'," he added.

The song was forgotten until one day during the second rock album sessions Grohl's manager, John Silva, came into the studio and asked him "What happened to that Best of You song?". The song was pulled out and worked on further, with the newer version deemed good enough to include on the record.

Another track recorded towards the end of the session was a bit of light-hearted fun for the band. Entitled 'That Ass', the rap style song featured such lyrics as "Ding dong, daddy's home, Time to get down and get this on." Moving back to more serious material the band pressed on with further tweaking the rock recordings and by late February all the basic tracks were deemed complete. Between the two discs, the band had around forty songs, or song ideas, which were then whittled in half down to the best twenty. All that remained for the band were a few overdubs before mixing could finally commence although there was still one song the band was working on right to the very end of proceedings - '7 Corners'. "There's always that stray song from eight years ago, and it's usually the same one. It's a great riff but it's not a great song", explained Grohl of the already long history of the track. "I've spent years trying to figure it out. I'm sure it'll come back out for the next album,"

Grohl believed. For now, though, it was left on the cutting room floor once again.

Mixing of the record began on February 28th, 2005. The rock songs were treated very differently from the acoustic songs, each requiring a very different approach. The rock tracks were mixed by Nick Raskulinecz in stereo to half-inch analog, Pro Tools at 88.2khz and DAT. He monitored with Yamaha NS-10 and ProAc studio speakers but also utilized a small pair of Realistic branded speakers that he had owned since he was a child.

Elliot Scheiner was placed in charge of mixing the acoustic tracks which he did at Capitol Studios in Hollywood using a Neve VR console. As he was a fair distance away and the band was still busy in the studio, he began mixing the tracks that he had received via the internet.

Scheiner mixed one track and sent the result to Grohl and Raskulinecz to listen to. "We just looked at each other, then said to him, 'Okay, which one do you want to do next?'," quipped Raskulinecz, obviously happy with what they had heard. Scheiner mixed in stereo to half-inch analog and also mixed in surround sound with a Studer A827 2-inch 8-Track, using a surround matrix fitted to the Neve console. For monitoring, Scheiner also used Yamaha NS-10s for the stereo mix and Yamaha MSP-10s for the surround sound mixes.

A rather strange piece of equipment brought to the studio towards the end of mixing was an Acura TL Sedan car. The vehicle was equipped with an ELS 5.1 surround sound audio system which Scheiner helped develop and he'd deemed it the perfect way to properly monitor the 5.1 mixes.

The album was released in June 2005 featuring twenty songs, split evenly between the two styles. Several songs from the session would also see release as B-Sides to singles from the album including 'FFL' and 'Spill'. A couple of covers the band recorded towards the end of the session were also released - 'I'm In Love With A German Filmstar' originally by The Passions and 'Kiss The Bottle' by Jawbreaker.

* * *

July 2005
Studio 606 West, Northridge, CA, United States

Foo Fighters
Hawkins, Taylor (Drums, Vocals)

Grohl, Dave (Guitar, Bass Guitar, Vocals)

Recording Credits
Terry, Mike (Recording)

Tracks Recorded
1. Skin and Bones

2. I Feel Free

Recording Equipment
Neve 8058 recording console

Studer A827 24-Track 2 Inch Tape Recorder

Foo Fighters began their world tour for fifth album 'In Your Honor' in May 2005 with a series of promotional shows at home in the United States as well as in Europe and Australia. A series of festival appearances were booked in July including a performance at the T-In The Park festival in Scotland, United Kingdom. On the day of their headline performance Dave Grohl was also scheduled to be interviewed for BBC Radio Scotland, as well as perform a song acoustically. Rather than pull out an old hit such as 'Everlong' or 'Times Like These' Grohl revealed he would be performing a brand-new song he'd written very recently.

"I just finished writing it ten minutes ago," he told the DJ. "It's called Skin and Bones".The band performed their full set later that night and following one further show the following night, returned home to the United States with a break of just over a fortnight before their next tour date.

Wasting no time Dave Grohl and Taylor Hawkins headed to Studio 606, wanting to make a quick studio recording of the new song before heading back on the road. Owing to the impromptu nature of recording neither Chris Shiflett nor Nate Mendel was present.

The song was recorded live with a single guitar track, the sound of Grohl sliding his fingers up and down the frets very clear throughout. With Mendel not around Grohl himself recorded a simple bass track before Hawkins added an equally simple, relaxed drum track. Grohl finished the song off with a couple of vocal takes and the recording was complete. As well as recording Dave's new song Taylor also wanted to record a cover whilst they had some free time, the Cream song 'I Feel Free'.

The session was recorded by Mike Terry who had recently helped engineer the recording sessions for 'In Your Honor'. Terry was surprised at how quickly both songs were recorded and in particular the Cream song, as Dave didn't really know the song well. "Dave came in that morning, learned the guitar part and they banged it out together. He learned the bass part and overdubbed it, then he learned the solo and even doubled it", Terry said of the speedy recording.

Both songs were recorded in a single day and then mixed by Terry the following day. The two tracks were also released quite hastily, first appearing as B-Sides on the 'DOA' single in September 2005.

March to June 2007
Studio 606 West, Northridge, CA, United States

Foo Fighters

Hawkins, Taylor (Drums, Backing Vocals)

Grohl, Dave (Guitar, Vocals, Piano)

Mendel, Nate (Bass Guitar)

Shiflett, Chris (Guitar)

Additional Musicians

Chen, Daphne (Violin)

Chipman, Lauren (Viola)

Dodd, Richard (Cello)

Gorfain, Eric (Violin)

Hester, Drew (Percussion)

Jaffee, Rami (Keyboards)

Kearns Jr, Brantley (Fiddle)

King, Kaki (Gutiar)

Riley, Audrey (Conductor)

Smear, Pat (Guitar)

Recording Credits

Bushby, Adrian (Engineer)

Lousteau, John (Assistant Engineer)

Norton, Gil (Producer)

Tracks Recorded

1. Bangin'

2. Seda

3. If Ever

4. Erase/Replace

5. Come Alive

6. Statues

7. Let It Die

8. But, Honestly

9. Home

10. Stranger Things Have Happened

11. Once And For All

12. Cheer Up, Boys (Your Make Up Is Running)

13. Long Road To Ruin

14. Summers End

15. In Silence

16. The Pretender

17. White Limo

18. This Will Be Our Year

Recording Equipment

Neve 8058 recording console

Studer A827 24-Track 2 Inch Tape Recorder

Following the release of the half rock, half acoustic double album 'In Your Honor' in 2005 Foo Fighters spent the following 18 months touring to support both discs of the album, playing rock and acoustic shows across the world. The tour finally ended in December of 2006 with two back to back shows for KROQ's annual 'Almost Acoustic Christmas' event at the Gibson Amphitheater in Hollywood, California. On both nights the band took advantage of the rotating stage at the venue to play a two in one set, part acoustic, part rock. The crowd didn't know it at the time, but this action would in a way be a sign of things to come for the band.

A month before those two shows the band had released their first live album, 'Skin And Bones'. The record (and companion DVD Video release) did not feature one of the bands many rock shows, it was instead an 'unplugged' release featuring a compilation of songs recorded during three acoustic shows in August 2006 at the Pantages Theatre in Los Angeles, California.

When asked what this release and In Your Honor meant for the future direction of the band and its records, Grohl was unsure. "That's the thing that makes it so confusing. Usually, when you have a string of rock records you think, 'Alright, let's make a rock record!' Now that we've split into two directions, we've hit this schizophrenic mark. We can do one of two things," Grohl explained. "We can make a beautiful, song-based album, or we can make the craziest, thrash-metal shit you've ever heard" he continued before joking "Who knows, maybe we'll make a folk record!"

On February 10th, 2007 Dave Grohl attended the annual pre-Grammy party hosted by Clive Davis, president of the RCA Music Group. In speaking with the host Dave was hit with something of an epiphany. Explaining how he was faced with the constant choice of rock vs acoustic, as separated shows, Davis told him quite simply that he could "do both together". As if the penny dropped, Grohl decided that the next record would not be half rock, half acoustic nor would it be one or the other. It would instead bring both styles together in one record, and even in the songs themselves.

Pre-production for the sixth Foo Fighters record was set to begin in March 2007 but before that, the band needed to hire a producer. Nick Raskulinecz had produced the previous two records but a change was desired and after some though that ended up meaning a look back to the past. Gil Norton, producer for their second album 'The Colour And The Shape' was considered as the man they were looking for.

With all the problems surrounding that record and the issues caused by Norton's punishing strive for perfection it seemed a surprising choice, but Grohl felt he may help them get out of the comfort zone they had been in ever since.

After building a studio in his basement and then upgrading to a newer facility in California the band had usually been able to record at their own leisure. The group would have barbecues, hang out with friends and record whenever the mood took them. Norton was also the first producer to really show Grohl the true meaning of pre-production - "honing the songs, compositions, and arrangement so that's it's just airtight when you go in to record," as Grohl described.

For this record the band leader didn't want to make their 'Back In Black' by AC/DC, instead he wanted to make a cross between a NoMeansNo (A Canadian punk rock band) album and 'Odessey & Oracle', the 1968 album by English pop rock band The Zombies. "We needed someone to break us out of our comfort zone, so we called Gil," remarked Grohl. With Gil in the hot seat pre-production got underway with the first action being to whittle down the "30 or 40 song ideas" Grohl had on the table to a more reasonable number. Over a week and a half, the band and producer selected what they felt were the "most powerful and dramatic" songs. "We wanted the stops to be pin-drop silent before exploding," explained Grohl. "If we had a beautiful melody, we'd throw a fucking string quartet in there. So, we did everything we could to really magnify all those elements and that was fun."

Unlike the previous record where songs were clearly divided into two groups, rock and acoustic, this time around everything was grouped together, with song ideas ranging from "wall-of-noise hard shit" to "mellow piano ballads", and some songs even combining ideas from either end of the spectrum. Songs were chosen not on the dynamics but "by their lyrics, structure or melody," a process Grohl felt came naturally.

Even with the best demos selected Grohl was still unsure of what the results would be once they all came together. "We didn't have a clue how the album was going to sound until it was done," he remarked. "We demoed so many songs before we went into the studio and all of them were so different. Some of them were really slow acoustic songs and others were really heavy songs with these big ass walls of guitars."

Final recording got underway in March 2007 and one of the first songs to be recorded was 'Erase/Replace', a track very much from the "wall-of-noise hard shit" category. The track was recorded with a strong focus on its main riff, something Grohl attributed to his repeated weekly plays of the 'Kill 'Em All' album by Metallica. "There's a part of me that will never lose the love of riffs, that's where a song like this comes in. As a drummer and a guitar player, the rhythmic quality of a decent riff is like a cannon to me. I can write riffs all day long because I look at the guitar like a drum set. So, just as I'll sit at a drum kit and play beats, I sit with a guitar and try the same thing. That's what I was doing here," he explained.

As well as the regular four band members the track also featured the first guest of the album, The Wallflowers keyboardist Rami Jaffee. Having joined Foo Fighters in the studio for the recording of their previous album Jaffee then linked up with them on the acoustic leg of the tour in support of it. Happy with his contributions the band once again invited him to the studio.

Another track worked on during the opening days of recording was 'Come Alive', the first track to feature a strong mixture of quieter and louder dynamics in one song. "On the last album, we split the acoustic side and the electric side into two albums. Here, we've split it into one song," explained Grohl. "This is about reawakening after becoming a father. Anyone who's a father understands how the world becomes a different place when your child is born. I just feel and see everything differently now," he added, describing the subject matter of the lyrics in the song. The track featured another guest musician who had also been a part of the extended band during the acoustic tour, multi-instrumentalist Drew Hester contributing percussion. Jaffee again featured on the track, recording keyboards.

'Statues' was recorded next, a simple melodic piano focused track written by Dave about him and his wife Jordyn. "To me, there's nothing more beautiful than seeing the headstones of a husband and wife side by side in a graveyard," said Grohl. For his 36th birthday in 2006 his wife had gifted him a piano and whilst he had previously briefly dabbled with the instrument his first feeling was intimidation – "I didn't really understand how they worked." The already talented multi-instrumentalist was willing to learn and after a quick crash course was soon up to speed - "Someone said, 'OK, see that there? That note is middle C.' I'm like, 'Oh that's a C? Oh well, that's an E... Fuckin' A, there's a chord!' And then I just started writing songs." As well as Grohl's piano work the song also featured Accordion from Rami Jaffee whilst another guest, Brantley Kearns Junior, recorded fiddle.

With the rough tracks for the song completed Grohl soon realized it was a vastly different performance to anything the band had done before, describing it as a "big departure". He had no reservations about including the song on the album though, echoing something Nate Mendel had told him about including vastly different songs on the previous record - "that's exactly why we should put it on the record!"

The next song the band started work on was entitled 'Let It Die', a song which Grohl described as being "written about feeling helpless to someone else's demise. I've seen people lose it all to drugs and heartbreak and death," revealed Grohl, also admitting that Kurt Cobain was "probably the most noted." Another Nirvana connection on the track came by way of yet another guest musician – former Foo Fighter Pat Smear. Having patched up any past grievances Grohl invited Smear to join the band on their acoustic tour the year previous and had no qualms about inviting him back to a studio session for the first time since 1997.

As well as contributing to 'Let It Die' Pat also worked with the band on 'White Limo', a track they had first attempted to record for previous album 'In Your Honor'. Still known at this point by the working title 'Flagger' only a little time was spent on this second version; Hawkins recorded drums but only partial bass and guitar tracks were completed before recording was abandoned, the band feeling the song was just too heavy for the overall tone of the record.

The band next recorded basic tracks for the song 'But, Honestly' however with only drums, bass and guitar laid down they then moved on to another song, electing to return to the track later in the session.

'Stranger Things Have Happened' was a song from the mellow side of their ideas, one Grohl described as a product of "sitting around and doing fuck all for weeks on end." The track featured two acoustic guitar tracks, recorded with the aid of a metronome. It was decided to include the sound of the device throughout the recording for artistic reasons, as well as Grohl winding it up before he started playing.

Drums and bass were not recorded for the song, but Drew Hester did record light percussion elements. It was however decided the song worked better stripped back, and so the final mix featured only acoustic guitar and Grohl's vocals.

One evening during recording Dave Grohl made good on a promise he'd made six months earlier. On April 26th, 2006 a small earthquake caused a gold mine collapse in the small town of Beaconsfield, situated in Tasmania, Northern Australia. Fourteen miners escaped the collapse, one was sadly killed, whilst two became trapped approximately one kilometer below the surface. The pair were located a few days after the collapse but the only access possible initially was via a small tunnel, large enough to send food and water whilst a rescue effort could take place. The pair requested several other small items, one of which was an iPod filled with music to help them pass the time and relax a little.

One of the two trapped men, Brant Webb, had a specific request when it came to the music included on the device – the latest Foo Fighters album. News of this soon spread in local media and via a member of staff at the Australian arm of the band's record label, Dave Grohl himself soon caught wind of the request. Unable to help in any practical manner Grohl sent a note of support to the pair, motivating them with the message "there's two tickets to any Foos show, anywhere, and two cold beers waiting for you. Deal?"

The men were successfully rescued from the mine a fortnight after the collapse and on August 31st Foo Fighters announced they were heading for Australia, with three acoustic performances set for October at the iconic Sydney Opera House.

Whilst the other trapped miner Todd Russell politely declined Dave Grohl's offer Brant Webb duly accepted, invited as a VIP guest. The night before the first show, with Grohl aware Webb would attend the following night's show, decided to write an impromptu song to play in dedication. "He definitely seemed like a hero. He gave me a gift that no one had ever given me before. He made me feel like my music is maybe more meaningful than just jumping up onstage after five beers and having lasers chop your head off," Grohl said of Webb.

The track he'd dubbed 'The Ballad Of The Beaconsfield Miners' was given its debut, describing it as a "folksy, instrumental song with banjo-picking style with hammer-ons and pull-offs." After the show the pair shared more than a few beers - "we went and got fuckin' wasted in the hotel bar and I was like, 'Dude, I promise I'm going to put this on the record." Despite his apparent lack of sobriety when making the promise he stuck by his word, recording the instrumental piece during this session.

The track had two distinct guitar parts which when played live were handled by Grohl and Shiflett but for the studio recording, yet another guest was invited. Kaki King is an American guitarist who rose to fame in the early 2000s with her unique abilities playing the guitar and other instruments, catching the eye of many musicians, including Grohl. "When Kaki came to our studio one evening, I had the feeling the piece was right for her," he said of his choice to include her on the track. Whilst almost every Foo Fighters song begins life as an instrumental this would be the first time one would be released in that form, with no vocals recorded. Grohl was very impressed with King's work on the track, noting that she "shredded it ten times better than I've ever played it."

Recording of 'Cheer Up, Boys (Your Make Up Is Running) got underway mid-way through the session, a song Grohl described as "A really bright, poppy, late '80s REM song that would have been off their Green album or something." Whilst aware many would believe the song title to be a negative dig towards certain demographics, the reality was quite different - "I gave it that title because it definitely seemed like the most light-hearted, melodic song of all that we had because there's some heavy, dark shit on the record and then there are some songs that aren't light and breezy and so we felt like we needed it on the album just to balance a lot of the other stuff out. I kept the title because I thought it was fucking hilarious! The title had nothing to do with the song."

In mid-April the band took a planned break from recording for ten days but before heading off they and producer Norton listened back to the rough mixes of what had been recorded to that point. The group liked what they heard but Grohl decided they needed "another up-tempo song", worried that the overall tone of the album was a little too light. During the break, Dave went back over some of the earlier ideas and songs that were left in pre-production, one of which was a track titled 'Silver Heart'. "Dave had the idea for the song for a while, and we played around with it in pre-production, but we never really developed it," said Norton of the track. "The chorus was there, but the verse and middle hadn't been written".

The song was also relatively low tempo initially and so with a newly reworked, more energetic version of the song in his head the band quickly recorded a demo version, which they then played for Gil Norton once he returned to the studio. "I loved [the demo] so we worked on it the next day and recorded it quite quickly", recalled the producer. The newly reworked track was fully completed with a vocal track and given the final title 'The Pretender'. It was, according to Norton, "exactly what we needed to finish the album."

With the final piece of the puzzle complete, the band was almost done. By the first week of May 2007, all that remained were some vocal takes, keyboard work by Jaffee and a few other overdubs. The following week the final guests of the album arrived at the studio, a fully-fledged string quartet. 'The Section Quartet' is based in Los Angeles and most well-known for transforming popular rock and pop songs into a classical music arrangement. Their role on this album was to compose and record strings for most songs on the album, featuring most prominently on 'Statues'.

Recording dribs and drabs continued throughout May with tracking finally completed by the end of the month, focus then switching to mixing. As this was taking place guest musician Jaffee almost "quit" the band, informing Dave Grohl that with his recording duties complete and forthcoming tours expected to be 100% rock affairs, he didn't believe his services would be required. Grohl had other ideas – "I want you in the band, and I don't know if you know how it works around here, but once you're in, you're in," he told the Wallflower. "So, I don't think you should go anywhere, because we have a lot to look forward to." Changing his mind rather quickly, Jaffee told him "I'm all good, I'm in", Grohl now considering him an important, permanent member of the band.

All the songs the band had completed during the main recording session were included on their sixth studio album, 'Echoes, Silence, Patience & Grace'. One of the tracks abandoned and not completed, 'Once And For All', did not see release however a complete demo version recorded in pre-production was included as a a B-Side.

Other songs recorded in pre-production without Norton were also released as B-Sides, including a demo version of the song 'Come Alive' as well as tracks 'Seda', 'If Ever' and 'Bangin'', which did not make the cut for the final recording session.

Shortly after the main recording for the album was completed the band returned to the studio to record a cover song, something they had always enjoyed doing after album recording sessions to wind down and let off steam. When talking about the musical direction for the album Grohl had mentioned that he wanted to make a record partially influenced by The Zombies' second album 'Odessey And Oracle' and evidently this vision was still on his mind, as the song they elected to cover was 'This Will Be Our Year', track nine on the album. Unlike the other extra songs this cover would not be released as a B-Side and it wasn't until 2011 that it saw release - featured on their covers compilation record 'Medium Rare'.

* * *

July 4th, 2007
Abbey Road Studios, London, United Kingdom

Foo Fighters
Hawkins, Taylor (Drums)

Grohl, Dave (Guitar, Vocals)

Mendel, Nate (Bass Guitar)

Shiflett, Chris (Guitar)

Recording Credits
Foo Fighters (Producers)

Tracks Recorded
1. Band On The Run

Recording Equipment
Neve 88 RS recording console

ProTools HDX

On July 5th, 2007 Foo Fighters played a secret live show at Dingwalls, a tiny club in the Camden area of London, United Kingdom. The show was booked to help the band shake off any rust before their appearance at Live Earth, a huge climate change music event taking place at the cities Wembley Stadium two days later. During the set they surprised the crowd by playing the Paul McCartney and Wings track 'Band On The Run' with Dave Grohl telling the crowd that he'd only learned the song the previous day.

The reason for learning the song was ultimately down to BBC Radio 1 as the radio station was celebrating their 40th anniversary of broadcast, having first hit the airwaves in 1967. The BBC had been broadcasting radio since the 1920s, but the Radio 1 channel was not created until several decades later to counter the prevailing number of pirate radio stations operating at the time. To commemorate the event the corporation reached out to several popular recording artists, asking if they would be willing to record a song for a compilation album. Each artist who agreed were given a year between 1967 and 2007 and asked to cover a song from that year. Foo Fighters were happy to participate and were allocated the year 1974.

The band chose the McCartney and Wings song and appropriately booked a day at the legendary Abbey Road Studios in London to record the cover, location for the recording of many of The Beatles albums. Recording on Independence Day 2007 the band tackled the historic track over the course of just a few hours. Guitar tech Joe Beebe was initially "a little skeptical" about the song choice but once the recording was complete believed the band "owned it".

A special guest arrived at the studio during the day with Paul McCartney himself getting wind of the recording session. "Someone told me they were down at Abbey Road recording it, so I dropped in and surprised them," recalled the former Beatle. "Dave was putting the guitar track down, it was great. I just busted in the session, ruined it I suppose, and said 'Hi' to everyone," he continued. "It kind of reminded me of a Wings session, which was good for me because they were doing Band on the Run, but Dave's wife had their baby there, which reminded me of how me and Linda would be. Often, one of the babies would be at the recording session or would be playing around on the floor. You don't see that so much now."

'Radio 1: Established 1967' was released on October 1st, 2007 featuring the Foo Fighters cover among thirty-nine others. The track was also later included on the bands 2011 compilation album 'Medium Rare'.

* * *

Fall 2008
Grandmaster Recorders, Hollywood, CA, United States

Foo Fighters
Hawkins, Taylor (Drums)

Grohl, Dave (Guitar, Vocals)

Mendel, Nate (Bass Guitar)

Shiflett, Chris (Guitar)

Recording Credits
Foo Fighters (Producers)

Tracks Recorded
1. Wheels

2. Rope

3. Word Forward

others

Foo Fighters toured in support of their sixth studio album, 'Echoes, Silence, Patience & Grace', throughout a large part of 2007 and most of 2008. As had become common ever since their very first tours in 1995 the band would not rest on their laurels, writing and honing new songs and ideas during soundcheck for the shows. The tour finally came to an end in September 2008 and with all the ongoing work the band found themselves in an unusual position, coming to the end of a traditional 'album cycle' with an entirely new collection of songs practically ready to go.

They needed to decide on their next move and with another 18 months of touring discounted, Dave Grohl first conceived a rather unconventional plan – record another album full of new material but do nothing for it – no real promotion, not go on tour to support it. Just release music, and then disappear. "I thought it'd nice just to silently put it out," he said of the idea, but it wasn't long before he changed his mind. "It didn't really feel like it was ready, and we wouldn't be able to just sit around at home if we had a new album out, and ultimately we just want to go out and play, so rather than jump back in to another cycle of things, it felt like a good idea to stop."

That left two options for the band and their stockpile of new songs. "Okay, we can do one of two things," thought Grohl. "We can not touch these songs until we're ready to make another record, or we can record them right now and forget about them." The band decided on the latter, heading to Grandmaster Recorders in Hollywood, California.

The band recorded fourteen songs and true to their word, simply tucked them away for future use. Three of those songs known to have been recorded were 'Word Forward', 'Wheels' and 'Rope', all of which would indeed be re-recorded and released in later years.

* * *

June 2009
Studio 606, Northridge, CA, United States

Foo Fighters
Hawkins, Taylor (Drums)

Grohl, Dave (Guitar, Vocals)

Mendel, Nate (Bass Guitar)

Shiflett, Chris (Guitar)

Recording Credits
Brown, James (Engineer)

Lousteau, John (Assistant Engineer)

Vig, Butch (Producer)

Tracks Recorded
1. Wheels

2. Word Forward

Recording Equipment
Allen Sides' custom API Recording & Mixing Console

Neve Console Module

Studer A827 24-Track 2 Inch Tape Recorder

With Foo Fighters deciding to take a sizeable break following the release cycle for 'Echoes, Silence, Patience & Grace' their record label was keen to see release of a 'Greatest Hits' record. When the band had signed a distribution deal with RCA Records in 1999 one of the clauses in that deal stated that the label would be able to distribute a compilation style release in a certain timeframe.

A Greatest Hits album had been tabled by the label in 2004 and again in 2006 but on both occasions the band had managed to put it off, instead releasing 'In Your Honor' and the live album 'Skin And Bones', keeping the label happy.

Now seemingly unavoidable with no new releases planned for a few years the compilation was penciled in for late 2009, whether Grohl really wanted it to or not. "It still seems premature because we're still a functioning, active band. Those things can look like an obituary," Grohl said of his reluctance to put out the release. "They started asking about four years ago, and we said, 'Don't we need some hits?'"

To make the release more desirable to the long term, 'hardcore' fans Foo Fighters decided to do what had become all too common with similar anthology style releases – record brand new songs to go alongside the hits.

With over a dozen new songs in their arsenal the band earmarked two of them for this release, aiming to record them in the summer of 2009. Shortly before the planned session Dave Grohl bumped into old friend Butch Vig at a party in Los Angeles. Having not worked with the producer since recording seminal Nirvana album in 1991 Grohl asked Vig if he wanted to produce these two new songs, an offer he felt he couldn't refuse.

The band rocked up to their private Studio 606 facility in June 2009 to record two songs, 'Wheels' and 'Word Forward'. The latter was a song openly written about Jimmy Swanson, Grohl's childhood friend who passed away in 2008. "Goodbye Jimmy, farewell youth" began the lyrics. The two had known each other for a long time, doing everything together right up to his passing. "He was my partner in crime from the time I was six or seven years old," explained Grohl. "The first time I smoked weed, he lit the bowl. The first time I went on tour, he was my roadie."

Whilst in interviews Grohl would claim the second song, 'Wheels', to be about "that feeling when the wheels touch the ground" after being on a flight it was in fact also about his friendship with Jimmy, albeit with more metaphorical lyrics.

Producer Vig greatly enjoyed working again with Grohl at the session, remarking that they "had so much fun doing it". Whilst he had no concrete plans to get started now, Grohl asked if Vig if he would be interested in producing the bands next full-length album, when they were ready. As with his acceptance of working on this session, it didn't take much convincing for the Garbage drummer to agree.

The two new songs were added to what the label decided were the bands thirteen "greatest hits". A final song included on the album was an acoustic version of arguably their biggest hit, 'Everlong'.

Despite having little desire to release the album the band did briefly return to the road to promote it, although Grohl would tell many media outlets the release was out of his hand and made it clear that these were the hits as selected by the label, not their best songs in his eyes. "I think there are better songs than some of those."

* * *

March 1st, 2010
Dave Grohl's Garage, Encino, CA, United States

Foo Fighters

Hawkins, Taylor (Drums)

Grohl, Dave (Guitar, Vocals)

Mendel, Nate (Bass Guitar)

Shiflett, Chris (Guitar)

Recording Credits

Brown, James (Engineer)

Lousteau, John (Assistant Engineer)

Vig, Butch (Producer)

Tracks Recorded

1. Dear Rosemary

2. 7 Corners

3. Better Off

Recording Equipment

Studer A827 24-Track 2 Inch Tape Recorder

Dave Grohl spent much of 2009 and 2010 on tour with Them Crooked Vultures, his side project supergroup with John Paul Jones, Josh Homme, and Alain Johannes. In January 2010 the band was touring Australia and it was there Grohl conceived a grand plan for the next Foo Fighters record. The main aspect of that plan was to record the entire album using classic analog equipment whilst the sub-plot was that rather than use their state-of-the-art Studio 606 facility to do it, they would occupy the garage of Dave Grohl's home in Encino, California.

On March 1st, 2010, with a short break in his Vultures touring commitments, Grohl and the rest of Foo Fighters convened at his house for some exploratory recordings. The garage had already been set up in the past for Grohl to record simple demos but for a full album recording, more serious equipment was required. Butch Vig had as promised joined the band to produce the eventual album and along with engineer James Brown everyone got to work at the house. To record these early demos Brown set up a Studer A827 24-Track tape recorder along with with a rack of Neve preamps removed from an old BCM 10 console previously installed in the old Studio 606 in Virginia.

Over the course of three days the band recorded three tracks. Each of the songs only took around three hours according to Brown, using just 16 of the 24 available recording tracks. "I threw up eight microphones, just to get a feel for what we were gonna be dealing with," he said, speaking of the investigative nature of the session.

The first of the three tracks was at this stage titled simply 'Rosemary', an early version of the song later known fully as 'Dear Rosemary'. The second song to be tracked was the now almost fabled '7 Corners'. The band had been attempting to record the song since 1996, for the album 'The

Colour And The Shape', but just weren't able to craft a song they liked around a riff that they did. They'd worked on it in some form during production and recording of each subsequent album, but still, it remained on the back burner. It was demoed once more during this session in the hopes that '7 Corners' might finally be ready for the public to hear on album seven.

The final track to be recorded on this day was titled 'Better Off' and in listening back to rough mixes of all three songs, the band, producer, and engineer were all suitably impressed with the sonic quality of the garage recordings, although a lot of work was still needed before the 'studio' would be ready for recording a full album.

Grohl soon went back out to finish off his duties with Them Crooked Vultures whilst work continued to prepare his garage and family home for full-blown recording, planned for later in the year.

None of these early test recordings have ever been released publicly although Grohl did tease fans by posting an image on social media platform Twitter which showed a CD containing all three songs.

* * *

* * *

September 6th to December 21st, 2010
Dave Grohl's Garage, Encino, CA, United States

Foo Fighters

Hawkins, Taylor (Drums)

Grohl, Dave (Guitar, Vocals)

Mendel, Nate (Bass Guitar)

Shiflett, Chris (Guitar)

Smear, Pat (Guitar)

Additional Musicians

Greene, Jessy (Violin)

Hester, Drew (Percussion)

Jaffee, Rami (Keyboards, Organ)

Mould, Bob (Guitar, Vocals)

Novoselic, Krist (Bass, Accordion)

Vig, Butch (Percussion)

Waybill, Fee (Backing Vocals)

Recording Credits

Brown, James (Engineer)

Lousteau, John (Assistant Engineer)

Vig, Butch (Producer)

Tracks Recorded

1. Miss The Misery

2. Dear Rosemary

3. These Days

4. Walk

5. A Matter Of Time

6. Bridge Burning

7. Better Off

8. White Limo

9. I Should Have Known

10. Arlandria

11. Back And Forth

12. Rope

Recording Equipment

AP1 1608 recording console

Two Studer A827 24-Track 2 Inch Tape Recorders

Except for a brief reprise to promote 2009s Greatest Hits album Foo Fighters were very quiet once touring for their album 'Echoes, Silence, Patience & Grace' was completed in late 2008. Dave Grohl told the media he thought it was time for a long break for the band as they had been working virtually non-stop since their inception in 1995.

That didn't mean a long vacation on a beach for the band members, though. The band leader instead formed supergroup Them Crooked Vultures, recording an album and touring across the world back behind the drum kit. The rest of the band similarly kept themselves busy – Chris Shiflett and Taylor Hawkins both recorded albums with their other bands, the Dead Peasants and the Coattail Riders respectively, whilst Nate Mendel joined his former band Sunny Day Real Estate for a reunion tour and also worked on material for his own future solo album.

In January 2010 Them Crooked Vultures were booked on a tour of Australia and New Zealand and before a show in Perth Grohl, sat in his hotel room, hatched an ambitious plan for the next Foo Fighters album. "OK, we should make a documentary about the recording of this new album and make it a history of the band too. Rather than just record the album in the most expensive studio with the most state-of-the-art equipment, what if Butch and I were to get back together after 20 years and dust off the tape machines and put them in my garage?" Grohl thought to himself.

The Vultures returned home in early February and Grohl

immediately began to put his master plan into action. "I literally backed the minivan out of the garage, pulled the lawnmower out, put a drum set in it and set up mics. We soundproofed the garage door so that my neighbors wouldn't call the fucking cops."

As with most previous albums demo recording began with just Grohl and Hawkins hashing out ideas. "I had maybe 20 or 30 rough ideas. And albums usually begin with Taylor and I, we'll go in and work on tempos and dynamic and rough arrangements of riffs, and then after we've narrowed it down to 20 song ideas, we ask the other guys."

Following his work producing two songs for Foo Fighters Greatest Hits record in 2009 Butch Vig had agreed to produce the next full-length record but was not entirely prepared for what Dave Grohl had in mind. "The first day we sat down and talked about it," said Vig. "He dropped one bombshell: 'I wanna do it in my garage.'" Following that first bombshell Grohl then revealed the next left field decision - recording on tape, entirely in analog. "What we'll do is we'll probably record on tape and then dump it into Pro Tools," thought Vig upon hearing the plan. That was indeed how the past couple of Foo Fighters records had been done, and it was relatively common in the industry. "No no no no, dude. No fucking computers. Not one computer. None" was the response from Grohl. This album was to be 100% analog, just as every band had done in the not too distant past. Whilst he had now adapted to the digital world Butch Vig was still very familiar with recording to tape, the "old fashioned" way.

He was happy to work that way again, but it came with words of caution for the band members - "That means you guys have to be razor-sharp tight. You've gotta be so well rehearsed, 'cause I can't fix anything. I can't paste drum fills and choruses around. This is gonna be a record about performance, about how you guys play" he told the band.

With exploratory recordings in March 2010 deemed a success work continued in the following weeks to fully prepare Grohl's house for recording. A single Studer A827 24-Track 2" tape recorder had been used during those test recordings and a second was brought in to enable the band to run up to 48 tracks. To keep track of which was which and avoid any confusion during recording they were given the nicknames Hal and Betty. A new recording console was also ordered, an API 1608 with 32 input channels. With no hope of fitting the huge desk in the garage itself it was instead installed in a spare room in the house, above the garage. "The API sound is great for rock," said producer Vig of the choice. "It's not subtle and it's not soft. When you turn the gain up on an EQ, you can really hear it. It's musical."

Engineer James Brown was similarly complimentary of the selected hardware. "I've always loved the API sound. I grew up as an engineer on a pair of API consoles back at RAK Studios in England. The sound is very open and musical. Heading into the project, I was glad to have the API sound as a known quantity. Also, I knew it would withstand the heavy workload day in and day out." Once the console arrived Brown kitted out the expansion slots with various API EQs – the 550A three-band, 550B four-band, and 560 Graphic EQs.

Equipment continued to arrive at the makeshift studio each day, all adhering to the analog only rules. A pair of Barefoot MM27s monitor speakers was installed as well as extensive outboard gear – two Chandler Little Devils, two Dramastic Audio Obsidians and five Universal Audio LA3As were used for compression whilst two Manley 'Massive Passive' and two GML 8200 boards were used in the EQ chain. For preamplifiers, a mixture of API and Neve racks were borrowed from Studio 606 across town.

For vocal recording a small isolation booth was created in a room just off the study with sliding doors to close it off from the main room. When it came to the garage space itself relatively little work was carried out other than the required soundproofing. Large four feet square baffles were placed behind Hawkins' drum kit, a further two placed near the door to stop sound leaking out and a large carpet was laid underneath the kit. "Initially, it was so loud and bright with no carpet in it, and the cymbal bleed was killing everything," said Vig of the reason for adding the latter. "To tame that space, we would've had to hang things everywhere" engineer Brown added, noting that lots of baffles and other noise isolation devices would've been required to get clean, pure results. "And y'know, the brief going into it was that Dave didn't want to do that. He wanted the record to have a trashy, aggressive quality to it."

The number of microphones in the garage was tremendous. Covering Hawkins drum kit was a Yamaha SKRM100 Sub-kick, an AGK D112 on the kick itself, A Shure SM57 on the top and bottom of the snare, an AKG 452 on the Hi-Hat, a Josephson ES22S on the toms and finally an AKG 452 on the ride cymbal.

Because of the unique challenge that came with recording in a room with no acoustic treatments and a concrete floor Brown spent a long time experimenting with the placement of overhead and ambient microphones in the small space. Eventually, he settled on a Neumann M49 for drum kit ambiance, a Violet Black Finger for overhead ambiance, a pair of Soundelux 251s at knee level against the garage door for main ambiance and a pair of Crown PZMs for floor ambiance. Finally, a Violet Designs Stereo Flamingo and a

Shure SM58 were used for overhead mics, the latter placed behind the drum kit at head height.

"I'd use the same mic placement in that garage, regardless of the mic," explained Brown. "Turning the Soundeluxes away from the drums and pointing them into a corner tempered the top end. The mic choices were more about choosing cymbals and asking Taylor not to hit so hard. That allows more room for the snare and kick to cut through in the ambient mics. That's when you can really hear the garage; the air isn't getting sucked up by cymbals and mid-range."

In terms of microphones on the amplifiers, most of the work was done by Shure SM7 and SM57 models although Royer R121s and two RCA BK5 ribbon mics were also used. "I had the RCA mics sent out from Smart Studios," explained Vig. "They're my favorite ribbon mic because they have higher end than normal ribbon mics, but they can also take a really intense sound pressure." Despite Grohl stating one goal of the album was to record away from a state-of-the-art studio, without the latest cutting-edge technology, all of the analog equipment purchased for recording did not come cheaply – the final cost came in at well over $150,000.

July 4th, 2010 saw Them Crooked Vultures play the penultimate show of their tour, with just one further show remaining at the end of the month in Japan. The band used this opportunity to head into Studio 606 for a week and work on some further Foo Fighters demos before final recording for the album would get underway later in the year. Seventeen songs were worked on at this time including 'Bridge Burning', 'Rosemary', 'Better Off', 'White Limo' and the long-standing 'Fuck Around'. The week was deemed a productive one by Dave Grohl as he headed off to play with the Vultures one last time.

With that side project at a close, the seventh Foo Fighters album now had Dave Grohl's full attention. August 16th saw official pre-production sessions begin at Studio 606 and for the following three weeks the band worked with producer Vig to reduce the thirty or so song ideas they had down to a reasonable number for an album.

Speaking of their choice to spend more time at 606 rather than just heading straight to his house, Grohl explained how beneficial he felt the extra time would be - "I thought the more prepared we are when we get to the house the less we have to worry about the songs and the more we can focus on the sound. Having never made a record in the garage, nobody knew what was going to happen." The band rehearsed at their base every day for up to eight hours, although he was conscious that they didn't over-work the songs too much - "Just to the point where there was still some mystery to them".

When the band was initially demoing songs earlier in the year they were playing around with ideas that Grohl considered "heavy shit" and in February he told Rolling Stone that the next Foo Fighters record was going to be "our heaviest record yet".

Despite many of those heavier songs not even making it to the final pre-production sessions Butch Vig had read the quote and told Grohl "Well, now it has to be 'cos you've already told everybody!" As summer started drawing to a close the band would play through each track with Vig deciding which were up to the billing. "This doesn't rock enough, no. Next," he would bluntly tell the group after hearing some of the ideas. The band continued to work through their material, re-arranging some songs until they had what they believed were the thirteen songs worthy of the 'heaviest record yet' label.

Pre-production work wound up on September 5th, 2010 and the very next day, Labor Day in the United States, operations moved straight to Dave Grohl's garage and recording of Foo Fighters seventh album was officially underway. When recording all their previous albums the band had always worked in the same manner – recording drums for the entire record first, then all the guitars, and so on. This time, a different approach was planned.

The aim was for one complete song to be recorded each week – start with the drums on Monday, the other instruments would then follow with a rough mix of the entire track competed by Friday. "We stuck to that and it was good because each song kinda had its own life." said producer Vig of the schedule. "Once we were focused on a song for a week, that's pretty much all we did. In a way, you had a sense of completion".

The first track the band worked on was 'Miss The Misery'. Hawkins began to lay down his drum track but immediately some teething issues arose - "when it came to recording the first drum track, it quickly became apparent that the cymbal bleed was still presenting a major problem" explained engineer James Brown.

"The cymbals are always a problem with the Foos because they wash a lot and they hit them so hard". In an attempt to solve the bleed issue the main crash cymbal was switched out for a Zildjian which had holes drilled in it to lower the pitch and shorten the sustain, the length of time it would ring out after being hit. The ambiance microphones in the garage were also turned away from the kit, instead facing outward towards the bottom corners of the garage.

Acoustics and bleed were not the only technical issues the band faced. With the first drum take on tape Vig started razor splicing edits only for the delicate magnetic tape to start shedding the oxide coating, a phenomenon known in recording circles as "sticky-shed syndrome". Concerned that audio would be lost to the process Vig suggested they also back up everything digitally but Grohl was having none of it. "If I see one fucking computer hooked up to a piece of gear, you're fucking fired! We're making the record the way we want to make it, and if you can't do it, then fuck you!" he playfully shouted at the suggestion. "What if something happens to the tape?" Vig asked. "What did we do in 1991, Butch? You play it again! God forbid you have to play your song one more time."

Sound problems averted and the 'no digital' ethos made crystal clear recording continued to plan with guitar tracks laid down for the first song. As well as Dave Grohl and Chris Shiflett a third guitarist was also at the house – Pat Smear. An original member of the band, Smear left in 1997 citing a lack of desire for constant touring, preferring to "Just do nothing". He'd first been invited back into the Foo Fighters family in 2006 as an extra guitarist on their acoustic tour and was then asked to record a small number of guitar tracks on their 2007 album 'Echoes, Silence, Patience & Grace'. Following recording Smear then joined the band on-stage throughout touring the for the album, performing on all the new songs but then leaving the stage for the old classics. This time, Grohl wanted him involved throughout the entire album and considered him the fifth full-time member of the band going forward.

With three distinct guitar parts recorded for 'Miss The Misery' next in the process was Nate Mendel laying down his bass track. For most songs, Mendel recorded with his Lakland Bob Glaub Signature bass guitar through an Ashdown ABM 900 EVO II Twin Bass Amplifier head. "I think we might have used a Fender on one song, I think we tried a Gibson Ripper on one song," noted Vig of some other selections. "But he's very fluid, he has a really good feel and that was almost more important sometimes than the sound — how the performance felt on the song".

It was then time to record the first vocals for the album. For much of the session Grohl would sing into a Bock Audio 251 Tube Condenser Mic which went through a Neve 1073 Microphone Preamp & Equalizer into an Empirical Labs Distressor Compressor. The majority of the vocals would be recorded in the small vocal booth to the side of the control room but on some tracks Grohl elected to perform out in the open control room, creating a more echoey sound. Speaking of the unique issues that the team was presented with recording in analog producer Vig noted "We were doing everything on the slave reel so by the time we got all the guitars on there, there were usually only four tracks left for vocals and two left for vocal bounces. So, Dave would just do these performances and we would work until we felt that we had four good takes that could almost be considered a lead. With Dave, once he got focused, the takes were very consistent. When we'd finish, I'd put all four takes up and listen to them all at the same time, and you could hear how tight it was. If he was off, phrasing-wise, especially on a chorus, then we'd go back in and do it. But really, though, it was so tight" explained Vig. "Then I would usually comp it in chunks — use take two for the first verse, take three for the chorus — and then we would record a double. The cool thing about live doubling is there's no Auto-Tune and it's not perfect and because it's looser, it sounds better. It's sort of wider and thicker sounding. Every now and then when we were bouncing, we'd have to punch in a word. Or sometimes I'd have to do, like, ninja fades, slight crossfades. It was a lot of work, but again I think when you hear it, it has character. It feels like a performance. It doesn't feel like something that was put together in a studio."

Grohl sang the lead on the song before Taylor Hawkins recorded backing vocals together with the first guest of the album — lead singer of punk rock outfit The Tubes, Fee Waybill. Dave Grohl first met Waybill several years earlier in a vintage cloth store whilst he and his wife were looking for costumes to wear to a party. Waybill went over to introduce himself to the couple and quickly hit it off, Dave and Fee both a fan of each other's work.

They soon became good friends attending parties and going to dinner together and so when the time came to record the album Grohl asked Waybill if he wanted to help. "He sent me a text and said 'We're doing this tune and the background vocal sounds like you, come over'" recalled Waybill. Speaking of the all analog, natural approach Waybill noted: "it was all real, no Pro-Tools, no flying in parts from here or there, we sang that chorus every time it came up".

Week two and work began on the next song, 'Dear Rosemary', previously titled simply 'Rosemary'. The process once again began with Hawkins recording drums, a routine already starting to form. Grohl would stand in the garage with his drummer, playing guitar and directing Hawkins. "Dave would just stand two feet away from him, just so they could communicate, especially if we were trying to figure out drum fills or some patterns that were not quite working. A lot of times with Taylor instead of tape editing, we would just punch in," explained Vig. Punching in/out is the practice of recording a new take directly over the previously recorded tape, replacing that section. A simple concept, but it meant whoever carried out the delicate work on the tape had to be very precise or risk losing something. "You can hear the punch ins and punch outs if you put headphones on. Especially if you soloed the drums, you would hear the cymbals change or the snare tuning change a little bit," the producer continued, adding that it indeed didn't always go swimmingly – "Sometimes we would fuck up — like James would punch in on a chorus and he'd clip a snare or something and we'd play it back for Taylor and go, 'Sorry, dude, you're gonna have to do it again'."

According to Butch Vig the three guitarists all brought something unique to each song - "They all kinda have different roles. Dave is kind of the glue, he plays most of the rhythm stuff and locks in really well with Taylor" he explained. "Chris is an amazing musician and normally he would play the riffy parts, the arpeggio parts, the lead breaks, things like that". The returning Pat Smear was described as "The X-Factor", coming up with "gnarly guitar tones" and adding smaller, unique parts to many songs. "For Pat's main rig we ended up using a Roland Jazz Chorus with these crazy pedals that would make the fillings in your teeth fall out" the producer revealed.

Smear also recorded several songs using a deeper Baritone guitar, finding a place in the songs lower than what Shiflett or Grohl had recorded. In terms of amplification the returning Smear used a low-end Peavey on some songs, with Vig believing it was the perfect antithesis – "Chris and Dave have all these great vintage amps and then Pat has like the crudest sound. It was perfect."

'Dear Rosemary' also saw the second special guest of the session, Hüsker Dü guitarist and vocalist Bob Mould joining the group. "I was a huge Hüsker Dü fan, and obviously Bob Mould's music has influenced the way I write music and the way I play guitar. A lot of what I do comes from [him]" said Grohl of Mould. "I met him for the first time last summer and said, You know I'd be nowhere and nobody without your music, right? And he very politely nodded and said: 'I know'. We swapped phone numbers and became friends. I had this song that I imagined would be a duet between us, and he obliged" Grohl said, explaining how the collaboration came about. When Mould arrived at the studio Grohl had purposely not written lyrics for the bridge of the song, preferring to do so whilst his special guest was there with him. The pair worked through the song, harmonizing together through much of it.

Recording continued in the same weekly routine with tracks 'These Days', 'Walk', 'A Matter Of Time' and 'Bridge Burning' all recorded, albeit not in the same order as originally written on their whiteboard. The next song due to be worked on was 'Better Off' and whilst all instrumentation was recorded as scheduled, the vocals were not completed. Grohl had intended for Shudder To Think frontman Craig Wedren to record backing vocals on the track but with Wedren unavailable the band moved on, hoping to complete it later in the session.

Next up was 'White Limo', a song the band had been working on for approximately eight years, occasionally playing an instrumental version of the song during soundchecks towards the end of touring for the fourth album, 'One By One'. For most of its life it was known by the working title of 'Flagger', owing to the fact the band believed it to be in a similar style to legendary punk rock outfit Black Flag.

Foo Fighters attempted to record the song for both 'In Your Honor' and 'Echoes, Silence, Patience & Grace' but for a multitude of reasons, it wasn't included on either album. "We've been trying to make that into a song for years," said Shiflett. "It has such a badass riff it's fucking insane. It makes you want to break into someone's car and steal their stereo," was Grohl's description of the track.

The instrumentation and structure of the song for this recording was largely the same as the version from pre-production in 2004, heard on the 'making of' DVD for the album 'In Your Honor'. This fresh version did though show clear signs of evolution with a much fuller sound, adding many layers of guitar. For the vocal performance, Grohl wanted to achieve a gritty, distorted sound similar to that of the song 'Weenie Beenie' from the 1995 debut album.

In an attempt to replicate that sound Grohl sang into a Shure SM57 microphone but rather than the usual clean signal path it was passed through a Pro Co Rat guitar distortion pedal. As far as the words Grohl sang, even he wasn't really sure - "I don't even know the lyrics to that song. I wrote them in two minutes," he quipped, comparing the hurried writing to the situation he found himself in when recording what would become the debut album. "Some of the lyrics weren't even real words" on that first effort according to Grohl and ever since then, he'd usually spent a lot more time on his lyrics.

For 'White Limo', he was reminded that it wasn't always necessary. "Dave, I don't want you to feel like you always have to write We Are The fucking World every time you write a song." wrote bassist Nate Mendel in an e-mail, referencing the charity song released in 1985 by U.S.A. For Africa, a huge collection of popular acts of the era. "That made me a lot more comfortable writing, a lot more laid back," said Grohl. With the song now finally deemed ready for release it was given a final title, 'White Limo'. According to Grohl, this was a code between the band members for "getting really fucked up", a description he felt suited the raucous song which he re-iterated was about "nothing at all". The band was well over halfway through recording by October 2010 and work began on the next track 'I Should Have Known'. Unlike many of the songs which had been first demoed several years earlier, this track was brand new - "That song happened halfway through pre-production," revealed Grohl. "We didn't enter into the recording with that song. I just did that in my bedroom. I sang it and played the riff, and everyone wanted to work on it."

Despite the strong positivity surrounding the song it almost didn't make it into the final cut of thirteen songs, the second take in pre-production sounding "like shit" according to Grohl, with "none of the passion or the energy or the combustion of the first take". Despite this the song did make the cut and was worked on over the usual week-long schedule. For the track Grohl's vocals were recorded through a Roland RE-201 delay effects unit creating a "spooky, distorted sound" according to Vig. Rather than head into the vocal isolation booth, he sang out in the main room sat next to the producer and he was astonished by the passion Grohl put into the performance - "At the end of that take, the hair on my neck stood up; I couldn't say anything. Dave looked like he was crying, 'cause he was singing so hard. He was obviously channeling something inside."

Butch believed the song was written about Kurt Cobain but Grohl in-part denied that. "At first I started writing it about someone specific, not Kurt," he told an interviewer. That specific someone he referred to was Jimmy Swanson, one of his best friends since childhood who passed away suddenly in 2008. "But then as I elaborated on it... I mean, I look at it and I think there are definite connections. And I definitely felt that way before, especially in Nirvana, with Kurt where, you know, I was afraid this was going to happen." Grohl added. Whilst most of the lyrics saw Grohl expressing feelings that he should've been more aware of the struggles Jimmy was facing before his death the reference to Kurt and others in the lyrics came explicitly with the line "I've been here before".

The track also saw yet another guest appearance, friend and former Nirvana bassist Krist Novoselic. "We've always been in touch. One of the things about the expanded Nirvana family, it doesn't matter how much time has passed, when you see each other you're immediately connected by that, by the good and bad things" said Grohl of his longtime friend. "It was perfectly natural for me to say,' Y'know, this would be such a cool opportunity to get Krist down into the studio.' He and Butch and I haven't hung out in the studio for 20 years. And I wasn't even thinking about the music, I was just thinking about the three of us coming together, and maybe without words just acknowledging that we survived, y'know?".

Novoselic recorded bass and accordion tracks for the song and it wasn't long before Grohl and Vig felt they were briefly back in the past - "When Krist plugged his Gibson Ripper into the Hi-Watt amp he played the bass line he came up with in his head and, I'm not kidding, it was so undeniably Krist Novoselic that Butch and I just looked at each other and laughed" said Grohl of the surreal experience. Recording continued into November with the tracks 'Arlandria' and 'Back & Forth' although for the latter only drums and bass were initially recorded, the band instead moving straight onto the penultimate song on the recording list, 'Rope'. The track had begun life in a way many Foo Fighters songs had in the recent past, with Taylor and Dave jamming together and bouncing ideas off of each other. "Taylor sometimes comes up with a rhythm on drums, and then bases a riff around that - that's how it happened with this song. I think he had that rhythm in his head and then figured out the chords and the structure" explained bassist Mendel on the origins of the track. "When we first heard it, it was just Dave playing it on the guitar; then we started jamming around with it. Taylor and Dave usually work on the drum parts together. Taylor comes up with ideas, and then Dave will say, "I want to hear it like this," or, "That's cool what you're doing there – try it this way," and we just build it up from there. Since Dave's a drummer, he has the advantage of rhythm being second nature to him. It allows him to do things that are a bit more complicated without having to think about it too much".

According to guitarist Shiflett, the song had evolved greatly since its early inception. "It is so different now than what it was when we were jamming it on tour". Grohl also noted that that the chorus was slightly different back then whilst Pat Smear wasn't sure on the merits of the earlier version of the song at all – "Somehow it didn't make sense to me when we played it at sound checks. I couldn't get a handle on it until we got into the studio."

The track featured irregular guitar work, something Shiflett had trouble getting his head around. "What my guitar is doing over the bass makes no sense in a way" he suggested. "It does, but you don't know how. A flat seventh, a fourth and a minor third; those seem like weird notes to put together in a chord and put in those places. I remember when we were learning that I was like, 'What the fuck? This is nuts.' They're all minor sevenths with a sus four. But it's in B minor, and then you move to a D, which is also a minor sus four. So that's kind of illogical, in a way, to your ear."

The drum track of the song featured what producer Vig described as one of his highlights - "there is an amazing, really ballsy moment on Rope where it just stops and it's dead space, and then they come back in and Taylor plays these crazy fills before it launches into the guitar solo. I think a lot of producers would probably have cut that out, but we wanted to leave it in because we felt we had captured something special. It had a great vibe, and it was fun, cool and completely unexpected". One further song remained on the song board hanging in the studio, 'To No End', but the band elected not to work on it at all, sticking with the twelve songs that had already been started.

With the exception of 'Echoes, Silence, Patience & Grace' every Foo Fighters album since 1997s 'The Colour And The Shape' had been in some way or another re-recorded. That wasn't the case with this album, but the band did go back to one song they weren't happy with, 'I Should Have Known'. "We tracked it and I thought it sounded good, but Dave thought it sounded too 'parted out' like I'd worked out the arrangement too much." said producer Vig.

Grohl thought the track was being turned into a radio single by Vig but that wasn't to Grohl's liking, instead desiring a "raw and primal" sound. "It sounded like some bad Coldplay B side. Fuck this! Why can't it be chaotic and out of control and why can't we let it explode? Don't try to rein it in. Let it go free" thought Grohl.

The band went back and listened to recordings of the track from pre-production and despite it sounding like "a complete train wreck" according to Vig he did prefer the general feel of the earlier, less polished version. "Taylor was playing all these wild fills and Pat Smear was playing noise and feedback, but I remember listening to it going, 'The vibe on that is really exciting'".

And so, in the final week of recording the band went back and re-tracked the song from scratch. Grohl told Hawkins to "Go bananas" and he duly obliged, adding fills that Vig described as "almost Keith Moon-esque". For Grohl's vocals, a lighter version of the setup used to record vocals for 'White Limo' was set up, a handheld microphone running into a guitar amplifier with tape echo applied. "It definitely has that John Lennon solo album vibe, dirty and mucky, but really primal sounding," said Vig of the resulting vocal capture. "The end of that song is all from the first take he did. He was sitting about four feet away from me and when he finished it nobody said anything for a few seconds and I could see tears welling up in his eyes and he had sung so hard he couldn't even catch his breath," he added, commenting on the emotion and power Grohl put into the vocal take. Krist Novoselic also returned to the studio, adding some further bass overdubs to the track.

With 'I Should Have Known' re-recorded and the band now happy with it recording was deemed complete, attention then shifting to mixing in mid-December. The group chose Alan Moulder for the job, a renowned British music producer who Dave Grohl had recently worked with mixing the Them Crooked Vultures record. Initially the master tapes were taken to Chalice Recording Studios in Los Angeles for Moulder to mix on their huge 72 Channel Solid State Logic SL9000 mixing desk, the same place and board he'd worked on the Vultures record, but neither Moulder nor Grohl were particularly happy with what they were hearing.

When comparing what he was able to do in comparison to James Browns original rough mixes, Moulder didn't feel he could make any improvements. "James hadn't done anything in particular – it just came off the API sounding like that. There was a certain top-end presence that when you threw it up on the SSL just wasn't there. Immediately it sounded a bit cloudier." Grohl was also keen for it to sound more like the rough mixes - "Make it sound like my garage" he told Moulder.

Grohl had initially wanted to mix the album back at the garage anyway and Moulder soon realized that was the only way it was going to sound the desired way - "You want to make it sound like your garage? Mix it in your garage!" he playfully told Grohl. "There seemed to be a theme and a story to the record and us being at Chalice didn't seem to be part of it. The whole record was done punk rock style in the garage, and it seemed a little odd to go from that to this other studio in Hollywood". Vig was surprised at how accepting Moulder was of the idea, noting "There's a lot of mixers I know who would not want to do that, who would not want to go to manually mix in this room where there's no acoustic treatment. But he did".

Moulder, Vig, James Brown and Grohl were all forced to squeeze together at the console in the study come control room back at the house, all their upper limbs required to complete the process. "We mixed manually on the API board, with me, James, Alan and Dave, all eight hands on board, all doing the faders, no automation; we couldn't even do mutes" Vig explained.

"I would do the vocal rides, Alan would man everything and effects, James would do the guitar, Dave would run the drums, but the drums were only four tracks and it was second generation. We didn't go back, we didn't have the inputs on the API to go back and lock up the A reel. So, all the drums are second-generation mixed to the B reel" he said, further detailing the process.

To this point the record had, as Grohl wished, been created using only analog gear and techniques. This was however broken slightly in the mixing phase, Moulder using an Eventide 2016 Reverb Unit on some tracks as well as two

Lexicon PCM 42 Signal Processors for delays and an Eventide Eclipse digital effects processor on the vocal tracks.

Despite mixing being well underway Grohl did have one vocal left to record at this stage, for the song 'Better Off' which was quickly taken care of.

On December 21st, 2010 the band played a secret live show at Paladino's, a small bar in the Tarzana neighborhood of Los Angeles. During the show, four tracks from the recording session were given their live debut - 'Back & Forth', 'White Limo', 'Dear Rosemary' and 'These Days'. Before playing the first of the four tracks Grohl told the crowd that they had just finished the record that day, clarifying in a later interview just how close it was - "Honestly, we finished the last mix and an hour later we got in Alan's car and drove down to the club and I walked right up onstage". With recording and mixing completed the last step of the process was mastering. After a short break for the holidays on January 3rd, 2012, Grohl took to Twitter to reveal that the task had been placed in the hands of Emily Lazar, a Grammy-nominated mastering engineer. Lazar worked on the record at The Lodge, a mastering facility she herself founded based in the Greenwich Village neighborhood of New York City.

Of the twelve songs fully completed during this session only the first take of 'I Should Have Known' has not been released. Eleven were released on all versions of the album 'Wasting Light' and the twelfth, 'Better Off', was included on a Best Buy exclusive special edition. Strangely for an album that had placed such a huge focus on analog recording two tracks were also made available as official dance remixes - Deadmau5 remixed 'Rope' and The Prodigy re-imagined 'White Limo'.

August 22ⁿᵈ, 2011
Art Farm Studios, Drabenderhöhe, Germany

Foo Fighters
Hawkins, Taylor (Drums)

Grohl, Dave (Guitar, Vocals)

Mendel, Nate (Bass Guitar)

Shiflett, Chris (Guitar)

Smear, Pat (Guitar)

Additional Musicians
Jaffee, Rami (Keyboards)

Recording Credits
Foo Fighters (Producers)

Tracks Recorded
1. Keep It Clean

Whilst on tour in Europe in the summer of 2011, supporting their seventh studio album, Dave Grohl hit upon an idea for a viral video to promote the North American leg of the tour later in the year. During a home tour many years earlier the band and crew had rested at a truck stop which among other amenities featured shower facilities. Whilst sitting in the dining area Grohl noticed that "big, burly truckers" were going in to take showers with a lady behind the counter calling out numbers to alert them when it was their turn, like a deli counter. Equal parts fascinated and amused by the experience he decided it was perfect for parody and mid-tour it was planned to quickly record a humorous song to accompany the video.

On August 21st, 2011 the band were booked to appear at the Highfield Festival in Erfurt, Germany and two days later at the Lanxess Arena in Cologne. The day in between was a day off for the band and touring member Rami Jaffee mentioned to Dave Grohl that he planned to use the day to visit a local recording studio owned by a friend to record some of his own material. Sensing an opportunity, Grohl decided this could a great chance for the whole band to have a little fun. Art Farm Studios, part of a larger complex that includes a club, restaurant and hotel is in Drabenderhöhe, a small locality of the city of Wiehl, 40 kilometers east of Cologne. Rami Jaffee had been friends with owner Robert Schuller for several years, even having a hotel suite in the room named in his honor.

The band were invited to the studio for the day and quickly got to work on their Tenacious D-esque ditty, 'Keep It Clean'. The lyrics of the song roughly followed the experience Grohl intended to parody, with such lines as "Driving all night, Got a hankering for something, Think I'm in the mood for some hot-man muffins".

According to Schuller the track was recorded and finished in just five hours, the band offering him backstage tickets to the Cologne show the next night by way of thanks. Two distinct vocal takes were recorded for the chorus of the track, one with the line "Maybe if we're lucky just a little butt fucking" and a second more PG version featuring "a little bear huggin'" instead.

Just six days later, August 27th, the 'Hot Buns' promo video was released online. The main part of the video saw the band lathering up in a truck stop shower to the soundtrack of the Queen track 'Body Language' but during the introduction, whilst the band was waiting their turn, 'Keep It Clean' was played in the background. The full PG-friendly version of the song was also shared via foofighters.fm, a now-defunct official website which made various Foo Fighters recordings available for fans to listen.

* * *

Late 2011 to September 2012
Studio 606 West, Northridge, CA

Recording Artists (Sound City Players)

Been, Robert Levon (vocals)

Commerford, Tim (Bass)

Goss, Chris (Guitar)

Greene, Jessy (violin)

Grohl, Dave (Guitar, Vocals)

Hawkins, Taylor (Drums)

Hayes, Peter (Guitar)

Homme, Josh (guitar, bass, vocals)

Jaffee, Rami (keyboards)

Johannes, Alain (guitar)

Keltner, Jim (drums)

McCartney, Paul (cigarbox guitar, vocals)

Novoselic, Krist (Bass)

Nicks, Stevie (vocals)

Nielsen, Rick (guitar)

Reeder, Scott (bass)

Reznor, Trent (guitar, synth)

Smear, Pat (Guitar)

Shiflett, Chris (Guitar)

Springfield, Rick (guitar, vocals)

Taylor, Corey (vocals)

Ving, Lee (guitar, vocals)

Wilk, Brad (drums)

Recording Credits

Brown, James (Engineer)

Lousteau, John (Engineer)

Vig, Butch (Producer)

Scott, Jim (Engineer)

Tracks Recorded

1. Heaven And All
2. From Can To Can't
3. The Man That Never Was
4. Time Slowing Down
5. You Can't Fix This
6. Centipede
7. A Trick With No Sleeve
8. Mantra
9. Cut Me Some Slack
10. Your Wife Is Calling
11. If I Were Me

Recording Equipment

Neve 8028 recording console

Two Studer A827 24-Track 2 Inch Tape Recorders

In late 2010 Dave Grohl and Butch Vig were hunting around the United States for equipment to kit out Grohl's garage studio, in preparation for the recording of the Foo Fighters 'Wasting Light' album. In search of vintage analog equipment, Vig suggested they call Sound City Studios, the location the pair had recorded Nirvana's seminal album 'Nevermind' in 1991. The studio had hit financial troubles and in a bid to survive Vig had heard they were selling all of the equipment from the smaller studio B at the facility. Fearing that complete closure may not have been too far away for the struggling studio, Grohl brought up the possibility of buying their historic Neve 8028 Recording Console from the main room. The board had been installed in the studio since 1973 and had seen countless classic albums recorded on it, including Nevermind.

Adamant they would survive, the studio manager informed Grohl that she would "sell my grandmother before

I'd sell that board". Sadly for Sound City, things did not improve and later in 2011 Grohl's prediction had come true as the studio faced full closure. With a heavy heart, they called Grohl back and informed him that if he wanted it, the board was his. Studio owner Tom Skeeter had chosen Grohl to take on the board knowing he would take good care of it but more importantly, he knew it wouldn't end up in a warehouse covered in plastic, that he would keep it in use. With a deal agreed for the console and some other equipment, Grohl headed to Sound City in November of 2011 to collect the board, with the intended destination being his own Studio 606 facility across the state in Northridge.

A large crew including family and friends helped to extract the console out of the Sound City control room, onto a van and then onto its new home in the Studio 606 control room. With the long and exhausting extraction and transportation taking most of the day Grohl and friends spent the evening relaxing, reminiscing about the studio and the board. As the beer flowed, so did some ideas on how to commemorate both. One of the friends with Grohl was James Rota, vocalist and guitarist for heavy metal band Fireball Ministry. As well as his musical endeavors Rota also had experience in video production and knowing that Grohl suggested they could make a short film celebrating the studio and on its 20th anniversary, Nirvana's album 'Nevermind'. Originally they planned to just upload the resulting video to YouTube but the idea spiraled and Grohl had decided on creating a full-length movie documentary on the studio.

One part of that documentary was going to explore the history of the studio, those who had recorded there and used its special recording console. The second part of the documentary would then invite back many of those artists to record a new album at Studio 606, using the Neve console for the first time since its move. Grohl contacted as many musicians as possible who had recorded at the studio and who he thought might be interested in joining his project. "I got a list of the big albums that were made there and got everyone's email addresses and started writing emails". Initially Grohl only planned to tell the story of the board and studio in his movie, before receiving words of wisdom from his mother - "She told me that I shouldn't start the movie by saying I bought the board - 'You tell the history of the studio, then you rescue the board and invite everyone back to make an album.' She's a writer – Thanks, mom!"

With the board freshly installed at Studio 606 the project got underway in early 2012 and Grohl was looking forward to working with such a diverse range of artists. "Why shouldn't Rick Springfield be on the same record as Lee Ving?" Grohl thought himself. "When I was a kid, I'd listen to Steel Pulse as well as Slayer. When you think about all the people who recorded at Sound City, It's like a virtual jukebox. To put all those people together in different configurations and make music together, it's pretty cool".

Butch Vig remained in the role of producer for the entire project with James Brown also again on hand to engineer. Most of the guest musicians did not have a lot of time to spare for recording and so Brown knew they would in turn not have much time to spend trying to find sounds for each song. "It became about creating a one-size-fits-all system," said Brown, with Grohl telling them to be "ready for anything".

Grohl's blue DW Drum kit was set up in the main live room at 606, microphones were strategically placed, everything ready to be played by whoever picked up the drumsticks. A bass cabinet was set up along with four guitar stations, mics connected to the board and ready to be placed in front of an amplifier. Several vocal booths were set up using Shure Beta 58 microphones, with provisions for other instruments such as keyboards also in place.

Naturally, the recording was entirely analog with the keyword for the whole project being "real", a carryover from the ethos behind recording of the Wasting Light record. "Pro Tools works just as well as tape for capturing those moments, but it also makes it incredibly easy to correct and perfect things," said engineer Brown. "Working in the analog domain, there's less temptation to correct idiosyncrasies or human flaws. Tape brings an honesty to the process – to the production side of things, too".

A plan was devised to invite musicians to the studio and a song would be worked on in a marathon 24-hour session. Many of the songs were conceived from scratch but according to Brown Dave Grohl arrived at each session with a demo or even just a riff, as an "insurance policy" in case what the musicians came up with on the day wasn't working.

Owing to busy schedules the recording sessions were scattered across several months. Some of the first musicians to arrive for their session were Robert Levon Been and Peter Hayes of Black Rebel Motorcycle Club. Whilst it might have been expected that the pair would've been nervous to work with Grohl, it was, in fact, the other way around - "It was terrifying working with [them]" said Grohl, highlighting the respect he had for the band.

As would be a recurring theme the song they recorded, 'Heaven and All", started out life as a loose jam that was then structured into a fully formed song over the course of the day. The final song was recorded as one live take with just a few guitars, tambourine and backing vocal overdubs added afterward. Barring the backing vocals, the song was left as an instrumental during initial recording, with Levon Been returning later in the year to record lead vocals, having written lyrics in the interim.

Corey Taylor of Slipknot arrived at the studio in February 2012. The song he was set to contribute to, 'From Can To Can't', was one of Dave's old demos and Grohl had already cut a basic track before Taylor arrived at the studio. The Slipknot frontman gave himself a few hours to write lyrics and then in just a few minutes recorded vocal takes for the entire song. "Corey blew us away by literally singing it top to bottom perfectly in a matter of minutes" recalled engineer Brown. Later in the month Cheap Trick's Rick Neilsen arrived to overdub his trademark guitar work on the song and finally former Kyuss and The Obsessed bass player Scott Reeder was at the studio to record a bass track, completing the song.

Also arriving at the studio in February was Rick Springfield. Pat Smear, Taylor Hawkins and Chris Shiflett were all called upon at 606 to work on the song earmarked for Rick 'The Man That Never Was', another old unused demo. Nate Mendel was not present, busy working on his own solo record. This was also the only song Shiflett would feature on, himself busy recording an album of honky-tonk cover songs with his side project The Dead Peasants. The core of the track was played and recorded as a band live in the studio with the rest of the day spent on overdubs and fleshing the track out in a standard manner.

Whilst Grohl and Springfield worked on vocals during the main session only rough scratch takes of the lead vocal were recorded at the studio, Springfield instead electing to go away and work on them more extensively before recording the final takes at his house and sending them in at a later date.

March 2010 saw the arrival of 50% of Rage Against The Machine, bassist Tim Commerford and drummer Brad Wilk. With Grohl on guitar, the three of them built up the core instrumentation of the song 'Time Slowing Down'. The following month Masters of Reality frontman Chris Goss was at the studio to perform lead vocals over the track, also adding piano and backward Mellotron.

April saw a slew of big names at Studio 606. First up was Stevie Nicks of Fleetwood Mac fame. When Grohl was digging through old demos and ideas to potentially use for the record there was one that immediately sprang to mind once he knew Nicks had agreed to participate. For the 2005 album 'In Your Honor' Grohl had written around forty songs with only twenty making the final cut. One that ultimately didn't make it was a track which Grohl believed sounded too much like Fleetwood Mac. "The song was just sitting there, so I sent it to her and asked what she thought" recalled Grohl. Nicks liked the track and so he and Taylor Hawkins got to work on recording a new version, working extremely quickly according to engineer James Brown - "[Dave] always works at the speed of light; you get a sound, find a balance that he's comfortable with, and he will literally throw it down in one take". Rami Jaffee was also on hand to record Keyboards for the song.

The instrumentation of the song was completed by the time Nicks arrived at the studio, allowing her to get straight to work on adding her vocals. Whilst the song was old, Nicks was asked to write entirely new lyrics, adding her own personal touch. She chose to write lyrics inspired by the life of her godson Glen B. Parrish Jr, son of Stevie's tour manager in the 1990s. Parrish Jr. died aged just 18 in November 2011 following a drug overdose. Nicks recorded both lead vocals as well as a backing accompaniment and the track was given the new title 'You Can't Fix This'.

Next through the doors at 606 were Josh Homme, Alain Johannes, and Chris Goss. Together with Grohl the four first recorded the track 'Centipede', the first half of which was another old Grohl demo. The first part of the song was recorded entirely live except for small tambourine and Urdu drum overdubs. The second section of the song was brand new, the four working off the first part to create a heavier section of music, also recorded live with little overdubs. Homme recorded lead vocals later in the evening but did also return at a later date to add further vocal harmonies. Grohl would also record his vocals for the track later in the year.

Whilst Johannes and Homme were at the studio that particular trio also started work on another song for the record, 'A Trick With No Sleeve', with Grohl on drums, Johannes playing guitar and Homme on bass guitar. Johannes soon had to leave but would return to the studio periodically to finish the song, as would Grohl.

Homme remained at the studio as the next guest arrived, Nine Inch Nails front-man Trent Reznor. Over the course of a single day the trio recorded the basis of an entirely new song, 'Mantra'. Born out of a jam which saw Homme switch from guitar to Bass the three laid down the core tracks of the almost eight-minute song, with Grohl on drums and Reznor recording both Wurlitzer piano and guitar tracks. Trent had limited time available at the studio and left the session with a ProTools copy of the basic tracks, electing to further work on it at his own studio. A month later he sent his finished work back to 606, having added further synthesizer and guitar tracks. The track was then finally completed with Grohl and Homme recording vocals, further bass guitar and an additional guitar track over the outro of the epic song.

The final guest at Studio 606 in April was arguably the biggest name so far, Sir Paul McCartney. McCartney had not actually recorded at Sound City and had originally only been invited to the studio to jam with Grohl as he was in town, with no end goal in mind. Not wanting them to miss out, Grohl also invited friends Pat Smear and former Nirvana bassist Krist Novoselic to the studio, an invitation the latter felt he couldn't turn down. The group got chatting and naturally the conversation turned to what they should play. With the Beatles originals off the table Grohl had considered they might just play some old classics by other artists but McCartney had a different idea. "No no no - let's write a song!" he told the group. "Let's write and record a new song in the three hours we have here".

Whilst he had brought with him his famous Hofner bass and a Les Paul guitar McCartney had also brought along a cigar box guitar - a gift from Johnny Depp - which is what he chose to play, surprising Grohl. "He walked in here with the bass and guitar, two of the most iconic instruments in music history. And he decides to play a cigar-box guitar in front of everyone, to record a song. Not a lot of people would do that", Grohl remarked.

Krist and Pat had never previously met McCartney and were not only nervous of playing with such a legendary musician but were also soon aware it was the first time they and Dave had properly played together since the passing of Kurt Cobain and resulting demise of Nirvana. "It was magic for me playing with these guys" McCartney later said. "During the session, I heard the guys talking - 'wow, we haven't played since Nirvana.' So, I found myself in the middle of a Nirvana reunion."

With Paul using an unorthodox instrument, Novoselic

suggested he might play his accordion but that idea was soon playfully shot down. Tape started rolling with McCartney playing some "mean slide" on the cigar-box. He told the others it was tuned to D and according to Novoselic his "grunge instincts" took over and he tuned the E string on his bass down to D. Paul started playing a riff and the rest soon joined in, a song starting to form. Once the basic instrumental track was laid down attentions then turned to vocals, with Paul and Dave deciding they would share the duties. A surreal moment came for Dave when Paul suggested he head into the vocal booth to double up a take he'd just recorded. "Ok, you mean put a harmony on it?" Grohl queried. "No, no just sing what I sang. Me and Lennon used to do it all the time" McCartney replied. "What's going on here! This Is crazy!" Grohl thought to himself, almost unable to believe the situation he found himself in.

All-in-all, recording of 'Cut Me Some Slack' took just three and a half hours. "Why can't it always be this easy?" Grohl asked the room rhetorically. "It is", replied McCartney. The only part of the song not recorded in the initial session was tambourine, added by Grohl at a later date. Whilst the recording session was kept a complete secret the foursome, later dubbed 'Sirvana' by the press, gave the song a live debut on December 12th, 2012 during a Hurricane Sandy benefit performance.

Another quick recording session for the album involved Lee Ving, lead singer of the seminal Los Angeles punk rock band Fear. Joining him and Grohl was fellow LA punk pioneer Pat Smear, Alain Johannes and Foo Fighters drummer Taylor Hawkins. The four quickly built up the track, a typically punk-rock up-tempo track and recorded much of the track in one live take with overdubs limited to the vocal harmonies and a few extra guitar parts. One further session yielded the mellow track 'If I Were Me', a recording that James Brown described as "magical". Prolific session drummer Jim Keltner was invited along, joined by longtime Foo Fighters collaborators Rami Jaffee and Jessy Greene. Along with Grohl, the musicians sat closely together in the live room at 606 to capture all of the energy and nuances of the live performance. "If you listen closely you can hear Rami's fingers scraping across the Hammond keys during the re-intro" noted Brown, referring to the Hammond B3 Organ Jaffee was playing on the initial live take. Piano was added to the basic take of the song, as well as Omnichord and a second Violin harmony by Greene. Finally, Keltner recorded a strangely emotional overdub with a hand shaker which reduced many of the men in the room to tears, including Brown.

Grohl recorded his vocals for 'If I Were Me' on the morning of September 30th, 2012. The night previous Foo Fighters had performed a live show at the Global Citizen Festival in New York and owing to Grohl's usual screaming performance, Brown believed the "weary, blown-out" quality of his vocals the next morning left a special mark on the song.

All eleven tracks were mixed that same day in September with James Brown taking the lead on all songs except for 'You Can't Fix This', which was overseen by Chris Lord-Alge. Mastering was carried out by Emily Lazar and Joe LaPorta at The Lodge in New York City. The completed soundtrack was released in March 2013, with Dave and many of the performers on the record playing a small number of special shows in the weeks leading up to release as the Sound City Players.

January 2014
Electrical Audio, Chicago, IL, United States

Foo Fighters
Hawkins, Taylor (Drums, backing vocals)

Grohl, Dave (Guitar, Vocals)

Mendel, Nate (Bass Guitar)

Shiflett, Chris (Guitar)

Smear, Pat (Guitar)

Additional Musicians
Jaffee, Rami (Clavinet, Organ, Mellotron)

Nielsen, Rick (Baritone Guitar)

Recording Credits
Brown, James (Engineer)

Norman. Greg (Assistant Engineer)

San Paolo, Jon (Assistant Engineer)

Vig, Butch (Producer)

Tracks Recorded
1. Something From Nothing

Touring in support of Foo Fighters seventh album 'Wasting Light' came to an end in September 2012 with a performance at the Global Citizen Festival in New York City. Grohl caused some alarm during the show by telling the crowd he "didn't know when the band would play together again". Whilst Dave had simply meant that it was the end of the tour and their future diary was empty for now, the media quickly ran wild with the quote, questioning if the band was splitting up. Quick to dispel those stories Grohl released an open letter days later clarifying the intent of his statement, noting that "I can't give up this band. And I never will. Because it's not just a band to me. It's my life. It's my family. It's my world."

Grohl also explained that his immediate priority would be finishing up his Sound City movie project, with Foo Fighters temporarily put on the back burner. The Sound City movie would see release in January 2013 and in the weeks that followed Dave Grohl took the music from the movie on a limited time tour. The band of musicians dubbed 'The Sound City Players' included several musicians featured in the movie, including Lee Ving, Krist Novoselic, Rick Neilsen, Rick Springfield, and Stevie Nicks. Backing a revolving door of musicians on the shows would be all five Foo Fighters, with the huge ensemble playing half a dozen shows in both the United States and the United Kingdom.

It was during that tour guitarist Chris Shiflett was first informed by Dave Grohl of his plan for recording the next Foo Fighters album. "I remember Dave saying that, for the next record, he wanted to go all over the world and record in different studios," recalled Shiflett.

Drummer Hawkins also acknowledged the connection to the Sound City project although he was unsure exactly when Dave came up with the plan - "I swear I feel like he had this idea to do the record like this before we did Sound City. Because they're so connected, it just makes sense that it was before, or around the same time. But I feel like it was before for some reason."

Whatever the truth, the plan was ambitious. The initial vision from Grohl was for the band to travel across the world, visiting up to fifteen recording studios in different cities. In each studio, the band would record one song and alongside recording a documentary would also be filmed, documenting the process and exploring the musical history of each city. As part of that documentary, Grohl planned to interview many contemporaries associated with the location, and from those interviews and experiences write the lyrics for each song on location.

According to guitarist Chris Shiflett it was not unusual for Dave to come up with several different ideas, many of which would not come to fruition. "He always got 10,000 ideas for crazy stuff. I personally try not to get too wrapped up in any until I see we're actually going to do one of them." When it became clear a scaled-down version of this idea was a goer, Shiflett was not too fazed - "It never seemed like a daunting idea, it always seemed very doable. If you have the resources to do something like that it's a great way to make a record."

Following several meetings between the band, their management and record label it was decided the original plan was just a little too ambitious, and not to mention costly. The project was scaled back, with the band now set to trek across the United States only, visiting eight different locations and studios. The final number was cut down to eight not only for cost reasons but also in a nod to the fact this would be the eighth studio album by the band. It was planned for the band to spend one week in each location, recording just one song as well as exploring the city for the documentary side of the project.

Writing and demoing of songs began soon after all Sound City commitments were complete and in Autumn 2013 serious pre-production work got underway at the band's Studio 606 complex. This was something the band did before recording all of their previous albums, a time for them to select their best material, flesh out the structure of songs and generally hone them, ready for the final recording session. Pre-production for this album was particularly intense according to guitarist Shiflett, owing to the pressures they would face in having to record each song in one week on location, no do-overs.

"We started learning the songs and working on demos probably around the beginning of last summer, so by the time we actually went out to record we were all pretty confident on the musical side of stuff" Chris recalled. "We did a lot of pre-production, more than we ever did in the past. We demoed these songs over and over and over and really hammered out everybody's parts, so musically we knew exactly what we were doing when we got in there."

Whilst the instrumentation of each song had been meticulously rehearsed no lyrics were written for any songs, their working titles only relating to their structure and style. As per the plan, Grohl was not going to write any lyrics until he'd arrived in each location on their studio tour.

Thirteen songs were worked on during pre-production and whilst eleven were finished, the number would then be whittled down to eight, ready for recording in each of the eight locations.

Recording of the album proper started in January 2014 with the first location on the schedule set for Chicago, Illinois. The band had booked time at Electrical Audio, a recording studio in the north of the city owned by famed recording engineer Steve Albini. An unsuspecting building from the outside, the studio is located just a few hundred yards from the Chicago River.

Drummer Taylor Hawkins believed Chicago was specifically chosen as the first location owing to the history Grohl had with the city. "I feel like Chicago was first because that's where Dave had his first eye-opening experience with music that drew him to become a full-on musician". It was a theory that Dave himself seemed to back up - "Chicago's the place where I saw my first show. The first time I ever saw a live band play was at this little bar called the Cubby Bear right across the street from Wrigley Field. It was just like 'I want to do this for the rest of my life.' So the idea of the song, and the episode, is that once you find that spark and inspiration, that begins your path in life, for whatever it is you want to do."

Whilst studio owner Albini was interviewed by Grohl for the documentary he was not directly involved in the recording session. "Steve wasn't recording the Foo Fighters" confirmed fellow engineer at the studio, Greg Norman. "He got interviewed, and the show kind of makes it look like they were recording with him, but they had their own crew," he added.

Butch Vig instead continued in the role he occupied in the recording of the seventh album, 'Wasting Light', with James Brown similarly continuing his role as an engineer. "I love Dave like a crazy brother," said Vig of Grohl. "I don't know anyone who has such infectious enthusiasm for life and for music". Also on hand were Electrical Audio engineers Greg Norman and Jon San Paolo, assisting Vig and Brown. Butch Vig described the first recording location as "not posh or super fancy, but really well appointed".

Whilst there was not the hubbub as with when promoting Wasting Light, recording for this session remained analog, at least initially. ProTools wasn't a dirty word this time around, used to manipulate tracks after the initial analog capture. As well as shipping all of their musical instruments and gear across the country, they also took Hal and Betty with them, their two Studer A827 tape recorders.

The track selected for Chicago was 'Something From Nothing', albeit only given that title at the end of the recording. Once all the equipment had been set up the band ran through the song together a few times before getting started for real. "The basic recording process was the same as the last record," explained Chris Shiflett. That process began with Taylor Hawkins laying down his drum track, followed by Chris, Pat Smear and Dave Grohl all adding their own unique guitar parts.

Nate was next to record his bass track before the now semi-permanent member of the band Rami Jaffee would add Clavinet, Organ, Mellotron onto the track, giving it an almost psychedelic feel. With the basic tracks down, it was then time for Dave Grohl to gather together all of his notes from interviews he'd carried out, including Cheap Trick's Rick Neilsen, to write the lyrics for the song. Whilst at the studio to be interviewed Neilsen was asked by Grohl if he wanted to take part in the recording and having agreed, recorded a deep baritone guitar part on the song. Chris Shiflett was almost starstruck by the visit to the studio of someone he'd looked up to as a kid, with the rest of the band similarly enthused by having the legendary Cheap Trick founder on their record.

Recording of the first song for the album had gone very well, Shiflett describing it as "a great way to make a record". In particular the guitarist enjoyed the one song at a time format, bemoaning that in the early days of his time in the band he'd spend weeks twiddling his thumbs waiting to record - "What we would do in the past is record all the drums and that would take a while, and then Dave would do all his guitars and that would take a while, then we'd throw some bass, so for me it would be a month into recording before I really did anything". The lyrics of the song written by Grohl heavily referenced among others the life of Buddy Guy, noting his move to Chicago with nothing to his name, meeting Muddy Waters and making his way in the Blues scene in the city. "It's basically about these people and how they all started with nothing," Grohl said of the song and accompanying documentary episode. "They were just inspired to follow their dream."

'Something From Nothing' was first released on October 16th, 2014 as a promotional single for the album.

* * *

February 3rd to 10th, 2014
Inner Ear Studio, Arlington, VA, United States

Foo Fighters

Hawkins, Taylor (Drums, backing vocals)

Grohl, Dave (Guitar, Vocals)

Mendel, Nate (Bass Guitar)

Shiflett, Chris (Guitar)

Smear, Pat (Guitar)

Additional Musicians

Jaffee, Rami (Organ)

Stahl, Pete (Backing vocals)

Thompson, Skeeter (Backing vocals)

Recording Credits

Brown, James (Engineer)

Vig, Butch (Producer)

Zientara, Don (Engineer)

Tracks Recorded

1. The Feast And The Famine

Stop number two on the 'Sonic Highways' recording tour would be a return home for Dave Grohl as the band headed for the US capital, Washington D.C. Whilst Grohl was born in Warren, Ohio as a youngster he moved to Springfield, a small area in the state of Virginia just 15 miles from the capital. Much of Grohl's teenage years were spent exploring the hardcore D.C. music scene, seeing dozens of shows at the hugely popular 9:30 club in the city. That scene stretched beyond the capital itself, with his own early bands playing shows in both the capital and across the state of Virginia, including Arlington Country. "I never tell anyone that I'm from anywhere. Well, I tell people I'm from Virginia, per se, and they say, "Virginia?" And I say, "Well, Washington, D.C." Grohl joked of how the two places felt like one. "But it's a huge part of who I am and I wouldn't be this person if it wasn't for that place and those people. I'm proud to say that. I'm proud to be a musician from the Washington, D.C. area. Musically, it's a lot richer and more vital than most people would ever expect."

Returning to the area for the Sonic Highways project was a no brainer and the studio Grohl had in mind was also an easy decision. Inner Ear Studio in Arlington was a legendary location in the hardcore D.C. scene with hundreds of albums recorded at the studio by artists such as Minor Threat, Fugazi, Bad Brains and Bob Mould.

Another previous client was Scream, the band including drummer Grohl visiting the studio in December 1989 to record what would turn out to be their final studio album. At that time the studio was located in the basement of owner Don Zientara's house, moving to the current location a short time afterward.

"I remember walking down into that basement as if it were Abbey Road," said Grohl of how much the studio meant to him. "Oh my god, Rites of Spring recorded here! It was like hallowed ground to me." Grohl had also visited the current incarnation of the studio a few years later to record demos of his own songs with his sister Lisa.

Grohl contacted Zientara to see if he'd be willing to host the band for their project, camera crew and all. For the longtime studio owner the decision to say yes was an easy one, remarking that he is always open for anyone to visit the studio, for any project. "There has been filming at the studio before, (although not of that size!) and I encourage it. Why not?" Zientara remarked rhetorically.

Foo Fighters and their huge crew arrived at the studio on February 3rd, 2014 and began loading their equipment in. The studio was already well equipped for recording but the band still brought a number of their own compressors and microphones, something Zientara totally understood - "I would have done the same in their situation - you've got to have some familiar tools with you." They did not bring their two Studer A287 tape recorders, however, happy to use the Otari MTR-90 II 24-track recorder already at the studio. "You really have to be a great musician and know your stuff really well," Don said of the challenge for the band recording in a new environment. "It's a new place, you're only doing one song here. You have to acclimate to the system. It's a crazy way to do it, but they took it all in stride."

With the gear set up, the band got to work on the song selected for this studio, 'The Feast And The Famine'. Spread out across two of the four main rooms in the studio the band ran through several live takes of the song, deciding which one they most preferred to work on further.

Whilst the band generally stuck to the standard process of working on the drums, bass, and guitar in that order, Zientara noted that they could "go freely back and forth" between the different instruments, iterating the song as they went on.

Despite the Otari tape recorder allowing a generous 24 tracks for recording this still became a limitation for Foo Fighters. Once all 24 had been used the tracks were bounced to a digital ProTools session with the tape then being re-used for further recording. This process continued throughout the recording, making all initial recordings to tape before transferring to the ProTools session. By the time the instrumental track was complete the track had evolved from "very good" to "the best" in the opinion of Zientara.

While he'd worked with Grohl on several previous occasions this was the first time the studio owner had worked with the rest of the band and had nothing but praise for the guys. "Professionals work efficiently and to a set routine. That routine is modified slightly by each group, but essentially yields in the best recording the group can produce" he explained. "It's so satisfying seeing this happen. Like a well-oiled and well-rehearsed machine, they incrementally but steadily get results".

When it came time to record vocals Grohl was backed up by former Scream bandmates Pate Stahl and Skeeter Thompson, the pair already at the studio for interviews.

The completed track was first released on October 24th, 2014 and included as the second track on the album 'Sonic Highways'.

* * *

Late February 2014
Magic Shop, New York, NY, United States

Foo Fighters

Hawkins, Taylor (Drums, backing vocals)

Grohl, Dave (Guitar, Vocals)

Mendel, Nate (Bass Guitar)

Shiflett, Chris (Guitar)

Smear, Pat (Guitar)

Additional Musicians

Hester, Drew (Tambourine)

Los Angeles Youth Orchestra (Strings)
Recorded at Ocean Way Recording, Hollywood, CA

Jaffee, Rami (Organ, Piano & Keyboards)

Young, Kristeen (Backing Vocals)

Recording Credits

Brown, James (Engineer)

Hermon, Kabir (Assistant Engineer)

Shurtleff, Chris (Assistant Engineer)

Vig, Butch (Producer)

Tracks Recorded

1. I Am A River

Location number three on the Foo Fighters tour of American recording studios was New York City, the band selecting The Magic Shop in the SoHo neighborhood of the City as the studio to record the third song for the record.

The studio had a long twenty-four-year history at the time of the bands visit with recording artists such as Lou Reed, the Ramones, Sonic Youth, and Arcade Fire all walking through the door at some point. Most recently prior to the Foo Fighters arrival the studio had been used by David Bowie to record his penultimate album, 'The Next Day'. "I considered a lot of studios in New York City. But rather than use an iconic studio that most people know about, I found this tiny place in Soho," said Dave Grohl of his choice. "This place is unlike anywhere else," he said of the city as a whole. "New York City has it all whether it's talking about inspiration or community or industry or gentrification or creativity or survival or starting over."

The song selected for New York was something of an epic, the band bringing along a seven-minute instrumental demo which Grohl was going to have to write lyrics for. "Write what you see. It's a different type of writing for me," said Grohl of his new approach to lyrics. "I've always gone inward, to discover things within myself. This time, it's more like reporting."

The studio was equipped with a Neve recording console allowing the band to continue their analog philosophy although as they'd already done in Washington D.C, transferring to digital after the initial recording was not something they were avoiding as they had for the recording of the previous album.

As well as layering several guitar tracks on the song building up to a large crescendo Grohl had also decided it would include a string treatment and towards the end of the session legendary producer and musician Tony Visconti arrived at the studio. Hired to arrange an orchestral accompaniment to the song, Visconti listened to a playback of the track and after just one playthrough told Grohl he already had an arrangement in mind. With the Magic Shop studio being far too small to house any kind of Orchestra the recording of the string section took place in California, at Ocean Way Recording.

The lyrics of the song once again referenced both the city and the stories Grohl had heard from those he interviewed. The first line of the song "There is a Secret. I found a secret behind a SoHo door" was in reference to the studio itself. Unlike many recording studios with grand entrances, or at the very least the name above the door, Magic Shop was located behind a completely unsuspecting grey door, daubed in graffiti. A tiny sticker below the bell the only indication on what was behind the door. "I found a reason, that's a Lou Reed reference," said Grohl of another lyric.

Much of the song's lyrics centered around the idea of a river, both literally and metaphorically. Beneath New York City was the Minetta Creek, a watercourse which used to run across approximately two miles of the city. Although it was filled in and covered over in the 19th century many historians to this day debate whether it still exists, running underneath the modern-day city in some capacity. "This song is mostly about that, this river that runs underground through the city," explained Grohl, evidently in the camp that believed it was still there.

"I thought it was just beautiful idea that there's something natural and prehistoric that runs underneath something monolithic and futuristic as New York City and that maybe we're all connected by something like that." As Grohl carried out more and more interviews with musicians and important figures that idea of everyone being connected would go on to be a key aspect of the entire album and documentary series. "When I interviewed all these people around the country for this project, I started to realize that everyone's connected and that it is like one big family tree. Whether it's Dolly Parton or Chuck D or Joan Jett or Zach Brown, everyone's kind of connected by something. So, I thought the underground river idea was very cool and turned it into a song," he explained.

Whilst New York was chronologically the third location the band visited when recording, 'I Am A River' was placed as the final track on the album and in turn featured as the last episode of the documentary series, closing out with the entire concept of people being connected by metaphorical rivers and "Sonic Highways".

* * *

March 3rd to 9th, 2014
Southern Ground Nashville, Nashville, TN, United States

Foo Fighters
Hawkins, Taylor (Drums)

Grohl, Dave (Guitar, Vocals)

Mendel, Nate (Bass Guitar)

Shiflett, Chris (Guitar)

Smear, Pat (Guitar)

Additional Musicians
Brown, Zac (backing vocals, guitar)

Recording Credits
Bell, Brandon (Assistant Engineer)

Brown, James (Engineer)

Mangano, Matt (Assistant Engineer)

Vig, Butch (Producer)

Tracks Recorded
1. Congregation

To record the fourth song for their eighth studio album Foo Fighters headed to Nashville, Tennessee. A few years earlier Dave Grohl had first met country music artist Zac Brown whilst out shopping in Los Angeles and Brown, being a big fan of Grohl, introduced himself. The pair chatted with Grohl telling him about the plans for recording his next album. Brown, in turn, revealed that he himself was a studio owner, running Southern Ground in Nashville.

The pair exchanged numbers and a short time later Brown called to ask Dave if he would be willing to produce his next record, with his band The Zac Brown Band. Despite still being only vaguely familiar with Brown himself and knowing nothing about his music Dave agreed, flying to Nashville in November 2013 and joining the band at their studio. A couple of years earlier Brown had bought the former Monument Recording Studio in the city, a converted Presbyterian Church which he had then further renovated into a state-of-the-art facility, re-naming it Southern Ground Nashville. Impressed by both the band and the studio during his time there Grohl took Brown up on the offer to return the following year on his 'Sonic Highways' journey.

The band were booked into Southern Ground in the first week of March 2014 and began their now familiar process loading in their gear, setting up the mics and getting to work. Despite spending several weeks in 2013 writing and rehearsing material the instrumental track which had been selected to record in Nashville, later titled 'Congregation', was not in a 'ready to record' format like many of the other tracks.

"When we first walked in on Monday and started rehearsing the song was not there 100% and I think all of were stressing a little bit," recalled producer Butch Vig. "Our first day here we were trying to figure out the arrangement, and we were kinda having trouble with it" added Grohl. Facing the troubles head-on Grohl soon found inspiration from the studio itself. Inside the former church was an arch which light shone straight through on a sunny day, showering the studio in beams of light. "I looked up at it and the light coming through there, and I totally had this moment where I'm like 'Oh my God, now I get it!'. I don't know if it was because the place used to be a church, but when that light hit me through that window, I felt inspired".

Following his epiphany-like moment Grohl headed into the control room where the rest of the band were discussing ideas and quickly pulled them out into the large live room, wanting to work on the new arrangement before the ideas left his head. "In 24 hours, we kind of overhauled the arrangement, and let the song breathe a little more," said Vig of the fast evolution.

Minor crisis averted the next day recording got underway with Hawkins laying down his drum track followed by bass from Nate Mendel. Guitar tracks were next to be recorded but Grohl was becoming concerned again, worried that the musical influences of the City were having an effect on the song. "It's kind of turning it into a bit of a country song," agreed bassist Nate Mendel. "I walk in the control room and everyone has cowboy hats on and they're playing a guitar lead that sounds like it's from The Good The Bad And The Ugly, I get a little nervous" recalled Grohl.

Guitarists Chris Shiflett and Pat Smear re-worked their guitar parts, Shiflett returning to a lead part he'd played earlier in the week rather than one that was now sounding straight out of a Garth Brooks record. As Grohl had been invited to Southern Ground by Zac Brown he chose to repay the favor by leaving space in the song for a guitar part by to be played by Brown. Whilst Grohl had a "machine gun-type guitar part" in mind what the Atlanta native ended up performing was "a little more melodic" according to Brown.

With all instrumentation recorded it was time once again for Grohl to get to work on the lyrics for the song, bringing together many hours of interview footage and his experiences in Nashville both during recording, and over the past year working with Brown. The final line of the song, '.and they're singing like a bluebird in the round', referenced Nashville's iconic Bluebird Cafe. "In Nashville, it seems like there are these rites of passage that you have to go through to become a star, whether you're a singer or a songwriter, and the Bluebird is really one of those. If you can get down at the Bluebird, you've got a gig," said Grohl having learned about the venue.

'Congregation' would be included as track three on the 'Sonic Highways' album, first released as a standalone track on October 31st, 2004.

* * *

Late March 2014
Studio 6A, Austin, TX, United States

Foo Fighters

Hawkins, Taylor (drums, backing vocals)

Grohl, Dave (Guitar, Vocals)

Mendel, Nate (Bass Guitar)

Shiflett, Chris (Guitar)

Smear, Pat (Guitar)

Additional Musicians

Clarke Jr, Gary (guitar)

Hester, Drew (tambourine)

Jaffee, Rami (Piano, Organ, Mellotron)

Recording Credits

Bolois, Charlie (Assistant Engineer)

Brown, James (Engineer)

Lousteau, John (Assistant Engineer)

Vig, Butch (Producer)

Tracks Recorded

1. What Did I Do?/God As My Witness

With four songs in the bag Foo Fighters were at the halfway stage of recording for their eighth album as they headed to their fifth recording location in late March 2014 – Austin, Texas. "The first time I came to Austin it was 1987," said Dave Grohl of the city. "I was like, 'Shit, we gotta go to Texas? We're dead fuckin' meat' – purple hair, all scruffy. Then we pulled into Austin and it felt like home. I thought it was filled with open-minded, beautiful, artistic people who like to get fucking weird."

Whilst Grohl had long selected the city of Austin as a stop on their recording tour the studio they would use was not locked down initially although he did have one in mind. Studio 6A, located within the University of Texas at Austin, was most well-known as the location for the recording of Austin City Limits, a musical Television show which has aired on public television in the United States for more than thirty years. "I was 7 or 8 the first time I saw it," said Grohl of the show. "I was just learning how to play guitar and there weren't too many shows like Austin City Limits back in the day. Here was a show that you could watch an entire live performance of a band – not just one song after Johnny Carson walks off the couch – in front of an intimate audience. Those experiences translate. When I was young, I was like, 'Wow, that's music! That's how it's done! Now it's in my living room and it makes me want to do that too.' You watch these brilliant musicians ripping on that stage week after week and it could only inspire young musicians. Maybe that's what it was for."

Intending to cover the studio and TV show in the documentary portion of Sonic Highways irrespective of where they recorded a song he arranged an interview with the current executive producer of the show, Terry Lickona.

That interview took place in December 2013 and one of

the topics covered was naturally the studio. Lickona explained to Grohl that whilst the television show had since 2011 been recorded in a new state of the art facility across the city, the old Studio 6A was still active. "Although we've moved out of the original studio, it's completely intact," he told an excited Grohl. "The stage is still there, the bleachers are there, the skyline is there, and nothing has changed."

Happy by the news, Grohl asked if it would be possible for the band to use the studio for recording. "It's totally possible" replied the producer. "The studio is there and even though the show is downtown in our new venue, we still do all of our post [recording processing] back at our old place. So, if you wanted to do everything in there, it'd be a thrill to work with you" he said in making an offer Grohl couldn't refuse.

The band booked a week at the studio in March 2014 and the session began as the previous four had, the first day spent setting up equipment and the following day setting up mics and finding a good sound for recording. This was a challenge for producer Butch Vig, engineer James Brown and the rest of the crew because despite the studio hosting a music show for thirty years it was never built with acoustics in mind. "James and I were a bit stressed before we came to Austin," said Vig. "We knew it wasn't set up like a professional recording studio." The main room according to Brown was "fairly dry" sounding, with very little in the way of natural ambiance. Once the crew arrived and started setting up, however, their fears were somewhat negated - "Once we got here and set up the mics, it actually sounded really good" revealed Vig.

Whilst the band was warming up on the historic stage proceedings started out like the previous four sessions for the album, working through the arrangement of the instrumental song selected for Austin. Then things got a little crazy. An impromptu jam session broke out among the band members, with Dave and Taylor first busting out the David Bowie track 'Rebel Rebel'. As the jam fizzled out the drummer said to the rest of the band that he had "lots of ideas for the next record", flippantly insinuating that what they had just played was an original piece of music. This theme continued, with new Foo Fighters song ideas including Black Sabbath's 'Paranoid', Queen tracks 'We Will Rock You' (Which Hawkins joked would "work well live") and Bohemian Rhapsody' which was then followed by Eric Clapton's 'Layla', Rami Jaffee leading that track. Dave then told the band he'd been "fooling around with this thing last night" before playing Nirvana song 'Smells Like Teen Spirit'. "I don't think that one's gonna work. B-Side," said Grohl in jest. Further brief jams on Nirvana songs 'Come As You Are' and 'Lithium' followed, the band enjoying themselves before they had to get down to more serious matters.

Fun shakedown over, the band returned to the song they were there to record. Following their familiar process recording went smoothly, with no major re-writes required as there had been during recording in Tennessee. Once the basic instrumental track was recorded Grohl laid down a guide vocal track, nothing more than phonetic sounds to aid the band whilst recording overdubs. In the meantime, he was out in Austin conducting further interviews which would help shape the real lyrics.

Once the members of the band had done most of their work a guest musician was invited to the studio to add his flair to the song – highly acclaimed local guitarist and performer Gary Clarke Jr. He was given no clear direction on what to play by Dave, producer Vig instead just asking him to listen to the song and play what came to him.

307

Once Grohl had returned from his interviews and lyrics had been crafted a number of vocal takes rounded out the song.

Unlike the first four sessions where the band focused solely on one song to record for their album in Austin they had another box to tick – recording a cover of the Roky Erickson track 'Two Headed Dog' for Austin City Limits' 40th-anniversary celebrations. With not much time left on the clock the band quickly learned the song and recorded the instrumental for the track almost entirely live out on the Studio 6A stage, with Grohl performing low-key vocals as a guide. A few guitar overdubs and proper vocal takes followed and the song was completed in just a few hours.

'What Did I Do?/God As My Witness' was included as the fourth track on the album whilst 'Two Headed Dog' got its debut in the 40th anniversary Austin City Limits show which aired on October 3rd, 2014 in the United States. The song was also released in a special flexi-disc format, a thinner type of vinyl record which was commonly used in the 1970s and 1980s to distribute records in magazines and music interest books; owing to their name, the records could bend along with the pages although that did come at the cost of audio fidelity, far worse than a traditional record.

* * *

April 18th to 26th, 2014
Rancho De La Luna, Joshua Tree, CA, United States

Foo Fighters

Hawkins, Taylor (drums, backing vocals)

Grohl, Dave (Guitar, Vocals)

Mendel, Nate (Bass Guitar)

Shiflett, Chris (Guitar)

Smear, Pat (Guitar)

Additional Musicians

Goss, Chris (backing vocals)

Jaffee, Rami (Organ, Mellotron)

Walsh, Joe (guitar)

Recording Credits

Bolois, Charlie (Assistant Engineer)

Brown, James (Engineer)

Schneeberger, Mathias (Assistant Engineer)

Vig, Butch (Producer)

Tracks Recorded

1. Outside

When Dave Grohl was choosing the final eight locations for his Sonic Highways project the selections usually boiled down to one of two reasons – either the band didn't have any strong connection to the city at all and wanted to properly explore them or the opposite, it was a city of huge personal significance to them. In selecting Los Angeles, it was certainly towards the latter. Whilst only guitarist Pat Smear could claim any real historical memories of the city having lived there most of his life, each member of the band had spent a lot of time in and around the famous city, with Dave living in Hollywood for a couple of years in the nineties and later moving to the neighboring Encino a decade or so later. The other members of the band also all now lived in the area and owing to that fact Foo Fighters would also set up base with their studio in the north of the city in late 2004. This lead to many in the industry today considering them a "Los Angeles Band", even though they themselves have never felt that way.

When planning out the episode and accompanying recording session Grohl was keen to explore not just the main city itself and all the famous haunts, but also travel slightly further afield. Joshua Tree is a small community approximately two hours east of L.A., situated close to the national park of which it is named. With a population of just 7,500 people the town is a far cry from the hustle and bustle of the big city, with just a few significantly built up areas.

Just outside the main residential areas and into the desert is Rancho De La Luna, the private home and recording studio currently owned and operated by Dave Catching, co-founder of the stoner rock band 'earthlings?' and occasional member of Queens of The Stone Age and Eagles of Death Metal.

Since the early 1990s, Dave and his friend Fred Drake had

operated the studio, allowing various artists the ability to record music away from the glamour and pressure of the big city. In 2002 Fred Drake died of cancer and ever since Dave has continued to live at Rancho and operate the studio.

Dave Grohl first experienced 'Rancho' and desert atmosphere in 1997 and returned several times in the following years, collaborating with Catching on his 'earthlings?' records among other projects. For Dave, it was deemed the perfect choice of studio for the documentary series, rather than just heading into one of the many professional studios in the heart of the city which everyone was already familiar with. "I didn't want to focus on all of those iconic studios like Ocean Way Recording or Record Plant and the decades of history and industry in the city," said Grohl of his choice. "I wanted to get outside of that because that's how I feel when I'm there. It can be overwhelming in Los Angeles. It can get to you. I didn't want to focus on the glitz and glamour because that's what people usually focus on."

Whilst Rancho De La Luna is now long established as a recording studio it is still a far cry from the professional installations found in the big city. "If you were to take a book, a home studio book of the do's and don'ts, Rancho literally has all the don'ts," claimed longtime performer at the studio, Josh Homme. The live tracking room is one of the smaller rooms in the house and no specialist acoustic treatment has ever been performed on the tiny space. Despite these drawbacks, recording at the studio had always been easy for Homme – "Recording there is somehow effortless and simple. You know, two wrongs don't make a right, but 40 wrongs do."

Foo Fighters arrived in the desert in mid-April 2014 and began the process of loading in their equipment, or rather what could fit. Just one of their Studer A827 24-Track tape recorders could be installed and with such a tiny 'live' room, most of their microphones and outboard gear simply did not fit, having to make do with what was already at the studio and whatever they could squeeze in.

Despite living in LA the longest guitarist Pat Smear had never been out in the desert before, an eye-opening experience for the city dweller. "I had never even been out in that general area before," said Smear. "So, I didn't know what to expect. And it was not something you could imagine, that's for sure!"

Inspired by the laid-back environment of the studio the band worked in a very casual manner, ideas being bounced around as they ran through live takes of the song selected for the studio. "Everybody just, kind of, let it flow. We didn't really think twice. We just made decisions really quickly," said Grohl. "There is something about this place that forces you to relax. Out here there's not a lot to distract you."

Like all the songs they'd recorded so far a guest musician was lined up to feature on 'Outside'. Through mutual friend Drew Hester the band had persuaded The Eagles legend Joe Walsh to contribute guitar to the track and spending two days out in the desert Walsh performed a trademark solo across the breakdown section of the song. Drummer Taylor Hawkins was a huge fan of Walsh, The Eagles, and his earlier band The James Gang and working with the man himself was a huge thrill. "I've had a few moments in my life where I've gotten to play with people who I think are just so fucking important," said Hawkins of the experience. "I'm sorry but how awesome does it sound to have Joe Walsh and the Foo Fighters? It's fucking rad! It's amazing!"

When it came to recording vocals no special isolation booths were set up, Grohl instead performing in the same small live room as they had laid down the initial instrumentals. Just a few takes were required to get the freshly written lyrics down with Grohl then heading off for some recreational activities outside the Ranch – shooting and a little off-road biking.

'Outside' was included as the fifth track on the 'Sonic Highways' album.

* * *

May 12th to 18th, 2014
Preservation Hall, New Orleans, LA, United States

Foo Fighters

Hawkins, Taylor (drums, backing vocals)

Grohl, Dave (Guitar, Vocals)

Mendel, Nate (Bass Guitar)

Shiflett, Chris (Guitar)

Smear, Pat (Guitar)

Additional Musicians

Braud, Mark (Trumpet)

Gabriel, Charlie (Clarinet)

Jaffee, Ben (Tuba)

Johnson, Ronell (Tuba, Backing vocals)

Jaffee, Rami (Organ, Piano)

Lousteau, John (Backing vocals)

Lonzo, Freddie (Trombone)

Maedgen, Clint (Saxophone, Backing Vocals)

Rota, Jim (Backing vocals)

Recording Credits

Bolois, Charlie (Assistant Engineer)

Brown, James (Engineer)

Lousteau, John (Assistant Engineer)

Vig, Butch (Producer)

Tracks Recorded

1. In The Clear

Foo Fighters continued their musical tour of the United States into May 2014, with their penultimate stop being New Orleans, Louisiana. With such a rich musical history visiting The Big Easy was an obvious choice to feature in the documentary side of the project but unlike some of the other cities the band visited during the recording of their eighth album, this wasn't one any of the band members had a strong connection with. Whilst they had all passed through many times over the years or tour, nobody had ever had a chance to stay around and really take it all in.

With New Orleans making the final shortlist it was then up to Grohl to once again select a suitable recording location in the city. With music flowing through the blood of so many residents and such a long history of making music, it was no surprise that he would be inundated with choice. Esplanade Studios, for example, is a large modern studio built inside an old church in the city whilst The Parlor is a similarly impressive bespoke facility which even houses a vintage Neve 8078 recording console.

What Grohl had in mind though was something rather different. Originally built as a tavern The Preservation Hall is a historic venue within the heart of the world-famous French Quarter in the city which since 1961 has hosted thousands of Jazz shows and events, bringing joy to locals and tourists alike. The venue has long been seen as a cornerstone of New Orleans music and culture but there is one thing it wasn't – a professional recording studio. For Grohl though, it made perfect sense. "When I think of New Orleans, I don't think of recording studios" he explained. "I just think of hundreds of years of music. Preservation Hall really took hold after the Hurricane [Katrina, 2005], when people realized that there was something to lose."

Usually open every night for performances, the hall was uncharacteristically closed to the public for an entire week in May 2014 to allow one of the biggest rock bands in the world record a song for their eighth studio album. Recording in such an unconventional building was naturally going to be a challenge but it's one that the band and crew were up for. "It was a little tricky because [the hall] is not used to a blaring rock band," said producer Butch Vig. "We moved the drums across the room from traditionally where they play, which opened up the sound a bit. Then we moved their amps and just baffled them enough, so it wasn't completely collapsing the room with volume."

As the hall was meant for performance and not recording there was little to no sound damping, with people walking by and other ambient noises outside the venue heard loud and clear inside. "Our microphones capture miscellaneous noises and that's part of the charm," said Vig of what other producers might've considered a serious problem. Likewise, people walking by outside could hear a Foo Fighters recording session, something of a rarity for members of the public. Despite several ceiling fans spinning at full strength the heat in the venue was another issue – if the band was going to record, they were going to have to suffer a little.

Once the historic venue-cum-studio was fully kitted out tape started rolling and the band got to work following their regular process, running through live instrumental takes of the song Dave Grohl had designated for the city. With the preferred take selected, work then got underway re-doing the different parts of the song, starting as usual with Hawkins' drums. "I had a blast doing the drum track," said Hawkins. "I did it quick, and it's exciting, and it pops".

Guitar tracks were then piled on by the three guitarists, followed by bass and finally organ and piano tracks from

Rami Jaffee. Whilst the track was already very busy at this stage, guests were once again invited along to the studio to contribute.

For almost its entire history the Preservation Hall has been home to a house band of sorts, the Preservation Hall Jazz Band. Many local musicians had played in the band over a 50-year period and were still going strong when Foo Fighters arrived in 2014. For Grohl, including the band on the song they were recording was something of a must, having learned about their history and prestige.

Foo Fighters sat patiently and taught the song to the members of the band and practically sat in awe as they watched the musicians on piano, saxophone, tuba, and trombone interpret the track. As they quickly burst into full-on performance engineer James Brown rushed to the console to hit record and capture the huge group of musicians in free flow. Taken by the moment, Dave Grohl suggested they open the doors of the venue and allow the public to hear and see what they were doing. Before they knew it, the huge swathe of rock and jazz musicians were out on the streets of New Orleans, playing and dancing down the road in an impromptu march the city was so famous for.

After heading back to the hall and once again closing the doors it was back to work, fleshing out the arrangement with all of the added instrumentation. The Jazz Band were not the only guests on the song, with local musician Troy Andrews, more known by his stage name of Trombone Shorty, also invited to participate after being interviewed for the documentary side of the visit.

Naturally, it was with the Trombone that he performed, giving the song an even stronger jazzy style. The final act of recording was for Dave to construct his inspired lyrics and add them to the track. A few vocal takes and overdubs later, and 'In The Clear' was complete. Owing to their less than private location and excursions out onto the streets of New Orleans Foo Fighters presence in the city was not secretive, as had been the case for the previous sessions. Locals were well aware of who was in town and thanks to an official press release in the middle of the week, they then knew why. Following several weeks of media and fan speculation, HBO announced the official details of the project, detailing the eight cities they had visited (or were set to visit) and revealing It was set to be both a documentary series and their eighth studio album.

Having had so much fun playing with the Jazz band out on the streets of New Orleans earlier in the week on the penultimate night of their stay at Preservation Hall, with recording complete, Grohl had hatched another plan – playing a live show that night at the venue. As the hall itself could only hold around 100 people at a push the band instead elected to open the doors and windows of the venue and play out into the street. A large crowd soon amassed leading to the road itself being closed temporarily for everyone's safety. The band played a ninety-minute set which naturally included cameos from the Preservation Hall Jazz Band and Trombone Shorty.

The final day in the city for the band was a day of leisure with everyone joining the regular Sunday parades through the streets of the city. Foo Fighters week in New Orleans had been a fun one, with each band member speaking positively of their time in the city and their experiences. "You go to New Orleans and you make 150 best friends in the first ten minutes," said Taylor Hawkins, whilst for Pat Smear it was "the only place I was sad to leave".

Nate Mendel later revealed it was also his favorite of the eight locations - "Because it's such a unique town and we just had fun there really, is what it came down to."

'In The Clear' was featured as track six on the 'Sonic Highways' album.

* * *

May 26th to 31st, 2014
Robert Lang Studios, Shoreline, WA, United States

Foo Fighters

Hawkins, Taylor (drums)	Shiflett, Chris (Guitar)
Grohl, Dave (Guitar, Vocals)	Smear, Pat (Guitar)
Mendel, Nate (Bass Guitar)	

Additional Musicians

Gibbard, Ben (backing vocals)

Jaffee, Rami (Organ, Mellotron)

Jones, Barrett (E-Bow)

Recording Credits

Armstrong, Justin (Assistant Engineer)

Brown, James (Engineer)

Fernandez, Marcel (Assistant Engineer)

Vig, Butch (Producer)

Tracks Recorded

1. Subterranean

Whilst some of the locations chosen for the Sonic Highways recording tour were because the band hadn't previously had a connection with that place, that was not the case for the very last stop – Seattle, Washington. Having only visited briefly once before Dave Grohl moved to the city in late 1990 when he joined Nirvana, although he would spend his first few months in Olympia, an hour further south. Later moving into the big city itself he would experience both highs and lows whilst living there. The high of success with Nirvana briefly becoming the biggest band in the world, followed by the lows of Kurt Cobain's tragic death. "Seattle is like my phantom limb" believes Grohl.

Whilst he had visited several studios in the city over the years there was one which just made the most sense for Grohl to return to for this project – Robert Lang Studios. "It's this strange underground studio in the north of the city that was right down the street from my house," said Grohl of the recording venue. By 1994 Dave was living in a house just down the street from the studio and on his recommendation, Nirvana booked into the studio in January 1994 to record what would be their last ever recording session. "Not long after we recorded there Kurt died, and I didn't want to make music anymore" explained Grohl. "Time went on and I thought 'Wait, music is the one thing that's gonna help me start over. It's gonna heal me, so that's what I have to keep doing".

As covered earlier in this book various circumstances led to Grohl returning to that same studio in October 1994, recording what would become the first Foo Fighters record - "My life started over again". That notion of starting over is what Grohl planned to focus the episode on, as well as the lyrics of the song they would eventually record at Robert Lang Studios.

For the final recording session of the album the process was now a well-oiled machine. Day one was spent loading in equipment and setting up whilst Dave conducted some initial interviews, then day two is when recording could begin. Coming off the back of recording at Preservation Hall in New Orleans, which was not a professional recording studio, things were far easier for engineers and producers being back in a place that very much was. With no problems finding an acoustic sweet spot and no concerns about outside interference, the band got right down to work laying down some live takes of the song chosen for Seattle, 'Subterranean'. With a base to work from, it was then the usual process of recording overdubs and tweaking the initial tracks.

When it came to drums on the song, Grohl had a very specific treatment in mind for the sounds and after some initial recordings, neither he nor producer Vig was entirely happy with what was being produced from the main room at Langs. Vig suggested they move the kit into one of the smaller rooms at the studio to potentially achieve the dryer sound they desired whilst Hawkins suggested they utilize a drum recording separation technique. "Cymbal separation technique is where you do the drums separately from the cymbals," explained Hawkins. "It gives you the ability to manipulate the sounds of the drums even more because you're not dealing with the bleed of the cymbals."

Hawkins' idea won out and his kit in the main room had the cymbals removed, with large insulation walls surrounding him on all sides to prevent sound leakage as much as possible. Towels were also placed on all the drum heads to further deaden the sound. Grohl was set up in a smaller isolation room, just three cymbals and a hi-hat in front of him.

The pair had fun with the notion of playing live in such a fashion before getting down to the task at hand. The results were desirable, with the separation allowing the drum sound to be tweaked and give the results they desired - giving 'Subterranean' a sound not found on the other seven songs.

Recording of the rest of the song was trouble free, and as had been the case throughout, lyrics came last. Whilst one of the ideas behind the Sonic Highways project was to write lyrics about other people's experiences and stories rather than himself, the lyrics in Seattle were unavoidably personal as Grohl reflected on his experiences in the city. Studio owner Lang believed the words (and song as a whole) were "very spiritual". One of the lines in the song, 'God In The Stone', was Grohl referencing a piece of marble in the studio that many believe has an image of Christ in the patterns.

With Barrett Jones playing such an important role in Grohl's Seattle story and early recording history, including his times recording at Robert Lang Studios, it was only right that he also featured on the song, recording a spacey guitar track utilizing an e-bow device.

The final guest musician to record for the album was Ben Gibbard of Death Cab For Cutie. He had, like many musicians, been invited to the studio initially just to conduct interviews with Grohl about the city and his experiences. The pair chatted extensively, Gibbard explaining among other things how he as a teenager had dealt with the death of Kurt Cobain. Moved by his honesty and emotion, Grohl invited him to perform on the song. Gibbard felt flattered, but initially concerned his "tiny, reedy voice" would not suit a heavy rock band.

His mind was put to rest when he heard the song, however, recalling that he and Grohl recorded some "Beatle-esque harmonies" which he was very proud of. "It's a really beautiful song," said Gibbard. "It reminds me of Notorious Byrd Brothers-era soft psych."

Gibbard was also impressed to see the way the band worked together in the studio, even after being together for over twenty years. "It's refreshing and cool to see a band that's been around as long as they have, and you get the sense they enjoy hanging out with each other," Gibbard said of his observations. "It's very easy for bands to get jaded. I'm sure they have things that they bitch about. But it's refreshing to see Dave be like, 'I'm gonna go do vocals now' and have Taylor and Nate go, "We've gotta go check this out!" As if they've never heard the guy sing a vocal before!"

Recording wrapped up in Seattle at the end of May 2014 and with that, work on Foo Fighters eighth studio album was almost complete. All eight tracks were taken to Atomic Sound in Brooklyn, New York for mixing, utilizing their Neve VR20 recording desk. The record was then mastered by Gavin Lurssen at Lurssen Mastering in Los Angeles. Whilst some of the songs had already been released as promotional singles to coincide with each episode of the documentary, the complete 'Sonic Highways' album saw release on November 10th, 2014.

* * *

* * *

October 1st to 3rd, 8th and 9th, 2015
Hotel Saint Cecilia, Austin, TX, United States

Foo Fighters

Hawkins, Taylor (drums, backing vocals)

Grohl, Dave (Guitar, Vocals, percussion)

Mendel, Nate (Bass Guitar)

Shiflett, Chris (Guitar)

Smear, Pat (Guitar)

Additional Musicians

Jaffee, Rami (Organ, Mellotron)

Kweller, Ben (backing vocals)

Recording Credits

Brown, James (Engineer)

Silva, John (Assistant Engineer)

Szymanski, Kevin (recording)

Tracks Recorded

1. Saint Cecilia

2. Sean

3. Fuck Around

4. Savior Breath

5. The Neverending Sigh

Following release of their eighth studio album in November 2014 the band planned to spend the next twelve months doing what they did best, touring the world playing shows to thousands of fans. In June 2015, whilst playing a show in Gothenburg, Sweden, Dave Grohl tripped and fell fifteen feet from the stage. The resulting impact with the ground caused multiple fractures to his right leg with Dave announcing to the shocked crowd "I think I just broke my leg". The show went on that night, but the injury threatened the remaining six months of the tour with uncertainty on whether Dave could perform.

Half a dozen shows were indeed canceled whilst Grohl's injury was evaluated and treated but on Independence Day, less than a month after the accident, Dave and the band returned to the stage for their scheduled event in Washington, D.C. Grohl had constructed a 'throne' that he could sit on throughout the shows and continued to use it for the rest of the tour.

By the end of September the tour was nearing its end with just a handful of shows in the United States during October followed by a final leg in Europe through November. Two of those performances in their homeland were set to take place at the Austin City Limits music festival, in Austin, Texas. The band was due to perform over two consecutive weekends with shows in Georgia and Tennessee sandwiched between.

Whilst in Austin the band had been booked into Hotel Saint Cecilia, a "lush retreat from the world" located in the heart of the city. Their transport arrived at the hotel in the early hours of September 30th, with two free days until their first performance across town.

It was upon their arrival at the hotel complex that Dave Grohl was struck by an impulsive idea – record a handful of songs as a thank you gift to fans for their support over the last eighteen months.

Just yards from the hotel was Arlyn Studios, a large, purpose-built recording studio that was even equipped with a one-of-a-kind Neve recording console like the one featured in the Sound City documentary. Recording some songs at the studio would have made perfect sense logistically but Dave Grohl is not one for conventional, easy solutions. In the previous few years, he'd recorded an album in his garage and another one touring the United States.

Enjoying a challenge, he instead considered the prospect of recording at the hotel itself. The owner of the hotel, Jenny Schipani, had heard what the band were considering and made the offer to let them use her facilities. Grohl was a little unsure initially, but it didn't take long for his mind to be made up - "After rolling it around in my head a few times, it made perfect sense!" exclaimed Grohl. "Returning to the city where the entire Sonic Highways concept was born, loading in one last time to a room that was never designed to be a recording studio a la Sonic Highways, and making some music! Fate? Destiny? I was too tired to figure that kind of shit out, so I hit the sack, woke up the next morning and started making some calls," he explained.

The band and crew got to work that next morning and the hotel was soon transformed into a makeshift recording studio. The office became a control room whilst the large bar and lounge area became the main recording space. "Amps were in the kitchen, Drums in front of the fireplace" recalled Grohl of the improvised setup.

Owing to the spontaneity of the session there was no time to ship any of their studio gear from Los Angeles to the hotel – that meant no analog tape recorders, no special outboard equipment. They instead had to make do with the equipment they traveled with whilst touring.

A Mac computer was set up running ProTools recording software and outboard gear consisted of just a few Neve EQs and compressors that they had with them. Microphones were set up around the lounge area and again, with no time to ship any of their preferred studio gear, the band would have to make do with their touring guitars, drums, and amplifiers.

By 6 pm on October 1st everything was in place and with acclaimed local producer Kevin Szymanski on hand to help with recording, the band picked up their instruments and started jamming. Rather than write brand new songs the band started exploring ideas from the Foo Fighters parts bin, revisiting older songs and ideas that they had previously worked on but then scrapped for whatever reason. "Riffs and ideas were thrown around, songs that were lost in the shuffle over the years, songs that were left unfinished," said Grohl. "Like a musical retrospective, we were going through decades of songs no one has ever heard, pieces left on the cutting room floor from every album. Our own sonic scrapbook."

The band worked without any pressures or expectations, playing around with whatever came to mind. To increase the fun factor the band decided to invite some friends to join them – local Gary Clarke Jr. arrived and reciprocating the hospitality shown to them 18 months earlier, Grohl invited the Preservation Hall Jazz Band along to what was essentially half party, half recording session.

With the relatively small lounge area full of bodies and instruments ideas and freeform jams were soon flowing. At one point, whilst the Jazz band was "doing their thing" Grohl jumped behind the drum kit and played through what an engineer at the session described as an "incredible moment that [I] won't forget any time soon, such smooth jams". The day soon turned into night, with Dave ensuring that the trusty laptop was capturing every moment. "As the hours passed, the atmosphere had reached exactly what every recording experience should be," said Grohl of what he described as a celebration. Not wanting to lose any moment of magic everything was recorded, even if it was unlikely to be released publicly "because you just might miss something that you'll never get back again. Moments that happen once in a lifetime."

The first fully fleshed out track they got into would later be named after the hotel, which in turn was aptly named after the patron saint of musicians, Saint Cecilia. Whilst both of the evening's guests would feature on initial recordings of the song, they were not included in the final mix of the track.

Recording continued over the weekend, the band getting as much done as they could before they needed to head out of the city to play shows. 'Sean' was a short, upbeat track and the third, 'Fuck Around', was the first of the older song ideas they worked on to retain an old title. The title had first been mentioned by Dave Grohl way back in 1998, whilst discussing ideas they were working on for their third studio album - "We have one new song called 'Fuck Around' – It's kinda like the summer anthem" he told an interviewer. Whilst the band did work on the song when recording for that album got underway in 1999, it did not make the final cut.

Persisting, the band would try to record it on several further occasions. It was attempted as an acoustic track for 2005s 'In Your Honor' album and was seen on planning boards during pre-production for their 2011 album 'Wasting Light'. It once again did not make the final cut, and so here once again they attempted the track. On this occasion, very little instrumentation was recorded for the song, Grohl playing a couple of simplistic acoustic guitar track accompanied by Rami Jaffee on piano.

The fourth track to be worked on was given the working title 'Save Your Breath (Cuz it's mine)', later simplified with the wordplay 'Savior Breath'. In comparison to the somber, acoustic 'Fuck Around' this was a heavy affair with a wall of heavy guitars in a frenetic, almost hardcore tempo.

A fifth and final track was then worked on - '7 Corners'. Like 'Fuck Around' it was a track that had been floating around for a long time, perhaps their most well-known unreleased track among die-hard fans, also giving this publication its title. The name for the song came from the Seven Corners area of Fairfax, Virginia, close to where Grohl had spent much of his youth. The area had got its name from an intersection of four highways – State Route 7, U.S. Route 50, State Route 613 and State Route 338. The coming together of these four roads at one time created an intersection with seven corners, although the later re-routing of one road means that is no longer the case today.

The track had first been recorded during sessions for their second album 'The Colour And The Shape' and fans first heard discussion of the title during recording for their third album, when the band once again attempted it. Since then Foo Fighters had pulled the song out at some point during recording for every subsequent album, but it always ended on the cutting room floor.

Explaining the reason why in 2005 Grohl described the track as "a great riff but it's not a great song - it could be though."

After recording the track once more during pre-production for 2011s 'Wasting Light' the band leader suggested in an interview that if they didn't use it for that album, they would finally put it to rest forever. Whilst it once again did not make the cut Grohl just couldn't let the riff die and decided to give it another shot in Austin. Guitarist Chris Shiflett recorded five different solos for the newest version of the song and when playing them back all at once an engineer at the session described the resulting sound as "a beautiful hurricane of guitars". For the final product, things were pared down slightly, Chris bringing the best parts of each into one cohesive solo.

The basic tracks were cut for all five songs over the weekend, with their first headline performance at Austin City Limits Festival squeezed in the middle. The band then downed tools and headed out on the road for shows in Georgia and Tennessee in the week. No vocals were recorded during the first weekend of recording, that process, as well as overdubs and any other final tweaks, were planned for their return the following weekend.

With their live commitments completed the band hurried back to the hotel and on October 8th got to work on finishing up the work they'd started the previous weekend.

A makeshift vocal booth was set up in the bathroom of one of Hotel Saint Cecilia's poolside bungalows. "The coffee table became a pile of guitar pedals and scribbled lyrics, beer bottles and ashtrays" recalled Grohl. Whilst recording vocals for the first song, 'Saint Cecilia', Ben Kweller arrived at the hotel, a singer-songwriter and multi-instrumentalist from Texas. He and Grohl had met in the 90s but this was the first time they had been together in several years.

Grohl noted that even without prompting Ben seemed keen to join in. "We hugged, hit play to listen to the last vocal take, and he instinctively started singing the perfect harmony to my line". Grohl quickly instructed Kweller to "get his ass in there and sing it right now!" Kweller picked up some hotel stationary with Grohl's hastily scribbled lyrics written on it and "banged his part out in two glorious takes".

Most of the lyrics were written by Grohl at the hotel and he spent the remaining day and a half committing them to the ProTools sessions, with Taylor Hawkins singing backing vocals for the tracks 'Sean' and 'Fuck Around'. As well as the vocal tracks a few guitar overdubs were recorded on the second weekend and everything was finished up before it was time to head across the city for their second performance at the Austin City Limits festival. Grohl teased the crowd during that performance, telling them about the music they'd just finished recording - "You know what I did last night? We recorded five fucking new songs in your beautiful city." The crowd may have expected them to debut some of the new songs but Grohl killed those hopes, telling them "We're gonna give it to you! But not tonight."As originally planned, it was intended to release the music after the last date of the tour on November 19th and soon after the session the band placed a countdown timer on their website, counting down to November 23rd, the selected day for release.

A few weeks before that date Dave Grohl penned a letter in a Berlin hotel room, shortly before the band played a show on the final European leg of their tour. The letter was written to the fans of the band, explaining how the EP had come about and that it was a gift to them, the fans.

On November 13th, ten days before the planned release, a tragedy occurred in Paris, France. A number of terrorist attacks occurred across the city, the worst being an attack on the Bataclan Theatre where friends of the band Eagles Of Death Metal were performing. 130 people were killed in the various attacks including ninety in the Bataclan, with hundreds more injured. On hearing the news Foo Fighters offered words of sympathy for the victims and announced they were canceling the remaining dates of their tour, one of which was scheduled in Paris. The band headed home in a subdued mood, the devastating attacks prematurely ending a tour which had seen many ups and downs.

On November 19th Grohl penned an addendum to his previous letter, discussing the attacks and explaining that their project for the fans had taken on a new meaning, hoping that the music they were about to release could help in any small way. "Now, there is a new, hopeful intention that, even in the smallest way, perhaps these songs can bring a little light into this sometimes-dark world. To remind us that music is life, and that hope and healing go hand in hand with song. That much can never be taken away."

'Saint Cecilia', 'Sean', 'Savior Breath' and '7 Corners' were all included on the EP, the latter given the new title of 'The Neverending Sigh', a nod to the long history of the track. The songs were mixed by James Brown back at Studio 606 and then mastered by Emily Lazar at The Lodge in New York. It was made available as a free download on November 23rd as planned but 'Fuck Around' was not included, the band once again deciding it was still not ready for the public.

* * *

October 20th to 23rd, 2015
Studio 606 West, Northridge, CA, United States

Foo Fighters

Hawkins, Taylor (drums, backing vocals)

Grohl, Dave (Guitar, Vocals)

Mendel, Nate (Bass Guitar)

Shiflett, Chris (Guitar)

Smear, Pat (Guitar)

Additional Musicians

Lousteau, John (percussion)

Recording Credits

Lousteau, John (Recording, Engineer)

Tracks Recorded

1. Iron Rooster

Following the impromptu recording sessions in Austin, Texas Foo Fighters returned home to California where they had just two further live performances left on the United States leg of the Sonic Highways tour. After that, there was a short break in the band's calendar before they were due to head to Europe for a series of shows starting in early November. Before that, the band decided to head into Studio 606. Whilst they were mostly happy with the work they'd completed in Austin, one song, 'Fuck Around', was not going to make the cut for the free EP they had planned.

Wanting to keep the release at five songs, the band got to work at their studio from October 20th to 23rd. Just one song is known to have been recorded, another acoustic song to replace the slow-tempo 'Fuck Around'. The band recorded the new song, 'Iron Rooster', predominantly live in the main room at 606 with overdubs then added afterward. In the initial live performance Grohl played an acoustic guitar but also added some clean electric overdubs, as well as playing the piano. He also experimented with a finger slider device on his electric, to generate some of the deep vibrato sounds on the track.

As the band had been globetrotting since its installation this would be the first song to be recorded by the band on the Neve 8028 recording console and given a release, the new song added alongside four from Hotel Saint Cecilia and released as the Saint Cecilia EP in November 2015.

* * *

* * *

December 2016 to April 2017
EastWest Studios, Hollywood, CA, United States

Foo Fighters

Hawkins, Taylor (drums, vocals)

Grohl, Dave (Guitar, Vocals, percussion)

Mendel, Nate (Bass Guitar)

Shiflett, Chris (Guitar)

Smear, Pat (Guitar)

Jaffee, Rami (Organ, Mellotron, Piano, Synthesizers)

Additional Musicians

Bacik, Kinga (Cello)

Grace, Rachel (Violin)

Greene, Jessy (Violin)

Greenwood, Taylor (backing vocals)

George, Inara (backing vocals)

Koz, Dave (Saxophone)

Kurstin, Greg (piano)

Lea, Thomas (Viola)

Luke, Ginny (Violin)

Mossheart, Alison (backing vocals)

McCartney, Paul (drums)

Stockman, Shawn (backing vocals)

Timberlake, Justin (backing vocals)

Recording Credits

Burg, Julian (engineer)   Rajabnik, Samon (engineer)

Dekora, Brendan (engineer)   Sexton, Chaz (engineer)

Pasco, Alex (engineer)   Thorp, Darrell (engineer)

Kurstin, Greg (producer)

Tracks Recorded

1. Run

2. La Dee Da

3. T-Shirt

4. Concrete And Gold

5. Sunday Rain

6. Arrows

7. Happy Ever After (Zero Hour)

8. The Line

9. Dirty Water

10. Make It Right

11. Soldier

12. The Sky Is A Neighborhood

2015 had been a year of mixed emotions for Foo Fighters. It had high points – huge stadium shows across the world and performing for David Letterman's last ever 'Late Show', but it also had low points – Dave's accident in Sweden leading to a broken leg, the resulting issues that it caused and the tour being cut short due to the horrific terror attacks in Paris, France.

It was also an exhausting year for the band which they would end by recording and releasing the 'Saint Cecilia EP', a collection of five new original songs. A free release for the fans, it was partly as a thank-you for their support, but also as something of a going away present. Alongside its release, Dave Grohl announced the band was going to take a hiatus from the limelight, get some well-needed rest and recuperate. "I thought the best thing for the band would be just to stop and get away from it for a while," decided Grohl. Keen to avoid any media frenzies about the bands future as had occurred the last time he announced a break, Grohl made it clear the band would be back – he just didn't know when.

Whilst he wouldn't put a time frame on the hiatus publicly, he had informed his bandmates and family that the goal was to take an entire two years out. "In order to take care of myself, I needed to get away from everything," said Grohl, adding that he also planned to not even pick up an instrument for the first year. The reception from his band was a mixture of surprise and disbelief, but in a positive sense – "I never really put too much faith in the whole 'hiatus' thing" said guitarist Chris Shiflett. "Because, you know, in this band it's usually shorter than is stated. I never really believed it".

Their last hiatus which started at the end of 2012 had lasted mere months and Shiflett was once again spot on this time around. Whilst still recovering physically and mentally at home Grohl soon started getting restless, thinking about his next project. At one point he received an offer to direct a feature-length film, something he'd never done before. Always up for a challenge, it was an offer he seriously considered but soon realized the time sink such a project would entail - "The great thing about being in the Foo Fighters is when we have an idea and we want to do something, we just go like that. We do it. The movie world isn't like that... It can take years and years and years." Passion was also a problem with some of the offers coming in. Without the personal attachment to a certain project, Grohl felt he would need to "manufacture the inspiration", something he'd never have to do with the band, or any of his own pet projects like 'Sound City'. Realizing that taking on the new challenge could jeopardize the Foo Fighters, and lacking true enthusiasm, he chose to respectfully decline the movie offers - for now at least.

Grohl knew that whilst he'd almost shunned it entirely once before, music was always going to be the art which kept him going. As his physical recuperation continued, he'd find himself regularly peeking into the recording studio in his garage – think about playing – and then walk out. The process continued until one day he decided to play the drums for a few minutes at a time if only to help in the rehabilitation of his injured limb.

Then came the inevitable step of setting up microphones, picking up some guitars and running a Pro Tools recording session. Adhering to the "always record" mantra Grohl would play anything that sprang to mind, laying down drum beats first before layering guitar ideas over time.

This process continued for several months, as Grohl bounced between family life, physical recovery and experimenting musically. "Six months went by, and I just hit this vein where riffs and melodies started coming out," said Grohl of the experience. One of the first new songs he would write was 'Run', a typically heavy, guitar-shredding Foo Fighters song. More followed, including the equally raucous 'La Dee Da', although at this stage the demos were merely untitled instrumentals. Grohl soon found himself sitting on half a dozen songs and ideas and so the next step was sending them to the rest of the band to see what they thought. Whilst he had many songs, Foo Fighters were still only six months into a supposed two-year break, and some members of the band were using the free time to work on their side projects. "Am I crazy? Or is this a record?" Grohl asked his bandmates. "Both" was their reply. For guitarist

Chris Shiflett the timing fell just right, having just completed recording for his solo record, 'West Coast Town'. "I remember being really happy that I'd gone and done that when I did. Had I waited another couple of months it wouldn't have been possible" noted Shiflett. Break or no break, Grohl was amped, the band was on board and it wasn't long before thoughts turned to actually heading into a studio to record another album.

Before that though, the so-far instrumental demos would need some lyrics. For the band's previous album, Sonic Highways, Grohl had written the lyrics for each song at the very last minute, taking inspiration from his experiences in each of the eight cities they recorded in, as well as interviews with influential people in each place. For this new batch of songs, it would be quite the opposite, as Grohl planned to get most of the lyrics written well in advance of any recording. There was still no clear plan for that recording at this stage but Grohl decided instead of writing at home, amongst the hullabaloo of three young children and daily family life, he would take a short solo vacation.

He didn't plan to go too far. Ojai is a small city in Ventura County, California, just over an hour's drive from his home. The surprisingly rural location is a popular getaway for creatives looking to escape central Los Angeles, a place of relative peace compared to the hustle and bustle of the big city. Grohl rented a house within an olive-tree farm in the city and got to work. "I spent most of my time just singing things off of the top of my head," said Grohl of the unstructured approach to writing. Much of the time he wouldn't even write anything down on paper - "I wasn't really playing the word game in a journal and cutting and pasting, like I had done before, but just really singing things unfiltered as I was drunk in my underwear." Following the different approach to writing for Sonic Highways for these songs Dave returned to more familiar ground, writing lyrics more personal to himself - 'Arrows' was another song he'd write about his mother Virginia, referencing her struggles raising two children alone. "As a parent now, I understand more how much of a struggle that must have been for her to keep the family not only together, but happy – which we were."

Just before Grohl headed away Donald Trump had been officially confirmed as the Republican candidate for the 2016 Presidential Election. The political climate at that time was therefore very much on his mind and whilst Grohl claims he isn't an outwardly political person, he believes it's "pretty easy to figure out" where his beliefs align. Indeed, Foo Fighters performed several times for President Barack Obama during his presidency and the band had also supported the 2004 Democrat candidate John Kerry. Clearly, Donald Trump was not a man he was likely to favor - "I'm looking at a candidate that has a blatant disregard for the future environmentally when it comes to women's rights, diplomatically" said Grohl of his concerns. "I have three daughters that are going to survive me for decades – how are they going to get on unless there's some positive and progressive change?"

Whilst several of the lines he was writing had political references, Grohl was keen to ensure that nothing too extreme crept in, adamant that Foo Fighters were not going to become outwardly political. "When I'm writing lyrics, I'm not so politically direct that it would sound like a Rage Against The Machine album, but what I'm trying to do is express frustration at how everyone is so divided."

Grohl experienced a feeling of "hopelessness and despair" upon hearing the news of Trump's nomination, feeling a desire to just run away it all, feelings that led to the lyrics for the song 'Run', echoing those desires to "find a place where you feel free, and there's peace".

There was, according to Grohl, a lot of other things to write about at this time other than politics – his experience as a father and family man, new musical experiences and other events that had impacted his life. "I look at all of the different periods of time where I've written lyrics and they all have their own references and different phases. This one came out pretty clear. I'm a father now, I have to consider a lot more than I used to, and I think I've realized we're not all as free as we were before."

The lyrics for 'La Dee Da' referenced the teenage years of his life, growing up in a blue bedroom in Springfield, Virginia. One of his friends at that time was a big fan of heavy, industrial rock bands and got Dave and their other friends into bands such as Coil, Whitehouse, Hunting Lodge, Psychic TV and Death In June. Unbeknownst to the youngster at the time Death In June had been linked to several far-right fascist groups, often using Nazi imagery in their live performances. To Grohl they were just a cool punk band and whilst he had learned of their ideologies in later years, it had slipped his mind again when he decided to reference them in the song. "Of course, I didn't think of that as I was writing the lyric!" he would later assure fans and critics. Another name mentioned in the lyrics Grohl penned for 'La Dee Da' was Jim Jones, a religious cult leader who in 1978 initiated a now infamous mass suicide event in Jonestown, Guyana. Whilst Grohl was certainly not a fan of Jones or supportive of what he did in any way he did find his story and the events of that day interesting. At one point during his youth, he decided to try and paint a portrait of Jones, using an old bedsheet as his canvas which he stuck to his wall to create a flat surface. When he was done, he removed the sheet from the wall only to discover the paint had bled through, leaving him with a crude mural of the cultist on his wall. This story is one of several he'd reference in the track.

For another song he would sing about 'drinking dirty water' but his words were not a literal observation of any sanitary issues in the world, instead the dirty water served as a metaphor for "that black cloud of oppression you feel sometimes" according to Grohl. "It's that feeling where you're bleeding dirty water and breathing dirty sky – you just kind of feel polluted by that sort of dark energy of the collective psyche of the world."

Dave Grohl's week in Ojai had been deemed a productive one by the man himself and so with around a dozen songs ready to go it was time for Grohl to round up the troops and begin the next phase of what had now clearly become the production of their ninth studio album.

As the band was publicly still on a hiatus it was decided that all future work on the album would remain as secretive as possible. No public announcements were planned until the recording was complete. Owing to the fact nobody was expecting an album any time soon, this meant the band was afforded similar freedoms as they had when recording the Saint Cecilia EP in similar secrecy in 2015.

To keep things under wraps rather than head to their own Studio 606 facility which had frequent visitors the group instead headed to the less well-known Fonogenic Studios, located in Van Nuys, California to start pre-production work. The studio is part-owned by Rami Jaffee alongside multi-instrumentalist Ran Pink, their creative partnership known as Pink Jaffee. Jaffee had been with Foo Fighters as a session and touring musician since 2005 and whilst Grohl had spiritually considered him a Foo Fighter for almost a decade by this point it was only now that it was decided to make it official. Going forward, Jaffee was to be considered the sixth full-time member of the band, which among other things meant he would be credited as a songwriter on many of the songs they worked on at the studio.

The band spent several weeks at Fonogenic in the fall of 2016, developing the songs Dave had recorded in his garage a few months earlier. According to guitarist Chris Shiflett, the band spent a lot of time shaping each song, recording lots of different demos, different versions of Dave's song ideas. "That's usually the method of this band, we just demo and demo and demo and do them over and over and tweak them along the way," said Shiflett of the iterative process.

Once the band was happy the songs were at an advanced enough stage, several decisions needed to be made to move things forward, one of which being how, and where, the final album would be recorded. Ever since the 2005 half acoustic, half rock double album 'In Your Honor' there had always been a grand scale idea behind each Foo Fighters album, a USP. Feeling that this trend should continue, shortly after completing recording for 'Sonic Highways' in 2014 Grohl began thinking up different ways the band could record their next record. A couple of years earlier he mentioned to the press that they wanted to record a future album in space, an "analog moonshot". He may have been joking on that occasion but the idea he initially settled on wasn't too many steps down on the craziness scale.

The grand plan centered around The Hollywood Bowl, a live amphitheater in Los Angeles which had in the past played host to hundreds of huge artists including The Beatles, Pink Floyd, Elton John, and Prince. The show Grohl planned to host at the venue was different from anything it had seen before, however. A recording studio was to be constructed on the stage, complete with a control room, isolation booths and all the associated equipment needed to record an album which would then be recorded live on stage. 20,000 lucky fans would be invited along to watch, giving the public a unique chance to see the band at-work as they put together the record. At the time he conceived of the idea he believed nobody else had ever attempted such a project, it would be a world first.

Grohl was very excited about the concept, although his bandmates were going to take some convincing - "Are you out of your fucking mind?" was their initial response. As it turned out though, he wouldn't need to get them on board as unfortunately for Grohl long before he could even think about carrying out the idea, he was beaten to the punch.

In January 2015 singer-songwriter PJ Harvey recorded her album 'The Hope Six Demolition Project' as an art installation at Somerset House in London, England. Over the course of the month members of the public were invited to the venue to watch Harvey perform, with the finished album released in April 2016. Grohl later caught wind of the project and whilst it was not the same as his idea, he decided it was close enough that he decided to scrap the Hollywood Bowl plans.

With that idea quashed, a new one was required. Perhaps reconsidering that space idea for a while, Grohl soon realized the strangest thing they could do after so many outlandish concepts was the most common – walk into a professional recording studio and just record an album. No flashy concepts, no world firsts, no garage - just create a record the old-fashioned way, as they had last done for a Foo Fighters album in 2002.

Whilst there would be no grand concept around the

album Grohl did have a couple of other changes in mind. The first was the producer. Whilst very happy to work with his friend Butch Vig on their past two albums, he felt a change was needed for the benefit of the music. That change came in the form of Greg Kurstin. Kurstin is most well-known in the music industry for his work as a producer, working with artists such as Adele, Sia, and P!nk. However, he also had his own band, The Bird And The Bee, which is how Grohl first became aware of him.

Driving in his car Dave heard the band on the radio, one he'd previously never heard of. The song he heard was "Again And Again", from their 2007 eponymous album and he was enamored by the track, dazzled by the melodies and harmonies. Like any regular music fan, he rushed out to buy the album as soon as he could.

Fast forward to 2013 and whilst on a break in Hawaii Grohl spotted Greg at a restaurant. Kurstin had a house on the island and despite his own huge fame, Grohl became a little star struck. "Oh my God, that's the guy from The Bird And The Bee, holy shit," he thought to himself before plucking up the courage to go over and introduce himself. His first point of inquiry was to ask about the status of Bird And The Bee, with Kurstin explaining that plans were at that time on hold as he had work to do producing. It was at this point Grohl became aware of his other work – Sia, Adele, and Beyonce were all upcoming clients at the time. After that first meeting, the pair became friends, meeting up whenever Grohl would visit Hawaii, talking music and discussing each other's latest projects.

Once the decision had been made that they were indeed going to record another album, Kurstin was the first name that came to mind when Grohl considered who might produce it. Greg had never made a rock record before, and

Dave was keen to bring his extensive knowledge and sense of melodies to the band's work. "I thought this might be a perfect match" recalled Grohl, planning to mix "our noise and Greg's big brain and all of his sophisticated arrangements and composition." The band had experimented with acoustic material in the past and brought the two together, but Grohl was keen to further explore a diverse sound and decided Greg was the ideal man to help them realize their grand ideas.

Dave invited Greg to the rehearsal studio to meet the rest of the band and listen to their demos, allowing both sides to understand whether the project could work. The rest of the band were not familiar with The Bird And The Bee, nor were they well-versed on pop music production, and so their first meeting with Kurstin was a step into the unknown. Indeed, when Grohl first discussed the idea with guitarist Pat Smear, it turned out he had never even heard Adele songs, never mind be aware of who produced them. After hearing the 2016 hit song 'Hello' for the first time, Smear was impressed with her talents but unsure of how relevant it was to their work - "OK, that's amazing, but how the fuck does this apply to what we do?" he asked.

Not every member of the band was too concerned with the potential new producer, however. For drummer Taylor Hawkins, he placed his trust in Grohl. "I just go with whatever Dave says. I just say, whatever, you're the boss. And I don't think anyone really knows how to steer the Foo Fighters better than Dave, and I wouldn't trust anyone else at the driver's wheel. We're like our own little Mafia family. Whatever he's got in mind we go out and we fucking do. Give it everything you've got."

Once Greg arrived at the studio, it didn't take long for any concerns to be put to rest with Pat Smear soon realizing he and Greg were not so different after all - "Oh, you're like us! You were some punk rock kid who played in weirdo bands, and somewhere along the line, you happened to do that thing that now everyone knows you for. So Greg may have veered off into other directions like jazz and pop and stuff, but I got it. And we immediately got along."

Kurstin entered the studio without any pre-conceived notions of what he would experience and was equally impressed with the band, and the material he heard. Kurstin agreed to work with the band and was looking forward to getting to work, particularly happy with the band's willingness to move out of their comfort zone, or as Greg put it, "how much they wanted to push the sound and go nuts."

Another new face would be involved in recording as Greg invited Darrell Thorp to assist him in engineering. The pair had worked together several times in the past and Thorp said he was "really excited to get the call" to join up with him again on a Foo Fighters record. Like Kurstin, much of his previous recording work had been with pop acts so he too was looking forward to the challenge.

With all personnel in place and a straight forward plan of action for recording, the last decision to be made was the matter of where they would record. At the suggestion of Kurstin they settled on EastWest Studios, a large state of the art facility in the heart of Hollywood which had seen hundreds of big names through the door in its 50+ year history. Pre-production and demo work continued through the fall with the band eventually moving to EastWest in late December 2016, a week before Christmas.

"There's a lot of stuff on this record that's been bouncing around in Dave's head for a long time – the super layered vocals and countermelodies and all that," says guitarist Chris Shiflett. "It was cool to see Dave let go and have somebody actually produce the record, usually it's tough for him to let go of the reins," added bassist Nate Mendel. "For the longest time we've been placing these restrictions round the band's boundaries," Grohl admitted.

"Not only in the recording process but also in the songs. Thinking, OK, we can't go that far because we'll never be able to reproduce that live, so let's keep it to the simplicity of the five or six guys in the band. And this time, I thought - fuck it. Just fuck it. I said to Pat and Taylor at one point, as we had stacked 32 vocals together, How the fuck are we gonna do this live? And Pat said, 'Just do what Queen did - do the live version.' So we sort of let all of that go."

Whilst any extreme concepts were off the table for this recording session, Dave Grohl did still have certain ideas which aimed to keep the band on their toes. One of those ideas was for the band to put aside their favorite, tried and trusted recording gear and instead experiment with equipment less familiar them. For guitarist Chris Shiflett that meant ditching his signature Fender Telecaster, instead electing to record much of the album with a 1968 non-reverse Gibson Firebird, equipped with P-90 pickups. "That to me is just a nice complement, I just love the P-90 sound," said Shiflett of the selection. "There isn't a lot of room for single coil stuff in Foo Fighters, it just tends not to work out. So usually I'm bouncing between guitars with humbuckers and guitars with P-90s."

Pat Smear similarly had to ditch his trusty Hagstrom guitars and instead dug through his collection to find some Les Paul models he'd never liked playing. Previously finding them a little heavy, and with inconvenient switch placement, Smear was surprised to find the models far more enjoyable this time around - 'Wow! holy shit, these things are great!' thought Smear. For Dave, his own rule meant putting down his beloved red Gibson Trini Lopez and instead also delving into his vast collection to try out some lesser used models.

Guitar amplifiers were also switched out, with Chris' Vox AC-30s replaced by the AC-15 model, as well as vintage models by Vibrolux, Deluxe and a Fender Champ. Pat recorded much of his guitar work with a custom solution created by the band's guitar techs that wasn't even technically a guitar amplifier. "I used an old '70s mixing board piped into some weird transistor amp. I can't even remember what it was, it didn't make any sense at all!" explained Smear. "It was like a PA plugged into a transistor amp, just a really cool-sounding thing."

In terms of drums, Taylor and Dave brought a variety of kits to the studio, including a Gretsch 'George Lake' kit with a 13-inch rack tom and a 16-inch floor tom." For bassist Nate Mendel he also put aside his signature models and played most of the record using custom shop Fender P-Bass models that were created for him in the late 1990s.

EastWest is a vast professional recording studio with four recording rooms including the main room measuring a huge 58 x 42 feet. The band took full advantage of this space setting up four full drum kits, a bass station, vocal booths, multiple keyboards and pianos, and over twenty guitar amps.

In terms of microphones engineer Darrell Thorp utilized a large number of Lauten Audio models, with the Atlantis and LA-320 models used on the guitar amplifiers, the LA-220 used to mic some of the drum kits and various other models used within the room. EastWest was equipped with an 80-channel Neve 8078 recording console which was first used at the studio to record Michael Jackson's 'Thriller' record in 1982. The band once again recorded to tape, but all tracks were then dumped into ProTools for further work, and the tape re-used with some tracks recorded straight to ProTools digitally.

Setting up the expansive collection of recording equipment was a challenge for Thorp. "Ultimately I came up with the idea to have two drum recording chains and patch all the kits across to the particular chain we wanted to use." explained the engineer. "Then a bass chain, and then a guitar chain for each player, a couple of vocal chains, one for lead and one for backing vocals." This recording chain was then fed directly to the 24-track tape machine, with the output finally ending up in a master ProTools session. According to Chris Shiflett, the "secret weapon" at EastWest were the echo chambers, large enclosures which allow sound to reverberate and create a big, open sound.

As had been the case since recording 2011s Wasting Light the band recorded the album one song at a time, aiming to complete one full song before moving onto the next. Right from the very start producer Kurstin played a huge role in recording, in particular when it came to vocal harmonies. "That was pretty amazing to watch," said Pat Smear. "He's definitely a guy who can visualize it. He'd play this part on the piano and Dave would sing it perfectly first time, always good - just a weird, doesn't make- any-sense melody, then Greg would say, 'Okay, here's another line I want you to sing.' It would have nothing to do with the first one!

One of the first songs to be recorded at EastWest was the title track, 'Concrete And Gold'. As the song was nearing completion Dave went out into the parking lot of the studio to finish up some lyrics and bumped into Shawn Stockman, singer in the 1990s R&B group Boyz II Men. The group were well-known for ballads which featured grand acapella vocal harmonies, something Grohl was well aware of. He originally envisioned a full choir to perform on the song but knowing Stockman's talents, asked If he would be interested in participating.

Stockman was surprised at being asked to perform on a Foo Fighters record, but up for the challenge he agreed and joined the band in the studio an hour later. Tasked with building an entire choir like performance as one person, Stockman began recording layer upon layer of vocal tracks, eventually completing twenty-six takes. Upon hearing the results Grohl and the band were suitably impressed, describing the sound as "huge". Grohl liked it so much he exclaimed to the rest of the band that he wanted the rest of the songs to be equally large. In the past the band had been wary of using too many layers in the studio, fearing they would never be able to reproduce the sound live, as five or six people. "For the longest time we've been placing these restrictions around the band, boundaries," said Grohl. "Not only in the recording process but also in the songs. Thinking, OK, we can't go that far because we'll never be able to reproduce that live, so let's keep it to the simplicity of the five or six guys in the band". But now, after hearing what Stockman had achieved, Dave had decided It was time to go beyond those boundaries. Answering the concerns as to how they would play the songs live, Pat Smear gave a simple solution - "Just do what Queen did – play the live version". With Greg Kurstin guiding them, the band pushed on, adamant they would create their weirdest record.

Another song recorded early in the process was 'Run'. Ironically when writing the song Grohl wasn't even able to walk unassisted, let alone run. "There's some catharsis there, that I get to scream my brains out," said Grohl. Whilst he'd said the same of several songs in the past, Grohl claimed that the track was "probably the heaviest thing we've ever recorded".

Whilst recording the song the band continued to believe it was a straight-up heavy rock song, and bassist Mendel, in particular, enjoyed the riff, believing it was so strong it would be the song they opened live shows with during the following live tour. As the song progressed and evolved during recording producer Kurstin pointed out that the band had unknowingly written a song with a strong reggaetón beat. "What the fuck is a reggaetón beat?" asked Grohl, with the producer playing several recent pop songs with a similar beat, such as the hugely popular Luis Fonsi & Daddy Yankee song featuring Justin Bieber, 'Despacito'.

In January 2017 the newly elected President Trump was officially inaugurated and a month later he gave a press conference which Dave Grohl described as "the one that turned into a screaming match", likening it to a promo appearance by a WWE wrestler. "All that gross ambition for power and control freaked me out," said Grohl, with the speech inspiring the introduction song on the album, 'T-Shirt'.

The last week in February saw the band take a short break as they headed to the United Kingdom to announce their appearance at the legendary Glastonbury Festival later in the year. To do this, the band booked a small venue near to the festival location and played a full-length show to a small number of lucky fans. During the show, the band played snippets of two songs they had already recorded at EastWest - 'Run' and 'La Dee Da'. Fans at the time speculated that they were new songs, but the general consensus was that they were just jams from the early stages of demoing. What they didn't know is that the band were mid-way through recording an album.

Recording of the track 'La Dee Da' began with just Dave

and Taylor player live in the main room, a track which called for heavy distortion and an overall deep, grungy sound. To achieve that on the guitars a pretty standard array of effects pedals were used including the Boss RE-20 Space Echo, as well as purposely overdriving the pre-amplifier on the microphones to "get it as buzzy as possible" according to Kurstin. This was nothing new for a Foo Fighters song but unusually the call for a non-clean tone also extended to the bass. Whilst it would've perhaps made sense to also use a distortion pedal to achieve the desired effect, Kurstin instead unleashed some of his technical wizardries. The dry part of the song was recorded in Pro Tools and then a second recording rig was set up with Logic Pro X, the Apple digital recording software which comes with a myriad of plugins. It was with these plugins Greg was able to manipulate the bass to achieve the gritty, distorted sound.

Another partial interruption in recording came when producer Kurstin was 'borrowed' by another artist – Sir Paul McCartney. The pair had previously worked together when McCartney recorded music for an animated movie and he invited Kurstin to again help him with his next solo album. When Dave Grohl got wind of the news and was told that his friend McCartney would also be recording with Kurstin at EastWest, he took the opportunity to call and ask for a favor in return for the producer-napping. Whilst McCartney is most well known for playing bass and piano, he is also a competent drummer and owing to the 'weird' theme of the record, Grohl asked the Beatles legend if he wanted to play drums on the song 'Sunday Rain'.

McCartney thought he was crazy but admitted that he would've said yes "Even if it had been banjo" that Dave wanted him to record. Grohl showed him the song on an acoustic guitar and McCartney very quickly understood what he had in mind. Just two drum takes were recorded, and amazingly, the one the band decided worked best was the very first take. "You don't generally think of him as a drummer," said Taylor Hawkins, "But he laid that track so fucking effortlessly". Dave had similar praise, simply stating that he was "so fucking good".

Once work on the Foo Fighters track was laid down McCartney couldn't resist hanging around and jamming with the rest of the band. With plenty of drums in the studio, both Dave and Taylor got behind a kit at one point, with McCartney on piano and the rest of the band joining in on their respective instruments, just recording whatever came to mind. This went on for several hours and the fact someone of McCartney's stature was still happy to just loosely jam like teenagers in a garage was particularly noteworthy to guitarist Chris Shiflett - "To see a guy who has done literally everything you can possibly do with the art form that we exist in, and he still just wants to make some noise with a bunch of guys in a room, just for the fun of the moment was amazing."

Another guest at the studio came with the track 'Dirty Water'. Harmonizing on the vocals with Grohl was Inara George, the other half of The Bird And The Bee. Following the lead of Shawn Stockman, the pair recorded a large number of harmonies, all layered together. "I love working out vocal arrangements, and Dave's guitar chords are so great, so there were a lot of possibilities for counter melodies and harmonies," said Kurstin of the vocal work on the track.

The start of the song featured something of a recording irregularity, Kurstin recording Dave playing his guitar in the EastWest parking lot into an iPhone, of all things - creating an intentional lo-fi start to the track. Towards the end of the track, a more hi-fi approach was taken, with Rami Jaffee mirroring the guitar tracks using a Minimoog synthesizer to create a "Gary Numan-ish" sound according to Kurstin. "The two parts play off each other. We loved how the song gets so much louder when it kicks in at the end and made sure to keep that in mastering."

EastWest is a very popular studio in the recording industry and during recording, many big names would visit the studio to work on their own music. Shania Twain and Lady Gaga were two of the names that dropped in whilst the band was residing there, usually stopping by to say hello to the band. Grohl even became the de-facto studio chef, regularly cooking on a grill outside the studio and feeding his musical colleagues. One of those big names was pop supremo Justin Timberlake. He and Grohl had already met a few times previously and appreciating each other's different crafts, became friends. Timberlake was booked into the studio for a few days and would spend time with members of the band, enjoying the songs he heard them recording.

On the eve of his last day at the studio, Timberlake put in a cheeky request - "Can I sing on your record?" he asked Grohl, eager to be able to tell his friends he was on a Foo Fighters record. Happy to oblige, the band were currently in the middle of recording the track 'Make It Right', a track that via Kurstin already had upwards of fifty guitar tracks on. Dave decided the track could also use some backing harmonies and so it came to be that Justin Timberlake sang some 'la la la's' on a Foo Fighters song.

Knowing the collaboration would be something of a surprise to fans, the band elected to keep it a surprise, planning not to reveal anything in future press interviews, nor credit him in the liner notes for the album. Whilst three unplanned guests in Shawn Stockman, Paul McCartney, and Justin Timberlake featured during recording, there was one name Grohl wanted to get on the record which didn't happen. "There was a song on the new record that I thought would be amazing if Roland Orzabal sang on or helped produce," Grohl revealed. "I emailed him - and never heard back. It would have been a dream come true, to get together with the singer from Tears For Fears. There's always next time."

By early March recording at EastWest was considered complete. Happy with their work, the band members took a well-earned break - guitarist Chris Shiflett had planned a number of tour dates in support of his solo record starting from March 21st, believing his work was done on the record. Dave Grohl headed off to Hawaii to relax before he was due to return to the studio in early April to oversee mixing and mastering of the record.

Whilst on his break, Dave had a feeling the album was missing something. "I got one more song in me," he thought to himself. One evening he found himself looking up at the Hawaii night sky, full of stars which reminded him of a Neil DeGrasse Tyson video he'd watched entitled 'The Most Astounding Fact'. In the video, Tyson unsurprisingly explained what astounded him most about the Universe we live in, giving an emotionally powerful answer. Looking up at the sky and remembering what Dr. Tyson had said, Grohl decided in his mind that "the sky is a neighborhood", believing like Tyson that humans needed to look after each other if the human race, and the planet itself, were to survive.

Whilst he'd come up with some basic lyrics for the song in Hawaii and had a rough idea of a melody, he hadn't yet written a cohesive song. Believing it could be the missing piece he felt the album needed Grohl returned to the studio in early April and informed the crew that mixing would have to wait a little while so they could work on the new song. He also needed to call the members of the band and let them know he had one last song to work on, although for Chris Shiflett this was something of an issue since he was out on tour.

As work on the album was supposed to be already complete Studio 1 at EastWest was not available, booked by another artist. Instead the song was recorded in the smaller, yet still impressive Studio 2. Producer Kurstin experimented with mic placement during recording to get the spacey sound the song called for. Initially, he tried to employ a technique called multi-latch gating, first known in rock circles when it was used on the David Bowie song 'Heroes'. A noise gate is used to modulate the volume of an audio signal and the multi-latch method involves multiple noise gates chained together in such a way that creates a unique ambient effect. In the end, it was instead decided to use a far simpler technique, placing microphones far away from Dave as he sang to pick up the "roomy" sound of the vocals bouncing around the studio.

The entire process of finalizing writing and recording the song was completed in a single day, resulting in a simple yet powerful song. In fact, Grohl would describe the finished track as "the biggest thing sonically that we've ever done" and believed that it was indeed the finishing touch required for the record.

Mixing got underway headed up by Darrell Thorp with Dave and producer Kurstin overlooking proceedings. Looking back philosophically on what they had done, Grohl felt they had accomplished their goal - "As we were mixing, I realized that we'd actually done what we set out do: to make this gigantic Foo Fighters record but with Greg Kurstin's sense of jazz and melody and arrangement, something that we'd never done before."

Thorp was also in charge of mastering, assisted by David Ives of 101 Mastering. The whole post-recording process was completed by late April and amazingly, the band and everyone involved in recording managed to keep it a secret. In May 2017 Grohl was pictured at EastWest with Red Hot Chili Peppers Chad Smith and session drummer Jim Keltner. The trio was at the studio recording for a Derek Smalls album, the persona of Harry Shearer in the cult classic movie 'This Is Spinal Tap'. Fans had no idea that Dave had already been at the studio the past four months, making the ninth Foo Fighters album.

Twelve songs were completed during the recording session and initially, it was planned for all of them to feature on the record. Listening parties were even held in the summer of 2017 which featured all twelve songs. However, in the end, one song, 'Soldier', was cut from the record. It was instead earmarked for a special release later in the year, a 7 Inch single supporting the Planned Parenthood organization.

The first song to be released from the session was 'Run', put out as a surprise single in early June. The existence of an entire album was revealed soon after, with 'Concrete And Gold' seeing release on September 15th, 2017.

* * *

January 2018
EastWest Studios, Hollywood, CA, United States

Foo Fighters
Hawkins, Taylor (drums, vocals)

Grohl, Dave (Guitar, Vocals)

Mendel, Nate (Bass Guitar)

Shiflett, Chris (Guitar)

Smear, Pat (Guitar)

Jaffee, Rami (Organ, Mellotron, Piano)

Additional Musicians
Sidley, Samantha (backing vocals)

Recording Credits
Urselli, Marc (producer)

Tracks Recorded
1. unknown T.Rex song

In January 2018 Foo Fighters were back at EastWest Studios in Hollywood for a special project. The band had been invited to perform a track for an upcoming tribute album to T. Rex, an English glam rock band of the late sixties and seventies fronted by singer-songwriter and guitarist Marc Bolan. T. Rex saw huge success in the 1970s with hits such as 'Ride a White Swan', 'Get It On' and perhaps their most famous track, 'Children of the Revolution'.

The band was considered one of the pioneers of the glam rock movement, but everything came to a premature end in 1977 with the sudden death of Bolan in a car crash.

A tribute album was conceived in mid 2017 by Sony BMG, planning to honor Bolan and the band alongside a visual documentary. Being on the same label, Foo Fighters were approached to contribute and as fans of the band (drummer Taylor Hawkins in particular), they agreed.

As well as all six members of the band guest vocalist Samantha Sidley was also present at recording. Sidley had been recruited by the band a few months previous to participate on their live 'Concrete And Gold' tour alongside two other vocalists, helping them to emulate the layered vocal harmonies that had been performed on the record.

The album and documentary were due to be released in the Spring of 2019 but at the time of publication no firm date had been revealed publicly and owing to this the track Foo Fighters performed was still considered confidential information. The unknown song was tracked entirely live in the main room at Studio A, with a very quick and relaxed attitude according to Hawkins - "We had fun. All of us sat in a room together and we just recorded it really quick, and live. We just sat in a room and had fun."

Grammy award-winning producer Marc Urselli was placed in charge of the session and he later enthused how much he enjoyed the process. "What a pleasure and honor to record these guys," said Urselli of his first experience with the band. "Great musicians, super nice people, and kick ass rockers."

March 11th to 17th, 2018
EastWest Studios, Hollywood, CA, United States

Recording Artist
Grohl, Dave (Drums, Bass, Guitar, Keyboards, Percussion)

Recording Credits
Matsumoto, Sydney (engineer)

Shields, Tyler (engineer)

Thorp, Darrell (recording)

Tracks Recorded
1. PLAY

As guitarist Chris Shiflett had noted when discussing how the band was going to record their Sonic Highways album, Dave Grohl always has many ideas rattling around his head at any given moment. Some of them a little crazy, some more orthodox.

In late 2017 one of the crazier ideas sprung into Grohl's mind. Ever since the late 1980s, Grohl had been recording his own music and had a special talent of being able to record an entire song himself, playing every instrument and singing vocals for a complete take. It was a technique he'd first developed as a youngster, utilizing two cassette recorders in his bedroom to build up a song with multiple instruments.

Of course, being just one man, he could only ever do that in a one-by-one process – usually drums first, then bass, guitar, and finally vocals. For this new audio-visual production, Grohl planned to change that limitation by cloning himself. Kind of.

The core part of the idea was to record a 23-minute instrumental piece of music he'd written over the course of ten days using old unused riffs and unfinished song ideas, as well as some new ideas. Laying out all the instruments in a recording studio, each would be recorded live in one take. Then would come the magic part. Using special video editing techniques, the finished product would blend all of the performances together into one video, giving the effect of five clones helping the original Dave Grohl to record the song in one harmonious take.

For Grohl, this was not just a vanity project to show off his recording skills. It was instead intended to serve as an inspiration for young children interested in playing music. He wanted to show "the rewards and challenges of dedicating one's life to playing and mastering a musical instrument," having been inspired by his own children going through that process just as he had. "Watching my kids start to play music and learn to sing or play drums, it brings me back to the time when I was their age listening to albums, learning from listening... and when I take my kids to the place where they take their lessons, I see these rooms full of children that are really pushing themselves to figure this out," Grohl said.

To carry out the project he once again returned to EastWest Studios in Hollywood in March 2018, almost a year to the day after initial recording for the album 'Concrete And Gold' had been completed there.

Grohl worked on musical production of the session himself although Darrell Thorp was again on hand to engineer, assisted by Tyler Shields and Sydney Matsumoto. On the video side of things, Grohl was also in charge alongside Mark Monroe, who he'd worked with on both the Sound City and Sonic Highways video projects. Therapy? Content also collaborated on the project, again returning from previous Grohl videos.

As he'd always done before, Grohl started with the drums. Whilst he would record the 23-minute track in one take, he did not do so on just one drum kit, deciding that certain parts of the music called for a different kit. His laser blue Drum Workshop Jazz Series kit was used for the first ten minutes of the track, which featured heavy, up-tempo beats. Alongside the first full kit, Grohl had set up what he considered a transition kit, consisting of just a single floor tom and two cymbals, to enable him to move to the second full kit without ever completely stopping.

The second set of drums was, in fact, a smaller Ludwig kit he'd bought for his daughter Harper to learn on, deciding it was perfect for the softer, slower-paced section of the instrumental - what he'd himself dubbed as a "mellow groove". Another transition station then allowed him to switch to the final kit for the remaining six or so minutes of the song. Dubbed the "big rock kit", it was actually the same Slingerland set that had been used for the One By One and In Your Honor album. The kit featured a large kick drum with two sound holes for microphones and was used for a section of the track in 3/4 time, followed by another heavy section, a 'dirge' section, and the big crescendo finale.

Grohl was serious about recording the music in one take, going right back to the start whenever he made a mistake. Once the first complete take was completed, he didn't start splicing in newer takes to create one perfect take, he went back out into Studio 1 and started over, repeating this until he was happy with one complete recording of his drum track.

Drums completed, he headed out of the performance room, changed into a new set of clothes for the purposes of appearing as a different Dave Grohl clone and started with the first guitar track. Guitar station one was set up with a black 1957 Gretsch Duo Jet, a guitar he'd been using since recording the third Foo Fighters album There Is Nothing Left To Lose in 1999. With this he could record some of the slightly deeper tones, using a relatively clean signal.

With one guitar track laid down as a guide, Grohl then switched clothes again to record Bass guitar, using a Fender P-Bass Elite model.

After another change of clothes, he then came to the second guitar track recorded with a 1967 black Gibson Trini Lopez with a Bigsby Whammy Bar. With these he played a mixture of distorted leads and cleaner parts, utilizing several effects pedals to do so.

At the final guitar station were two guitars, his favorite red Gibson Trini Lopez and a maple bodied Gibson Dove acoustic guitar. The latter was used for the mellow sections six minutes into the track with the Trini Lopez filling out the big rock sound in the rest of the song. An E-Bow was also on hand at the third guitar station which Grohl used with the Trini Lopez for a very brief part of the 'dirge' section of the track.

With the core elements of the track laid down, he then moved on to his weakest instrument, keyboards. Grohl sat surrounded by several different models, utilizing four in the final take – a Yamaha DX7 synthesizer, a Nord Wave Synthesiser, a Rhodes Piano, and a Wurlitzer Electric Piano. With playback of the track in his headphones, Grohl bounced between the four, each offering a different sound for each part of the track. The Rhodes was used for the clean piano whilst the DX7 gave Grohl some funkier, distorted sounds.

Finally, the finishing touches were added with some percussion. A Yamaha Xylophone, tambourines, plastic Cowbell, Timpani drums, and wooden shaker were all used during the lengthy track.

The final product was completed in seven days with seven different Dave Grohl's involved. One drum track, three guitar tracks, a bass track, percussion, and keys.

When Grohl initially discussed the project with the music press before recording he teased that he might not even release it, just doing it for his own amusement. That statement was something of a tease, as barring any disasters Grohl had always planned to release the project and attempt to build on it, supporting workshops around the world in helping youngsters learn the trade.

The project, entitled 'PLAY', was first revealed to the public in August 2018 with a website set up allowing fans to watch the spliced video of the completed recording featuring Dave and his six clones. Fans were also given the ability to isolate the camera feeds and watch an entire take of each of the seven tracks, from start to finish. A special 12-inch Vinyl edition of PLAY was released in September.

* * *

Whilst I've done my absolute best to research all of Dave Grohl and Foo Fighters studio recording there were some sessions where despite my best efforts, I was not able to glean enough information to properly present as an entry in the main book. I didn't want them to be excluded entirely however, so below is a list of those sessions along with a brief description of events. Hopefully, in a future edition of this publication, I will be able to cover these sessions in greater detail.

March 1993 – Ocean Way Recording, Hollywood, CA (Backbeat Band)

With some rare free time in Nirvana's schedule, Dave Grohl headed to a recording studio to join a large collection of musicians as they recorded material for the soundtrack to Backbeat, a 1994 drama film which chronicled the early days of the Beatles before they were famous. The Backbeat Band had been assembled by producer Don Was, who was tasked with putting together a soundtrack album featuring some of the Beatles earliest tracks. As well as Dave the band featured Thurston Moore of Sonic Youth, Mike Mills of R.E.M., Greg Dulli of The Afghan Whigs and Don Fleming of Gumball.

Starting from an initial list of 200 songs, the group eventually ended up recording twenty over a period of three days. Fourteen of those twenty were included on the album.

Summer 1994 – Robert Lang Studios, Shoreline, WA (Mike Watt)

After Kurt Cobain's death in 1994, Dave Grohl's first musical performance was with The Backbeat Band at the MTV Movie Awards in June 1994. There he met Mike Watt and the pair discussed Watt's upcoming solo album. Grohl was asked to play drums on some tracks and accepting, he headed with

Mike to Robert Lang Studios in the summer of 1994. He played drums on the tracks, 'Against The 70's' and 'Big Train' as well as lap steel guitar on the latter.

September 6th 1997 — New York City studio (Puff Daddy)

In a more unlikely collaboration, Dave Grohl was invited by Puff Daddy to perform on a rock remix version of his track 'All About The Benjamins' in 1997. Grohl performed guitar and drum tracks for the new version of the song. "I did a remix with Puff Daddy because he wanted to get some funk music, so he called the whitest guy in the world," Dave joked about his contribution. "It's hard to write a new-sounding song to a song that's already been written. So I just went in and did something that I thought wound up sounding like Rage Against the Machine, in a weird way. It just took one night, and it went pretty well."

1998 — Rancho De La Luna, Joshua Tree, CA (earthlings?)

After his first visit in early 1997, Dave Grohl was invited back to Rancho a year later to hang out with owners Dave Catching and Fred Drake. Whilst there he would also contribute to their band earthlings?, along with former Scream bandmate Pete Stahl. He would add backing vocals and a guitar track to the song 'The Dreaded Lovelies' which appeared on their eponymous debut album as well as drums on 'Rock Dove', which would be on their second album 'Human Beans'.

January 2000 to 2003 — Various Studios (Probot)

Probot began life at the turn of the millennium with Dave heading to Studio 606 with producer Adam Kasper wanting to record some "heavy stuff", following the somewhat mellow recording of Foo Fighters album 'There Is Nothing Left To Lose'. After recording several instrumental songs the next few years would see Dave contacting various metal/hardcore style vocalists to ask if they would be willing to perform on the project. Dave would usually send the instrumental tracks out to those that agreed, getting a finished track back in return. The finished project was released as Probot in 2004.

Mid 2000 – A&M Studios, Hollywood, CA (Iommi)

Partway through his Probot recording project, Dave was contacted by Black Sabbath guitarist Tony Iommi who was himself putting together a solo project and wanted Grohl to contribute (it was this that gave Dave the basic idea for Probot). Dave headed to a Hollywood studio in mid-2000 to record Drums and vocals for the song 'Goodbye Lament', a track which also featured Queen guitarist Brian May.

Early 2002 – Various Studios (Cat Power)

Grohl became aware of Chan Marshall, the woman behind Cat Power, in the late nineties. "She's kind of cool. She's a girl with the most delicate, seductive, bluesy gospel voice and she sings these fucking heart-wrenching songs, so amazing," he said of the singer-songwriter. Her 2003 album 'You Are Free' was engineered by Adam Kasper and it was via this connection she was able to invite Grohl to guest on the record. He would record drum tracks for the songs 'Speak For Me', 'He War', and 'Shaking Paper', also playing bass on the latter. The album was recorded sporadically over 2002 and saw release in February 2003.

Late October 2001 & Late April 2002 (Queens Of The Stone Age)

Following release and touring of their second album 'Rated R' Queens Of The Stone Age parted ways with their drummer Gene Trautmann. Dave Grohl had long been a fan of the band and had known frontman Josh Homme since the early 90s. He had wanted to feature on their second record but with Trautmann now out of the picture the road was clear for him to help with recording for their next record. He first recorded with Queens in October 2001, laying down initial drum tracks for many of the songs and returned to the studio in April 2002 after Homme had decided some of the tracks needed more work.

In the end, Grohl drummed on all songs of 'Songs For The Deaf' except for 'You Think I Ain't Worth a Dollar, But I Feel Like a Millionaire' which still featured Trautmann. For this short time, Grohl was effectively the permanent drummer in the band, playing live shows with them between March and July 2002. The album was released in August 2002.

March 2003 – Grandmaster Recorders Ltd, Hollywood, CA (Killing Joke)

After performing on the same bill at a festival in January 2003 Killing Joke frontman Jaz Coleman invited Grohl to join the band and record their eleventh studio album. With the band not having a drummer at the time it was planned for several guests to feature on the album including Tool's Danny Carey and System Of A Down drummer John Dolmayan. However, once Grohl had heard the tracks they were working on he was adamant he would do everything.

He joined the band at Grandmaster Recorders in March 2003 and unusually with most of the recording already complete by that point he had the challenge of adding drums last, whereas in his entire musical past he'd always recorded them first. Grohl overcame that hurdle and recorded on all ten songs on the album which was released in July 2013.

2004 – Sound City Studios, Van Nuys, CA (Garbage)

2004 saw Dave once again working with Butch Vig as he joined up with his band Garbage during the recording of their album 'Bleed Like Me'. As had been the case with Foo Fighters recording of their album 'One By One' recording of the album had been troubled, lead singer Shirley Manson undergoing surgery on her vocal cords after initial recording. There was a lot of tension among the band members and Grohl was one of several guests brought in to try and re-energize recording, Vig calling in a favor from his old friend. The track he recorded drums for was 'Bad Boyfriend', Vig not happy with his existing drum track. Grohl "brought a different energy level to the song", according to Vig.

July 2004 – Sound City Studios, Van Nuys, CA (Nine Inch Nails)

Grohl was back at Sound City later in 2004 for another guest musician slot, this time with industrial rockers Nine Inch Nails. Frontman Trent Reznor invited him to the studio to record drum tracks for six songs and percussion on a seventh. The songs were included on their fourth studio album, 'With Teeth'.

Early April 2006 – Jim Henson Studios, Los Angeles, CA (Juliette & The Licks)

The drummer for hire was busy again in 2006 working on a full album with Juliette And The Licks, the band headed by Juliette Lewis. Lewis and Grohl had met a year or two earlier and when he heard the band was looking for a drummer, he volunteered. Dave recorded the drums on all twelve tracks featured on their second studio album, 'Four on the Floor'.

Early 2009, April to July 2009 — Pink Duck Studios & Chalice Studios (Them Crooked Vultures)

Them Crooked Vultures began life in secrecy, recording an entire album without anyone knowing. Recording took place over the first half of 2009 with action split between frontman Josh Homme's own Pink Duck Studios and Chalice Studios in Los Angeles. Grohl recorded drums on all thirteen songs of their self-titled album as well as percussion and backing vocals.

Spring 2012 — Fairfax Recording Studios, Van Nuys, CA (RDGLDGRN)

After Sound City closed its doors in 2011 it became known as Fairfax Recording and one of the artists to record there was RDGLDGRN. Before recording the bands' producer had envisioned Dave Grohl drumming on their album and after putting in some calls, Grohl. He first joined them at the studio to record the track 'I Love Lamp' and enjoying what the indie rock/hip hop act was doing, asked if they had any more tracks. Over the course of just two days, Grohl recorded drums for their self-titled debut album released in 2013.

November 2012 — Pink Duck Studios, Burbank, CA (Queens Of The Stone Age)

Partway through recording for their sixth studio album QOTSA once again found themselves without a drummer, Joey Castillo leaving midway through the process. Dave Grohl once again stepped in, recording drums for five of the eleven tracks on '....Like Clockwork'.

June 2013 – Southern Ground Recording, Nashville, TN (Zac Brown Band)

As already covered earlier in this book, Zac Brown first invited Dave Grohl to his studio not long after first meeting, the Foo Fighters frontman heading in practically blind. As well as producing four new songs in the summer of 2013 he also participated, playing drums on the track 'Let It Rain' which was included on the aptly named 'The Grohl Sessions, Vol. 1' released in December 2013.

Late 2013 – Studio 606 West & Regret Chamber Studios (Birds Of Satan)

Just before Foo Fighters headed out on the road to record their eighth studio album across the country drummer Taylor Hawkins formed his own new band, 'The Birds Of Satan'. The members were all at the time part of Hawkins cover band 'Chevy Metal' with the original project being a natural evolution. Hawkins decided to call in a favor from several members of Foo Fighters to help with the recording of their first album with Pat Smear, Rami Jaffee and Dave Grohl all contributing. In the case of Grohl, it was with guitar tracks, Hawkins taking care of drums. The self-titled album was released in April 2014, featuring seven tracks.

Bibliography

In writing this book I have referenced hundreds of articles, books, interviews and conducted many interviews myself. Listing them all here would take up several dozen pages and so wanting to do my little bit to save some trees, you can instead find the complete bibliography online at the following location:

https://7corners.foofighterslive.com/bibliography

"The Neverending Sigh is 20 years old! Was once called 7 Corners for all you die hards out there..."

Printed in Great Britain
by Amazon